16.

Ulysses in Progress

Ulysses in Progress

Michael Groden

Princeton University Press
Princeton, New Jersey

*to my mother, Mickey Groden, and
in memory of my father, Sheldon Groden*

Acknowledgments

In *Finnegans Wake* Joyce describes his "ideal reader" as "suffering from an ideal insomnia"; his sleepless students need ideal friends as well. This book has benefited immeasurably from many friends and colleagues who have read it at various stages in its development and offered encouragement, advice, and correction: Hans Walter Gabler, Peter K. Garrett, Philip Gaskell, Phillip F. Herring, Hugh Kenner, A. Walton Litz, and Michael Seidel. Philip Gaskell and Phillip Herring sent me detailed suggestions for revisions. None of these people will be entirely satisfied with the changes I have made (and have not made); I can only paraphrase the words that appear on most pages of this kind to the effect that these people can all take credit for the improvements in my text, and I alone am responsible for the errors and weaknesses that remain.

Michael Seidel and Phillip Herring allowed me to read typescripts and proofs of their important new books. Michael Seidel and I had each begun investigating Joyce's use of Victor Bérard when we met and discovered that we were looking at the same problem through opposite ends of a telescope. While I was studying Joyce's precise use of Bérard in "Aeolus," Seidel was investigating the broad patterns of epic geography and movement. Each of us was able to supply the other with the vital support that only an opposite approach could provide. Similarly, Phillip Herring prepared his edition of Joyce's "Cyclops" copybook as I was considering its role in Joyce's progress on *Ulysses*. My "Cyclops" chapter, and eventually my entire book, have been greatly aided by the several years of correspondence that have resulted from our common interests. I was able to use a typescript of *Joyce's Notes and Early Drafts for* Ulysses while I revised my own manuscript; my debts to it will be evident in the many references throughout the following pages.

My interest in Joyce and *Ulysses* was first aroused and then sustained by four teachers, whom I would like to thank: Peter Bien of Dartmouth College; Richard Cross, formerly of Dartmouth, now of U.C.L.A.; A. Walton Litz of Princeton University; and Peter Garrett, formerly of Princeton, now of Illinois.

I am grateful to Jerry Sherwood of Princeton University Press for her suggestions and guidance as I tried to turn this mass of detail into a readable study. The maps were drawn by R. L. Williams of the Yale University Map Laboratory, and Ines Lottbrein performed the heroic task of typing the final manuscript.

I acknowledge my greatest debt with much pleasure. First as teacher, then as dissertation director, finally as friend, A. Walton Litz has offered advice and support that have affected these pages in ways far beyond those suggested by the references to his published works. The dissertation out of which this book has grown began in response to a suggestion of his, and he has never lost interest in its welfare since that time. For me he will always be an expression of the true meaning of the words "scholar" and "teacher."

I wish to thank Miss Anne Munro-Kerr of the Society of Authors, acting for the James Joyce Estate, for granting me permission to use the many quotations from Joyce's published and unpublished works included in this book and to reproduce pages from the prepublication documents. These publishers have allowed me to quote from their books: Random House and the Bodley Head (*Ulysses*), Viking Press and Faber and Faber (*Giacomo Joyce, Letters*, and *Selected Letters*), New Directions and Jonathan Cape (*Stephen Hero*), and the Librairie Armand Colin (Victor Bérard's *Les Phéniciens et l'Odyssée*). The many quotations from the unpublished documents at Buffalo are included with the kind permission of the Poetry Collection of the Lockwood Memorial Library, State University of New York at Buffalo; the fair copy of *Ulysses* is cited with the permission of the Philip H. and A.S.W. Rosenbach Foundation; the proofs at Harvard University are quoted by permission of the Houghton Library; Joyce's unpublished letters to John Quinn are used by courtesy of the John Quinn Memorial Collection, Manuscripts and Archives Division, The New York Public Library, Astor, Lenox and Tilden Foundations; the list of characters for "Cyclops" on page 134 is published with the permission of the Cornell University Library; and the note Joyce sent to his printer, quoted on page 165, is used by courtesy of the Humanities Research Center, University of Texas at Austin. The libraries at Buffalo, Harvard, Cornell, Texas, Yale, Southern Illinois, and Wisconsin—Milwaukee, and the New York Public Library, sent me photocopies and microfilms of their holdings, thus greatly facilitating my work. The Princeton University library allowed me regular access to the holdings in its Sylvia Beach Collection.

In a somewhat less developed form this book was a doctoral dissertation at Princeton University. The "Cyclops" chapter, again in a slightly different form, appeared in the *James Joyce Quarterly*, Vol. 12, Nos. 1-2, 1974/75. My work during the summer of 1975 was made possible by a grant-in-aid from the American Council of Learned Societies, for which I am very grateful.

Princeton, N.J.-London, Ont.
1973-1976

Contents

Illustrations

Abbreviations

Bérard Victor Bérard, *Les Phéniciens et l'Odyssée*, 2 vols. (Paris: Librairie Armand Colin, 1902-03)

Budgen Frank Budgen, *James Joyce and the Making of* Ulysses (1934; rpt. Bloomington: Indiana Univ. Press, 1960)

Gilbert Stuart Gilbert, *James Joyce's* Ulysses: *A Study* (1930; rpt. New York: Vintage, 1952)

Goldberg S. L. Goldberg, *The Classical Temper: A Study of James Joyce's* Ulysses (London: Chatto and Windus, 1961)

Goldman Arnold Goldman, *The Joyce Paradox: Form and Freedom in His Fiction* (London: Routledge and Kegan Paul, 1966)

JJ *Richard Ellmann, James Joyce*, Galaxy ed. (New York: Oxford Univ. Press, 1959, 1965)

Letters *Letters of James Joyce*. Vol. I, ed. Stuart Gilbert (New York: Viking, 1957, 1966). Vols. II and III, ed. Richard Ellmann (New York: Viking, 1966)

Linati Schema Joyce's 1920 schema sent to Carlo Linati is transcribed and translated in the Appendix to Richard Ellmann, *Ulysses on the Liffey*, Galaxy ed. (New York: Oxford Univ. Press, 1972, 1973)

Litz A. Walton Litz, *The Art of James Joyce: Method and Design in* Ulysses *and* Finnegans Wake, Galaxy ed. (New York: Oxford Univ. Press, 1961, 1964)

LR The *Little Review* (New York), which serialized *Ulysses* from March 1918 to September-December 1920

MS   Ulysses: *A Facsimile of the Manuscript*, 3 vols.
                      (New York: Octagon, and Philadelphia:
                      The Philip H. and A.S.W. Rosenbach
                      Foundation, 1975)

Notes and   Phillip F. Herring, ed., *Joyce's Notes and*
  Early Drafts   *Early Drafts for* Ulysses: *Selections from the*
                      Buffalo Collection (Charlottesville: Univ.
                      Press of Virginia, 1977)

Notesheets   Phillip F. Herring, ed., *Joyce's* Ulysses
                      Notesheets in the British Museum (Char-
                      lottesville: Univ. Press of Virginia, 1972)

Selected   Richard Ellmann, ed., *Selected Letters of*
  Letters   *James Joyce* (New York: Viking, 1975)

Ulysses   James Joyce, *Ulysses* (New York: Ran-
                      dom House, 1961)

1921 Schema   Joyce's 1921 schema is reproduced photo-
                      graphically in *A James Joyce Miscellany:*
                      Second Series, ed. Marvin Magalaner
                      (Carbondale: Southern Illinois Univ.
                      Press, 1959), opposite p. 48. It is tran-
                      scribed in Stuart Gilbert, *James Joyce's*
                      Ulysses: *A Study* (1930; rpt. New York:
                      Vintage, 1952), p. [30], minus the
                      column of "correspondences," and in
                      many other studies.

Ulysses in Progress

Introduction

I've put in so many enigmas and puzzles that it will keep
the professors busy for centuries arguing over what I
meant, and that's the only way of insuring one's immortality.

—James Joyce, in conversation
(*JJ*, p. 535)

CONSIDERING the activity that has surrounded *Ulysses*
since its publication, James Joyce seems to be over fifty
years on his way toward the immortality he imagined—an
eternity of scholarly perplexity and squabble. By conservative calculation, my book is at least the thirtieth full-length
study of *Ulysses* alone, not to mention the more general
books on Joyce (well over one hundred) and the thousands
of articles and chapters on *Ulysses*. Such a production con-
jures up images of a flourishing "Joyce industry" but, more
importantly, it testifies to the continuing vitality of *Ulysses*
itself. Despite the millions of words, there is much yet to be
said.

One major aspect of *Ulysses* that has remained obscure is
its complicated and bizarre prepublication history. It is not
just that Joyce spent eight years on the book; also, he radically changed his artistic goals during the last few years and
reworked some of the book's early parts to conform with
these new goals. The book was published twice: once in a
serialized version while it was very much a work in progress, and later (much revised) set in book form by French
printers who knew no English. By the time of its final publication as a book, Joyce's desires for encyclopedic com-
pleteness had become so dominant that every set of proofs
occasioned further revision and addition, with the result
that for some pages there are as many as thirteen different
stages of development, beginning with the manuscript
from which the typescript was prepared and ending with
the published text.

In Ulysses *in Progress* I have investigated four different
aspects of Joyce's making of his book. The opening chapter, *"Ulysses*: The Three Stages," looks at the finished book
from the point of view of Joyce's processes of composition.
Critics have often emphasized only one side of *Ulysses'*
many dualisms, the "novelistic" story of Stephen and
Bloom, for example, or the "symbolistic" pattern of parallels and correspondences. Recent attempts to incorporate
these dualisms into a unified reading have led to the argument that the book's meaning is essentially a multiple or
ambiguous combination of novelistic and symbolistic tendencies. This view is strongly supported by Joyce's methods of composing. Between 1914 and 1922 he passed
through three distinct stages (rather than two, as has been
thought) in his writing, with the middle stage serving as a
bridge between his early interest in character and story and
his late concern with schematic correspondences. In the
first stage ("Telemachus"—"Scylla and Charybdis") he developed an interior monologue technique to tell his story.
In the middle stage ("Wandering Rocks"—"Oxen of the
Sun") he experimented with the monologue and then
abandoned it for a series of parody styles that act as "translations" of the story. He balanced his growing attraction to
stylistic surface with a continuing interest in the human
story. Finally, in the last stage ("Circe"—"Penelope") he
created several new styles and revised the earlier episodes.
He only partly reworked the episodes, however, as if to
present *Ulysses* as a palimpsest involving all three stages. A
complete reading of *Ulysses* must accommodate Joyce's different artistic intentions during his eight years of work on
it, since his methods of composition show that he never entirely abandoned a set of aesthetic principles, even when
new ones dominated his writing.

The chapters that follow detail the three stages of composition. "The Early Stage: 'Aeolus' " discusses the development (from the first extant version to the final publication) of the early episode that Joyce revised most
dramatically to conform with his late intentions. In many

ways, the composition of "Aeolus" serves as a microcosm of the entire book. "The Middle Stage: 'Cyclops' " focuses on that point when he abandoned the interior monologue. An unusually complete set of early "Cyclops" drafts shows Joyce's first attempts to create a new style for *Ulysses*, and his use in the process of numerous notes. Finally, "The Last Stage: 1920-1922" documents his work from his arrival in Paris (during the early work on "Circe") to the time of the book's publication. During these eighteen months, he engaged in an elaborate combination of new episodes and revision of earlier ones, a process that became even more complicated when his French printer began to pull proofs in mid-1921.

The prepublication evidence in all four chapters comes from letters, notebooks, drafts, the autograph fair copy, typescripts, proofs, and the early version of *Ulysses* that was serialized in the *Little Review*. Because I will refer frequently to specific documents and their interrelationships, I think it best at the start to outline Joyce's progress on the book, differentiate the documents involved, and indicate the ways in which I will cite these documents.

Joyce's early years of work on *Ulysses* are not very clear; few materials survive to chart the story.[1] As early as 1906 and 1907 he planned a modern version of Odysseus' wanderings, first as a *Dubliners* story and then as a short book (*Letters*, II, 190, and *JJ*, pp. 238-39, 274-75), but he presumably never wrote either. He apparently thought of the long novel *Ulysses* while he worked on the last chapter of *A Portrait of the Artist as a Young Man* in 1914. His earliest efforts on *Ulysses* were combined with work on several other projects: correcting proofs for *Dubliners*, which was finally being published; molding Chapter V of *A Portrait* while faircopying the earlier parts for the *Egoist* serial publica-

---

[1] The best discussion of Joyce's early work on *Ulysses* is in Rodney W. Owen's doctoral dissertation, "James Joyce and the Beginnings of *Ulysses*: 1912 to 1917," Diss. Kansas 1977, especially Chapter 2. The following paragraph is based on Owen's research.

tion; faircopying *Giacomo Joyce*; and drafting and then completing the play *Exiles*. These projects were finished when he left Trieste for Zurich in June 1915 (though *A Portrait* would not be published in book form until the end of 1916), so from then until February 2, 1922, his creative energies were directed solely toward *Ulysses*.

Joyce's first explicit reference to *Ulysses*, probably written in 1914, appears in a dream he describes toward the end of *Giacomo Joyce*: "Gogarty came yesterday to be introduced. *Ulysses* is the reason."[2] On June 16, 1915, he told his brother Stanislaus that he was working on a new novel (*Selected Letters*, p. 209); the announcement, written on the day the finished book would immortalize as Bloomsday, is his first mention of *Ulysses* in the surviving letters. Occasional references to it appear in 1915 and 1916. In October 1916 he told Harriet Shaw Weaver that he had nearly completed the first three episodes, the "Telemachia," and had done some work on the "Wanderings" and the "Nostos" (*Letters*, II, 387). In April 1917 he offered to send Ezra Pound excerpts of "the Hamlet chapter" (*Letters*, I, 101), and on August 20, 1917, he was "prepared to consign it [*Ulysses*] serially from 1 January next, instalments of about 6000 words" (*Selected Letters*, p. 227).

It is only toward the end of 1917 that we can begin to document Joyce's progress closely. When Ezra Pound became the European editor of the *Little Review*, he arranged for the serialization of *Ulysses*, and Joyce, probably prodded by the monthly deadlines, began to complete the early episodes in regular succession. To finish each episode, he prepared a holograph manuscript, from which a typescript was made. After correcting errors on the typescript and usually making some changes and additions on all copies, he sent two copies to Pound, one for submission to the *Little Review* and one for Harriet Shaw Weaver of the *Egoist*. He retained a third copy. The *Little Review* published "Telemachus" in its March 1918 issue and had printed one part of "Oxen of the Sun" in the September-

[2] *Giacomo Joyce*, ed. Richard Ellmann (New York: Viking, 1968), p. 15.

December 1920 number when a New York court ordered it to cease publishing *Ulysses*.

The book publication process began in the summer of 1921, by which time Joyce was ready with revisions and additions for the episodes that had already appeared in the *Little Review*. He took unused copies of the typescripts prepared and corrected several years earlier for the serial publication, and made his new changes in ink.[3] He sent these doubly emended typescripts to Maurice Darantiere, his printer in Dijon. No new typescripts of the first fourteen episodes were prepared for the book publication. Thus, in 1921 the *Little Review* version of *Ulysses* drops out of the line of transmission. It has no textual significance, except in those cases where it differs from both the fair copy and the later published versions, and where the typescript is not extant to provide holograph evidence of Joyce's intentions. The last four episodes were not published in the *Little Review*; the typescripts of these episodes were prepared directly for the eventual book publication.

Joyce's writing of *Ulysses* hardly stopped when he submitted the typescripts to Darantiere; indeed, for some parts of the book it had barely begun. Darantiere pulled the proofs in two stages: *placards* and page proofs.[4] Joyce received three copies of most pullings, writing his corrections and additions onto one copy. He returned this copy to Darantiere, who used it to reset the type for the next set of

[3] The copy of the typescripts used by the *Little Review* was lost, but Joyce had the other two copies available at this time. One he had retained all along; the other traveled an Odyssean route from Joyce to Pound to Harriet Shaw Weaver to B. W. Huebsch to John Quinn and back to Joyce. See Clive Driver, "Bibliographical Preface," MS, 1, 24. For further discussion of the *Ulysses* typescripts, see the Appendix.

[4] The *placards* (*épreuves en placard*) consist of eight unnumbered pages printed on one side of a large sheet, four pages wide by two high. The second page is printed below the first, the fourth below the third, etc. The page proofs are printed on both sides of a sheet of the same size as the *placards*; each gathering contains sixteen numbered pages. I have included a census of the proofs, with library locations, as an appendix to my doctoral dissertation, "The Growth of James Joyce's *Ulysses*," Diss. Princeton 1975, pp. 314-45.

proofs. Joyce's reading of each set of proofs acted as such a powerful stimulus to revise and add that many sections required five or six sets of proofs; some needed eight or nine.

The prepublication transmission of *Ulysses* can best be summarized in chart form, but the single stemma offered here is necessarily a gross oversimplification. Joyce's unit of composition was the episode, not the entire book. In general, he began each episode with notes and early drafts, eventually producing a holograph manuscript from which a typescript was prepared. He considered each episode finished when the typescript was ready for submission to the *Little Review* (for the first fourteen episodes) or to Darantiere (the last four). Each episode was subsequently revised and augmented on the proofs. This general pattern, however, breaks down at some point for almost every episode. For example, the only extant holograph manuscript, the autograph fair copy owned by the Philip H. and A.S.W. Rosenbach Foundation (known as the Rosenbach Manuscript), was for several episodes the manuscript from which the typescript was made, but for many others it seems to be a fair copy made from another draft (presumably a holograph manuscript not extant) from which the typescript also was prepared. Likewise, for some pages of one episode ("Ithaca"), more than one typescript was made, each deriving from the previous one. The Appendix discusses the relationships between the prepublication documents and considers the transmission of each episode, but the chart offered here will serve as a general stemma of *Ulysses*.

The many transcriptions had a significant effect on the text of the book. First the typists and then Darantiere's compositors made numerous errors. Joyce caught many of them, but four major factors—the printers' lack of English, Joyce's difficult handwriting and weak eyesight, and the pressures of time—made complete accuracy impossible. As a result, errors have persisted through all editions published since 1922. For example, the angle-bracketed words in the following passage appear in the fair copy of "Lotus

A STEMMA OF *ULYSSES*

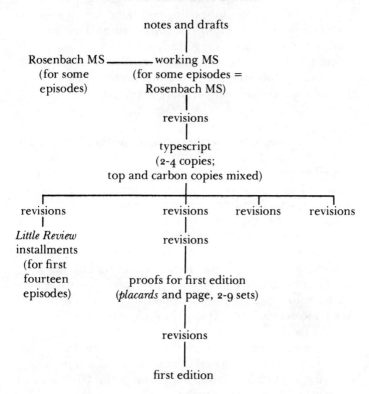

Eaters" (MS, fol. 1) and in the *Little Review* (5, iii [July 1918], p. 37), but in no later editions: "So warm. His right hand once more more slowly went over ⟨his brow and hair. Then he put on his hat again, relieved: and read⟩ again: choice blend, made of the finest Ceylon brands" (cf. *Ulysses*, 71.33-34). The printer must have skipped an entire line of the typescript, as he did at the end of "Nausicaa" in the images that pass through Bloom's mind as he falls asleep (again, the angle-bracketed words do not appear in the first or later editions): "young eyes Mulvey plump ⟨bubs me breadvan Winkle red slippers she rusty sleep wander⟩

years dreams return" ("Nausicaa" TS V.B.11.a, p. 21; cf. 382.17).[5] Many errors in spelling and punctuation were introduced in this way. However, considering all the complications involved in writing and publishing *Ulysses*, it is amazing that the text is not more corrupt than it is. Still, there is no doubt that the numerous prepublication transcriptions introduced unfortunate errors that were never corrected.

Many of the relevant prepublication documents have survived. Sets of notes are owned by the British Museum (edited in 1972 by Phillip F. Herring) and the Poetry Collection of the Lockwood Memorial Library, State University of New York at Buffalo (catalogue numbers V.A.2 and VIII.A.5, both edited by Herring in 1977).[6] The Buffalo collection also contains early drafts of several episodes, and the Cornell University Library has a draft of half of one episode. John Quinn began to buy the autograph fair copy in March 1920, but to Joyce's great annoyance he auctioned it in 1924. It is now owned by the Philip H. and A.S.W. Rosenbach Foundation in Philadelphia, which published a facsimile of it in 1975. Typescripts for twelve of the first fourteen episodes (five of them partial) and for the last four episodes have survived; almost all of these now belong to Buffalo. The *Little Review* collection at the University of Wisconsin—Milwaukee has the portion of the "Oxen of the Sun" typescript sent to the *Little Review* but never printed. The typescripts actually used by the *Little Review* have not survived.

The proofs are now housed in several libraries. Joyce's corrected and augmented *placards* are at Harvard; the page

[5] I have discussed these and other omitted passages in "Toward a Corrected Text of *Ulysses*," *James Joyce Quarterly*, 13 (1975), pp. 49-52. See also Jack P. Dalton, "The Text of *Ulysses*," in *New Light on Joyce from the Dublin Symposium*, ed. Fritz Senn (Bloomington: Indiana Univ. Press, 1972), pp. 99-119.

[6] The Buffalo collection has been catalogued by Peter Spielberg, *James Joyce's Manuscripts and Letters at the University of Buffalo: A Catalogue* (Buffalo: Univ. of Buffalo, 1962).

proofs are at Buffalo (catalogue number V.C.1), except for the final set of proofs, which is owned by the Humanities Research Center at the University of Texas at Austin. Unmarked duplicates of these proofs are at Buffalo and Princeton: the proofs at Buffalo run through the middle of "Sirens" (both *placards* and page proofs: V.C.2, V.C.3, V.C.4), and those at Princeton cover the rest of the book.

Wherever possible I have used Joyce's own words to support my statements. I have given parenthetical references to all works included in the list of abbreviations. In referring to drafts, notebooks, and typescripts (most of which are at Buffalo), I have provided Peter Spielberg's catalogue number and folio or page number. I have followed Phillip F. Herring's page numbering for the documents he edited in *Joyce's Notes and Early Drafts for* Ulysses: *Selections from the Buffalo Collection*; this should facilitate tandem use of my discussion with that volume. In the autograph fair copy, Joyce returned to number 1 at the beginning of each episode; I have followed this practice, citing episode name and folio number. I have referred to notebook and typescript sheets as "pages" and to loose manuscript leaves as "folios," using "r" and "v" (recto and verso) when necessary to indicate front (on which Joyce usually wrote out his text) and back (usually reserved for additions to the facing recto). For the notesheets at the British Museum, I have used Phillip Herring's page and line notations (e.g., "Cyclops" 9:13).

Despite its lack of textual authority, I have occasionally referred to the *Little Review* version of the first fourteen episodes. This happens primarily when there is no typescript to provide more authoritative evidence, or when the context calls less for textual accuracy than for the version of his work that Joyce released to the public. In referring to the major stages of Joyce's progress, I have often called the first stage "fair copy-*Little Review*"; in discussing later revisions in relation to this stage, I have used the phrase "post-*Little Review*."

A final point requiring clarification is my method of transcription from the prepublication documents. Unless stated otherwise, all angle brackets in my transcriptions indicate additions to or changes in the document's original text. An angle-bracketed passage following crossed-out words is a substitution; otherwise it is an addition. Double angle brackets indicate an addition or substitution within an addition. I have placed a question mark before any word I could not decipher with certainty.

Ulysses: The Three Stages

IN October 1916, well over two years into his work on *Ulysses*, James Joyce provided one of the first progress reports on his new book:

> I am working at it as well as I can. It is called *Ulysses* and the action takes place in Dublin in 1904. I have almost finished the first part and have written out part of the middle and end. I hope to finish it in 1918.
>
> *(Letters, II, 387)*

In fact, Joyce never really "finished" *Ulysses*. Rather, since he was determined that it should be published on his fortieth birthday, February 2, 1922, he had to stop writing it. By that time he had spent eight years on the work, lived in three cities, changed his address nineteen times, suffered several eye attacks and subsequent operations, and, at a distance, experienced a world war. More important, during this time his artistic goals changed to such an extent that a book that in some aspects began as a sequel to *A Portrait of the Artist as a Young Man* ended as a prelude to *Finnegans Wake*.[1]

Ulysses lies between *A Portrait* and *Finnegans Wake* in ways beyond mere chronology. To a large extent it is a novel in the traditional sense: it features three major characters, Leopold and Molly Bloom and Stephen Dedalus, and it introduces a technical device, the interior monologue, that

---

[1] See Robert Scholes and Richard M. Kain, eds., *The Workshop of Daedalus: James Joyce and the Raw Materials for* A Portrait of the Artist as a Young Man (Evanston: Northwestern Univ. Press, 1965), pp. 106-08, and Litz, pp. 132-41, for passages Joyce apparently rejected for use in *A Portrait* but incorporated into the opening pages of *Ulysses*. At the other end, Joyce used several of his *Ulysses* notes during his work on *Finnegans Wake*; see *Notesheets*, pp. 525-26, and Buffalo *Finnegans Wake* notebook VI.C.7, pp. 136-269.

contributes to the illusion of verisimilitude in these characters; it contains several developing themes and conflicts, including the movement of Stephen and Bloom toward each other in a "spiritual" father-son relationship, Bloom's need to deal with Molly's adultery (an act consummated during the course of the book), and Stephen's anguish over his mother's recent death and his refusal to obey her dying wish that he pray for her. On the other hand, from the start *Ulysses* contained elements that set it beyond the realm of the novel, and toward the end of his work Joyce emphasized these elements much more than the novelistic ones. The characters and events are determined not solely by the logic of their story but also by the external parallel with Homer's *Odyssey*. Before he stopped work on the book, Joyce filled it with countless minute correspondences to the *Odyssey* and other configurations. Furthermore, the last nine of the eighteen episodes transfer concern from character to technique and feature what has been called "the drama of the alternatives" of telling a story (Goldman, p. 78). There was thus a shift in Joyce's writing of *Ulysses*, a change of direction that expanded the book and made his prediction of a 1918 completion comically optimistic.

With uncanny faithfulness to his prediction, though, Joyce did finish the first major phase of the book in 1918. From the start he constructed each episode as a parallel to an incident in the *Odyssey* with a unique set of symbols and metaphors, but these variations existed within distinct limits. In 1918 he explained the stylistic differences to his Zurich friend Frank Budgen:

> "Among other things," he said, "my book is the epic of the human body. . . . In my book the body lives in and moves through space and is the home of a full human personality. The words I write are adapted to express first one of its functions then another. In *Lestrygonians* the stomach dominates and the rhythm of the episode is that of the peristaltic movement. . . . If they [the characters] had no body they would have no mind. . . . It's all

one. Walking towards his lunch my hero, Leopold Bloom, thinks of his wife, and says to himself, 'Molly's legs are out of plumb.' At another time of day he might have expressed the same thought without any under-thought of food. But I want the reader to understand always through suggestion rather than direct statement."

(Budgen, p. 21)

Changes like these occurred as variations on a basic style, which in 1919 Joyce called the book's "initial style" (*Letters*, I, 129). It involved a combination of third-person, past-tense narration and direct first-person, present-tense depiction of the characters' thoughts. The relationship of the narration to the interior monologue of Stephen or Bloom is not constant. At times, the narrator serves as an adjunct to the monologue, a method of placing the thinking character in time and space:

He halted. I have passed the way to aunt Sara's. Am I not going there? Seems not. No-one about. He turned northeast and crossed the firmer sand towards the Pigeonhouse.

(41.11-13)

Sometimes the narrator aligns himself with the perceptions and point of view of the character:

Mr Bloom gazed across the road at the outsider drawn up before the door of the Grosvenor. The porter hoisted the valise up on the well. She stood still, waiting, while the man, husband, brother, like her, searched his pockets for change. Stylish kind of coat with that roll collar, warm for a day like this, looks like blanketcloth. Careless stand of her with her hands in those patch pockets.

(73.32-38)

At other times, the narrator occupies a more distanced position from which he can report conditions or perceptions outside the characters' minds ("He [Mr. Power] glanced

behind him to where a face with dark thinking eyes followed towards the cardinal's mausoleum. Speaking";
101.36-37) or describe impressions or biases that are distinct from the characters' ("—Ah, poor dogsbody, he [Mulligan] said in a kind voice"; 6.2). The monologue, too, varies from episode to episode, from the lethargy of "Lotus Eaters" to the hunger of "Lestrygonians":

> Nice kind of evening feeling. No more wandering about. Just loll there: quiet dusk: let everything rip. Forget. Tell about places you have been, strange customs.
>
> (79.11-13)

> Hungry man is an angry man. Working tooth and jaw. Don't! O! A bone! That last pagan king of Ireland Cormac in the schoolpoem choked himself at Sletty southward of the Boyne. Wonder what he was eating. Something galoptious. Saint Patrick converted him to Christianity. Couldn't swallow it all however.
>
> (169.22-27)

These differences do not begin to approach the degree of variation among the later episodes, between, say, the "gigantism" of "Cyclops" (in which the happenings in Barney Kiernan's pub are related in the first person by an unnamed debt collector and the narration is frequently interrupted by parodies of such forms of expression as newspaper accounts and legal briefs) and the "tumescence-detumescence" of "Nausicaa" (where half the episode is told from Gerty MacDowell's point of view in the literary equivalent of her sentimental cast of mind, and half reports Bloom's thoughts in a return to the initial style).[2] The original monologue technique, even with its built-in Homeric parallels, is basically concerned with character, verisimilitude, and a continuing human story involving three main characters (one present only in Bloom's mind throughout most of the book) and many subsidiary ones.

---

[2] The descriptions of the techniques are Joyce's; they appear in the famous schema (1921 Schema) he distributed among selected friends beginning in late 1921 and permitted Stuart Gilbert to publish.

In the later episodes, technique seems to dominate over content, parallels and correspondences override specific incidents, and the story seems buried under the surface.

Joyce wrote the first nine episodes—through "Scylla and Charybdis"—in the initial style (third-person, past-tense narration; first-person, present-tense monologue). Then in "Wandering Rocks" he used this initial technique to depict the minds of other characters besides Bloom and Stephen, and in "Sirens" he distorted the style practically beyond recognition. Finally, he abandoned it as the book's exclusive narrative device in "Cyclops," using it again only in the second half of "Nausicaa." (In "Penelope," he closed *Ulysses* with another monologue, this time a pure one lacking the third-person narrator.) Joyce finished "Scylla and Charybdis"—hence the book's original style—at the end of 1918, and he indicated this clearly on the fair copy of that episode. On the last page of "Scylla and Charybdis" he wrote "End of First Part of 'Ulysses' " and the date, "New Year's Eve 1918" (MS, fol. 37), as if to indicate that one phase of *Ulysses* was ending and something new was about to begin. In this way at least, he validated his original prediction.

Because of Joyce's changes in intention and technique after half the episodes, an approach to *Ulysses* by way of his composition processes inevitably points to the many provocative dualisms that permeate the book: given the epic parallel with the *Odyssey*, is *Ulysses* heroic or mock-heroic? Is it ultimately a realistic drama of human characters or a static Poundian "image" whose significance is carried through its symbols? What is the meaning of the ambiguous ending? The conclusions of both "stories"—of Stephen and Bloom and of Bloom and Molly—have been variously interpreted as conclusive and positive, conclusive and negative, and indeterminate. The study of Joyce's composition processes elicits questions of its own: what kind of book was he originally writing, and what kind did he later write? When and how did the change occur? What prompted it?

Joyce's first biographer, Herbert Gorman, ignored the

idea of a change in his writing midway through *Ulysses* and claimed that from the start "the idea was clear in his mind and so was the variegated yet unified technique through which he intended to present it."[3] It is now clear that this was not the case. Richard Ellmann's 1959 biography and A. Walton Litz's 1961 study of Joyce's notesheets and late revisions demonstrate that he markedly altered many of his artistic goals while he was writing *Ulysses*, to such an extent that he wrote later episodes in a method vastly different from that of earlier ones (and different from the way he originally intended to write them) and reworked earlier episodes to conform more closely with later ones. If "in the space of three or four years he travelled most of the distance from *Dubliners* to *Finnegans Wake*" (Litz, p. 35), then there are opposing tendencies in *Ulysses*—compression and expansion, verisimilitude and literary parody, "centripetal" and "centrifugal" writing[4]—that achieve a state of resolution, remain locked in unresolved conflict, or are simply thrown together in a witches' brew that is proudly termed "allincluding" (423.26).

A prominent critical approach to the problem of *Ulysses'* dual tendencies has been to subordinate one aspect to the other. Two major unilateral interpretations are those of Stuart Gilbert and S. L. Goldberg. In *James Joyce's* Ulysses, Gilbert treats the entire book as if Joyce had not begun to write it until after the 1918-19 change. In defining his approach, Gilbert also provides one definition of the change:

> The meaning of *Ulysses* . . . is not to be sought in any analysis of the acts of the protagonist or the mental make-up of the characters; it is, rather, implicit in the technique of the various episodes, in nuances of language, in the thousand and one correspondences and allusions with which the book is studded.
>
> (Gilbert, pp. 8-9)

[3] *James Joyce* (New York: Rinehart, 1939, 1948), p. 227. Richard Ellmann, *JJ*, p. 370, makes the diametrically opposite claim.

[4] The phrase "centripetal writing" appears in Joyce's 1904 Pola notebook. *Workshop of Daedalus*, p. 87.

Prompted and aided by Joyce himself (and authorized to publish the famous schema for the first time), Gilbert emphasizes the parallel with the *Odyssey*, the minute correspondences from the schema, the expression of meaning through symbols, and Joyce's use of esoteric lore. He attempts to present "a clue to the mystery, a thread of Ariadne to guide a modern Theseus through its labyrinth" (p. 43); thus he outlines major themes, often derived from the episodes of the *Odyssey*, that subsume the details of plot and character. (His introductory chapter titles provide a sketch of his approach: " '*Met-him-pike-hoses*,' " "The Seal of Solomon," "The *Omphalos*," "Paternity," "Dubliners-Vikings-Achaeans," and "*Ulysses* and the Odyssey.") The *Ulysses* Gilbert presents is a vast Poundian image, a book of "static beauty" (p. 9).

For Gilbert the elaborate pattern of symbols and correspondences, that is, the *Ulysses* of 1919-22, completely absorbs the possible human conflicts in the *Ulysses* of 1914-18. For example, "Sirens," a transitional episode that would upset any reader approaching *Ulysses* with rigid novelistic expectations, presents no problems for Gilbert; it represents a "complete 'atonement' between subject-matter and form . . . the musical rhythm, the sonority and counterpoint of the prose are evocative of the theme itself, the Sirens' 'song of enthralment' " (p. 257). No conflict exists for Gilbert between the early and the late *Ulysses*, partly because he avoids the inherent conflicts in the characters and reduces the meaning of an episode to a phrase like "song of enthralment," partly because, like Joyce devising the schema late in his work on *Ulysses*, Gilbert seizes on the aspects of the book that best support his argument. The themes and patterns he discusses certainly exist in *Ulysses*, but by denying the possible importance of "the acts of the protagonist or the mental make-up of the characters," he can present no more than a partial, distorted reading of the book.

An approach exactly opposite to Gilbert's is that of S. L. Goldberg in *The Classical Temper*. Gilbert discusses the

"meaning" of *Ulysses* in terms of symbols and correspondences (pp. 8-9); Goldberg considers the "value" of
Ulysses through "its *dramatic* presentation and ordering of
human experience" (Goldberg, p. 30; Goldberg's italics).
Gilbert rejects the importance of the characters' minds or
actions; to Goldberg, "what is of permanent interest . . . is
what always interests us with the novel: its imaginative illumination of the moral—and ultimately, spiritual—
experience of representative human beings" (p. 30). For
Gilbert, Joyce only began to write *Ulysses* in 1919, but for
Goldberg he should have stopped (with few exceptions)
after 1918.

Goldberg thoroughly recognizes the dichotomy in
Joyce's intentions, but he damns most of the last nine
episodes (and, of course, all of *Finnegans Wake*) as "precari-
ous intellectualization of structure" (p. 281). He rejects
seven of the last nine episodes; only "Circe" and "Ithaca"
successfully merge form and content, or "structures" and
"values" (pp. 248, 289). The novel that Goldberg reads in
the first nine episodes is almost exclusively the fair copy-
Little Review Ulysses; most of his examples tend to be passages that were in the book by the time of the serial publication. Because of Goldberg's rigidly defined concept of what
Ulysses, as a novel, should be—the dramatic rendering of
character and human action—he is extremely sensitive to
all Joyce's deviations from this norm. Gilbert and Goldberg
thus represent two one-sided approaches to the inherent
problems *Ulysses* poses; the one ignores the human drama
to find a coherent structure of symbols, the other dog-
matically rejects the expanding symbolic structure in a determined effort to make *Ulysses* a dramatically rendered
novel gone wrong.[5] Both miss much of the reality of *Ulysses*
and its unique achievement.

[5] Despite the enormous blind spot in Goldberg's critical attitude, *The
Classical Temper* is filled with valuable insights about the parts of *Ulysses*
with which he is in sympathy, particularly the dramatic function of
Stephen's aesthetic theory (chapter 3), the general problem of irony in
Ulysses (chapter 4), and the relationship of Joyce's book to the *Odyssey*
(chapter 5).

There have been several responses to such one-sided readings. The most valuable have been attempts to incorporate both the human drama and the symbolic structure into a unified theory of the book. Such a synthesis has been made by critics like Arnold Goldman and Peter K. Garrett. In *The Joyce Paradox*, for example, Goldman argues that the interrelationship of *Ulysses'* many styles precludes a single interpretation on either the realistic or the symbolic level; as he says of the numerous styles of "Cyclops," "where so many are available at all times, the choice of one mode of vision . . . is demoted in importance" (Goldman, p. 93). The human drama of the opening episodes is gradually replaced by a "drama of the alternatives," the various methods of presentation; thus, the poles of realism and symbolism, the problematic relationship of *Ulysses* to the *Odyssey*, and the book's ending all partake of a "radical ambiguity" that Joyce built into the book and that itself, rather than any one of the alternatives, constitutes the book's ultimate meaning. "We do not wish to strike through the mask to discover which of the alternatives is right, we wish to enjoy the drama of the alternatives."[6]

Critics who enter Joyce's "workshop" through his notesheets and drafts and through his revisions of *Ulysses* repeatedly find themselves in trouble with a unilateral interpretation of the book, since they find evidence of a dichotomy in Joyce's intentions that a single approach cannot subsume. In *The Art of James Joyce*, A. Walton Litz studies the notesheets and late revisions in detail and thus documents the change in Joyce's writing after 1919; nevertheless he wishes to emphasize the "novel" in *Ulysses* and to de-emphasize the conclusion his own carefully presented evidence points to—that after 1919 Joyce was no longer writing a novel based primarily on human actions:

Many of these detailed schemes ["the detailed working-

[6] Goldman, p. 78. Garrett presents a similarly strong argument for *Ulysses'* deliberate and meaningful ambiguity in *Scene and Symbol from George Eliot to James Joyce: Studies in Changing Fictional Mode* (New Haven: Yale Univ. Press, 1969), pp. 245-71.

out of a 'correspondence' "] lurk in the background of
the novel, like the discarded scaffolding of a building
which reflects its external form but tells us little of the
essential nature. It would be a grave mistake to found
any interpretation of *Ulysses* on Joyce's *schema*, rather
than on the human actions of Stephen, and Molly, and
Mr. Leopold Bloom.

(Litz, p. 40)

In *Surface and Symbol*, Robert Martin Adams deals with
the processing of factual raw material in *Ulysses*—personal
history, Dublin history, Dublin residents and geography—
to determine if Joyce's use of it is consistent, and if it regularly functions as "surface" ("surface in fiction invites us to
repose in the object itself as represented") or "symbol"
("symbol invites us to transpose, to see the object as a key to
some meaning other than itself").[7] Adams finds a
hopelessly frustrating inconsistency in Joyce's use of the
details, and his reluctant conclusion adumbrates the position later developed by Goldman and Garrett:

> By showing the variety of Joyce's practices upon his ma-
> terials and the diversity of his objectives, this study may
> foster a measure of healthy skepticism about the extent
> to which any single view of his novel can be deduced
> from or imposed upon its details.[8]

Both Litz and Adams assume that *Ulysses* should be one
thing (a novel primarily concerned with human action; a
transformation of realistic detail into a consistent symbolic
structure) but is often another, or that it began as one thing
but became something opposite. A close study of Joyce's
writing of the book can shed light on these either/or problems. The notebooks, drafts, and early versions, and *Ulysses*
itself, suggest that his work progressed through three,
rather than two, major stages, and that the middle stage in

---

[7] *Surface and Symbol: The Consistency of James Joyce's* Ulysses, Galaxy ed.
(New York: Oxford Univ. Press, 1962, 1967), p. 83.
[8] *Ibid.*, p. 249.

many ways served as a bridge between the opposed tendencies of the earlier and later work, exhibiting both a continuing concern with character and realistic detail and a
growing interest in symbolic correspondences and stylistic
elaboration. Litz describes the change from the early to the
late *Ulysses*, that is, from the Joyce of *Dubliners* to the Joyce
of *Finnegans Wake*, in terms of revolution rather than evo-
lution (p. 35), but if we allow for the short period of time
involved, we can see Joyce moving through discernible
stages in a way that supports the idea of a stylistic development. (The concept of stages must remain a flexible one or
it may imply a more schematic process than was actually
the case. He never planned to end one stage and move on
to another; one evolved into the next without a clear
break.) He retained the results of each stage he passed
through, even after he had progressed into the next, so
that he presented *Ulysses* as a palimpsest of his development from 1914 to 1922.

The Early Stage

The first stage of Joyce's work on *Ulysses* is the most easily
defined; it comprises the book's first nine episodes, or, in
terms of the total number of episodes, the first half.[9] He
noted the end of the first half when he finished the "Scylla
and Charybdis" fair copy, and he continued to emphasize
the division of *Ulysses* into halves as an alternate pattern to
the three-part Homeric structure, as in his September 1920
letter to John Quinn (*Letters*, I, 145). He wrote the first nine
episodes in the initial style; they contain the grounding of
character and setting that Arnold Goldman has called
"norms" for Stephen and Bloom, a necessary "gradual *lead
into*" the later "extravagances" (Goldman, pp. 81, 89;
Goldman's italics).

The readers of the early published version of *Ulysses*—

[9] For the stages to which I have given sequential labels throughout this
study, Hugh Kenner has suggested descriptive terms: for the early stage,
"Initial," for the middle stage, "Transitional," and for the last stage, "Radical."

the first thirteen episodes and part of the fourteenth were serialized in the *Little Review* from the March 1918 to the September-December 1920 issues—were presented with a much more novelistic work than were the readers of the final version. In the *Little Review*, the first nine episodes proceed without radical changes in style (Joyce had not yet added the major disorienting feature of the final version, the "Aeolus" subheads) and the interior monologues are not filled with the numerous elements from the schema that he added before the final publication (references to flowers in "Lotus Eaters," to the heart in "Hades," to wind in "Aeolus," for example). All the details of the early part of the "story" that Joyce ever included in *Ulysses* are present in the fair copy-*Little Review* version, but compared to the published book, the early *Ulysses* is much less rich in detail in terms of the range of Bloom's thoughts, the specific events in his life, and the Dublin he experiences on June 16, 1904.

The version of the episodes that Joyce published in the *Little Review* was less dense than the final version, but this does not mean that it provided easy reading. As to the reader of the final version, Joyce gave the early reader no help—no introductions or guides to Stephen's and Bloom's minds; no hint of the Homeric parallels (the *Little Review* episodes are numbered but not named); not even a Roman II, as in the book version, to indicate the break between Stephen's and Bloom's episodes. In the 1920s, when Edmund Wilson saw the schema Joyce had prepared during his last months of work on *Ulysses*, he described it as "a scheme which we could scarcely have divined except in its more obvious features";[10] the early reader, guided only by the title, must have had great difficulty in seeing even "the more obvious features" of either the realistic or the mythic elements of the unfolding book.

As he prepared the fair copy for the *Little Review* serialization, Joyce was concerned only with the "obvious fea-

---

[10] *Axel's Castle: A Study in the Imaginative Literature of 1870-1930* (New York: Scribner's, 1931), p. 211.

tures" of the Homeric parallel. He had established the basic parallels between Bloom, Stephen, and Molly, and Odysseus, Telemachus, and Penelope, and he had worked out a rough draft or outline of the ending to correspond to Odysseus' return (see *Letters*, III, 31), but he was much more concerned at this time with the characters of Stephen and Bloom.

The fair copy-*Little Review* version of the first nine episodes contains practically the entire basic outlines of both Stephen and Bloom. Reacting to Ezra Pound's suggestion that Bloom be relegated to the background and Stephen brought forward, Joyce told Frank Budgen, "Stephen no longer interests me to the same extent [as Bloom]. He has a shape that can't be changed" (Budgen, p. 105). In the late revisions to the first nine episodes, Joyce added a few important supporting details, but Stephen's "shape" was indeed fixed.

The Stephen Dedalus of the opening pages of *Ulysses* bears many resemblances to the Stephen of the fifth chapter of *A Portrait of the Artist as a Young Man*—he is lonely, isolated, arrogant, engaged in an intellectual revolt against the Catholic church that dominated his emotions in much of *A Portrait*. There are two major developments in his personality, the failure of his stay in Paris and his guilt over his refusal to obey his dying mother's wishes. The introduction of the interior monologue, the major technical difference between *A Portrait* and *Ulysses*, adds an entirely new dimension to the characterization of Stephen. (Joyce moved toward the interior monologue technique in the excerpts from Stephen's diary at the end of *A Portrait*.) Whereas in much of *A Portrait*, especially in Stephen's discussion of aesthetics with Lynch, we saw Stephen from the outside or in summarized accounts of his mind, now in the thoughts that balance his new aesthetic discussion in "Scylla and Charybdis" or in his solo musings in "Proteus" we can observe the self-doubts behind the facade of assurance, the soft edge of "Kinch, the knife-blade" with his "dagger definitions" (4.21, 186.13).

Without knowing it, the Stephen of *Ulysses* is a Telemachus searching for his father, and Joyce needed to establish in him a new openness to experience, a willingness to
participate in the Dublin around him. The city and its inhabitants contain much that is alien to Stephen, but among
the Dubliners is Leopold Bloom, the unexpected Odysseus.
Stephen's aesthetic discussion in the library episode differs
from that in *A Portrait* in that it insists on the crucial importance of the artist's experiences—all of them—in shaping
his art. Several of Stephen's thoughts indicate his growing
awareness that he must deemphasize the distinction between himself and his surroundings and recognize the
common nature of both. For instance, while he walks on
Sandymount strand, he sees cocklepickers, his thoughts
turn to Dublin history, and he realizes, "Famine, plague
and slaughters. Their blood is in me, their lusts my waves"
(45.17-18); and while he listens to John F. Taylor's words
about "haughtiness" and "pride," a passage from St. Au-
gustine enters his mind concerning the middle state between perfection and corruption, a state that, within or beyond the book, Stephen needs to recognize in Leopold
Bloom (142.16-24).

In his first version of the opening episodes, Joyce established Stephen's potential openness, but in the late revisions he added a few phrases to intensify both Stephen's
guilt over the past and his possible receptivity to the future.
In "Aeolus" Stephen listens to the windy talk in the newspaper office and to the noise of the newsboys. His initial
reaction to the yelling of the exiting newsboys was simply
"Dublin," but Joyce added the thought, "I have much,
much to learn" (144.31). Also, he picked up a phrase that
Stephen used in the library discussion to describe the wan-
ton Ann Hathaway's late turn toward religion—"agenbite
of inwit"—and developed it into a leitmotif for Stephen's
own guilt. (In the final version Stephen uses a phrase in the
Shakespeare discussion that has been in his mind all day.
However, in a typical sequence in the development of *Ulysses*, Joyce first wrote what is now the recurrence of a word

and only later added the preparations for the recurrence.)[11] Finally, he added several references to the search for a father to the words Stephen thinks, speaks, and hears; he did this in Mulligan's description of Stephen ("Japhet in search of a father!"; 18.17), in Stephen's memory of Kevin Egan's conversation ("You're your father's son. I know the voice"; 43.10), and in Stephen's thoughts during the Shakespeare discussion, specifically his initial response to Best's concern about the author of parts of *Hamlet*, Shakespeare the father or Shakespeare the son ("He is in my father. I am in his son"; 194.39-40). These additions do not change the character Joyce had already developed, but they serve to emphasize aspects crucial for the movement of *Ulysses*.

The situation was somewhat different with Bloom. Unlike Stephen, most of whose history from *A Portrait of the Artist as a Young Man* Joyce treats as assumed knowledge in *Ulysses* (see 7.14, for example: "Cranly's arm. His arm"), Bloom presented no ties to the past. In revising, Joyce did much to expand details about Bloom's past life, the information he remembers, the facts he knows or almost knows, and his general inquisitiveness and responsiveness. But as with Stephen, Bloom's outline existed intact from the start.

The elements that were present in the fair copy and *Little Review* and the degree to which Joyce expanded Bloom's monologue are both evident from a typical passage in one of Bloom's early episodes. Here is the fair copy version:

> Mr Bloom put his face forward to catch the words. Glorious and immaculate virgin. Joseph, her spouse. Peter and Paul. More interesting if you understood what it was all about. Wonderful organisation certainly, goes like clockwork. Squareheaded chaps those must be in Rome: they work the whole show. And don't they rake in the money? Bequests too: to say so many masses. The priest in that Fermanagh will case in the witnessbox. No

[11] The original use is at 206.26. Joyce added it at 16.7-8, 17.3, 189.26, 243.27, and 243.31.

browbeating him. He had his answer pat for everything. Liberty and exaltation of our holy mother the church. The doctors of the church: they mapped out the whole theology of it.

(MS, "Lotus Eaters," fol. 12)

This passage occurs in "Lotus Eaters," the episode of forgetfulness and drugged lethargy. In a church, Bloom hears part of a mass, as Stephen heard Mulligan's parody of a mass in "Telemachus." The man who envisions a more efficient tramline and dreams of the perfect advertisement here admires the "wonderful organisation" of the Roman Catholic church. The priest's words filter through his mind, and he responds in his idiosyncratic way, untouched by them but fascinated by the efficiency and power they symbolize.

When Joyce stopped revising the passage, it had doubled in length:

Mr Bloom put his face forward to catch the words. English. Throw them the bone. I remember slightly. How long since your last mass? Gloria [*sic*] and immaculate virgin. Joseph her spouse. Peter and Paul. More interesting if you understood what it was all about. Wonderful organisation certainly, goes like clockwork. Confession. Everyone wants to. Then I will tell you all. Penance. Punish me, please. Great weapon in their hands. More than doctor or solicitor. Woman dying to. And I schschschschschsch. And did you chachachachachacha? And why did you? Look down at her ring to find an excuse. Whispering gallery walls have ears. Husband learns to his surprise. God's little joke. Then out she comes. Repentance skindeep. Lovely shame. Pray at an altar. Hail Mary and Holy Mary. Flowers, incense, candles melting. Hide her blushes. Salvation army blatant imitation. Reformed prostitute will address the meeting. How I found the Lord. Squareheaded chaps those must be in Rome: they work the whole show. And don't they rake in the money too? Bequests also: to

the P. P. for the time being in his absolute discretion.
Masses for the repose of my soul to be said publicly with
open doors. Monasteries and convents. The priest in the
Fermanagh will case in the witness box. No browbeating
him. He had his answer pat for everything. Liberty and
exaltation of our holy mother the church. The doctors of
the church: they mapped out the whole theology of it.

(82.38-83.20)

Without changing the passage's basic outline, Joyce has
fleshed it out in many ways. For one thing, he ties it to the
lotus-eating theme by emphasizing the narcotic effect of
the mass: "English. Throw them the bone"; "Confession.
Everyone wants to"; "Flowers, incense, candles melting."
(The last example includes one of the many references to
flowers in "Lotus Eaters.") In Bloom's thoughts about confession, Joyce introduces the theme of masochism, an underlying aspect of Bloom's personality that dominates one
of the "Circe" fantasies; "Punish me, please" also echoes
the letter from Martha Clifford that Bloom has just read
(78.4-6). The idea of confession leads Bloom to the main
thought that will occupy his mind all day: "Woman dying
to. . . . Husband learns to his surprise." Because of the
lotus-eating atmosphere, Bloom is not upset by the thought
of adultery; he does not even connect it with his own situation. In the next episode and throughout the rest of the
book, such evasion proves much more difficult (as at
92.19-33).

The revised passage allows much greater play to Bloom's
mind. As he assimilates the priest's words, his thoughts
move to the church's organization, as in the fair copy, but
then other ideas follow—confession and its psychological
benefits, lustful wives, and finally the Salvation Army with
its public confessions—before his mind returns to the
church's organization in Rome. The subsequent addition,
"Masses for the repose of my soul," not only suggests the
prayer Stephen refused to offer for his mother but also
looks forward to Bloom's acquaintance with Stephen's
aunt, Mrs. Riordan ("Dante" in *A Portrait*), whom Bloom

aided hoping that she would remember him in her will but who left all her money for such public masses (305.40-306.4, 738.5-6). The passage thus reveals Bloom's mind to a greater extent than it originally had, without in any way changing its basic outline.

In style as well as character, the fair copy-*Little Review Ulysses* is more "novelistic" than the final version. When he first wrote the episodes, Joyce was far less concerned with stylistic extravagances than he was later. There is little in the early versions of the first nine episodes to prepare the reader for the developments that begin in "Wandering Rocks." The early episodes vary in their dominant metaphors and rhythms, in the ways Joyce explained to Budgen, but compared to the *Ulysses* Joyce published in 1922, a striking feature of the fair copy or *Little Review* version of the first nine episodes is its stylistic consistency.

Joyce always planned the first six episodes as a unit, since Bloom's first three episodes take place at the same time as Stephen's three. From the start Joyce planted linking devices in the paired episodes, such as the indication that both Bloom and Stephen observe a cloud (9.32, 61.7). Joyce built two different structural principles into these opening episodes. One connects Bloom's and Stephen's simultaneous episodes; Joyce emphasized this pattern in his 1921 schema for the book. The entries under "Hour" emphasize the time parallelism, and the techniques of the first and fourth episodes, "narrative (young)" and "narrative (mature)," undescore their linkage. (The exact parallelism in the episodes was apparently a late idea, since in the schema Joyce sent to Carlo Linati in September 1920, "Proteus" takes place between 10:00 and 11:00 A.M., whereas "Hades" occurs between 11:00 A.M. and noon; Linati Schema.) As David Hayman has observed, though, another pattern also exists, one that connects the first and sixth, second and fifth, and third and fourth episodes:

"Telemachus" and "Hades" are social or group chapters which might be qualified as dramatic units. . . . "Nestor" and "Lotus Eaters" present Stephen and Bloom in the center of a larger dramatic frame and give their voices and reactions clear precedence. . . . "Proteus" and "Calypso" are the protagonists' most isolated performances.[12]

"Telemachus" presents Stephen primarily from the outside. The narrator is often clearly distinct from Stephen; when he describes Mulligan, he seems to assume that visual surface constitutes the entire reality, as if Mulligan's words and tone had no underlying motives. For example, Mulligan offers Stephen "a pleasant smile" (3.35); he points "in friendly jest" (3.39); he agrees with Stephen "frankly" (4.16); and he speaks "in a kind voice" (6.2). Perhaps it is the narrator's lack of insight, as well as his eagerness to report everything he sees with precise accuracy, that Joyce means by "narrative (young)." All of "Nestor," on the other hand, is presented from Stephen's point of view, like *A Portrait of the Artist as a Young Man*, and in "Proteus" the external description serves to locate Stephen precisely on the strand, to follow his movements, and to introduce his thoughts. Bloom's first three episodes reverse this pattern, moving from his relative solitude in "Calypso" to his occasional meetings with acquaintances in "Lotus Eaters," and finally to his "public" self in "Hades," where he finds himself among unfriendly Dubliners who themselves usurp a great deal of the narrator's time and attention and where, for the first time since he entered the book, he moves out of the narrator's range of perception (101.28-37, 106.12-107.32). In this second grouping of the opening episodes, the first three move progressively inward; then the second three move out again.

"Aeolus" continues Bloom's outward development. He is in an even more hostile environment than in "Hades," and his progression into the city continues until he disappears into it halfway through the episode. Stephen, on the other

[12] Ulysses: *The Mechanics of Meaning* (Englewood Cliffs: Prentice-Hall, 1970), p. 79.

hand, is now "public" after the extreme privacy of "Proteus." Dublin becomes as important as either of the main characters, and so the final version of "Aeolus" (but not the fair copy or *Little Review* version) begins "In the Heart of the Hibernian Metropolis," as if the action proper is about to begin after six introductory scenes.

Of all the early episodes, "Aeolus" exhibits the most pronounced differences between the fair copy-*Little Review* and the final versions. In its early form the episode in no way stands apart from those preceding or immediately following it. The lethargic rhythms of "Lotus Eaters" give way to the carriage wheels of "Hades"; in "Aeolus" there are first the rhythm and noise of the newspaper machines and then the wind of human bombast. The episode continues Bloom's outward progression, but when Joyce added the newspaper subheads he superimposed a new function on the old one. The final "Aeolus" is an abrupt stylistic departure, another reason that it seems to be a new beginning after six introductory episodes. The subheads call into question the relationship between the episodes' narrators and the characters, since their speaker is distinct from any of the characters or from the narrators; in doing this they boldly assert Joyce's omniscient authorial powers. (These powers have functioned all along in the excursions into the characters' minds and in the Homeric parallel, but the first six episodes do not proclaim their existence in the prominent manner of the "Aeolus" subheads.) The subheads shatter the comfortable uniformity of the early-stage episodes, and they make the later developments much less surprising.

In the early version, "Lestrygonians" and "Scylla and Charybdis" continue (and in the final version they return to) the initial style, although signs of Joyce's impatience with the technique begin to show. Inspired perhaps by Stephen's playful mood, perhaps by his own impatience, Joyce experiments with the form of the page to reflect Stephen's view of the library scene—he introduces musical notation (197), free verse (203), and dramatic dialogue

(209). The narrator exhibits a new boldness as he duplicates Stephen's mocking attitude in describing the other
men in the library: "—A shrew, John Eglinton said
shrewdly" (190.26); "—It is clear that there were two beds,
a best and a secondbest, Mr Secondbest Best said finely"
(203.39-40). In retrospect, these liberties with the initial-
style narrator signal the beginning of the end of the
method.

Although Joyce may have known all along that his book
would change decisively after an initial group of episodes,
it seems much more likely that he gradually decided to
alter his technique. Two facts suggest this gradual change.
As late as May 1918, seven months before he finished
"Scylla and Charybdis," he still planned *Ulysses* in seventeen
episodes (*Letters*, I, 113); this means that he had not yet
thought of "Wandering Rocks," a crucial episode in terms
of the change in *Ulysses'* techniques. Second, in the schema
for the book that he sent to Carlo Linati in late 1920, long
after he had written drafts or rough versions of the last
three episodes but before he had done any work on them,
he described them in terms appropriate to the initial style:
"Eumaeus" is in "relaxed prose," with "nerves" as the organ; "Ithaca" is in "dialogue, pacified style," with "juices" as
the organ; "Penelope" is in "monologue, resigned style,"
with "fat" as the organ (Linati Schema). The decision to
move beyond the monologue technique thus seems not a
preconceived plan but a result of his episode-by-episode
progress on his work, progress that never extended very
far beyond the immediate episode at hand. When Joyce
noted on the last page of the "Scylla and Charybdis" fair
copy both the end of the "first part" of *Ulysses* and the eve
of a new year, he announced a new step in *Ulysses*, the im-
plications of which he was only beginning to realize.

The first nine episodes of *Ulysses* give the illusion of a
narrative limited to the thoughts and perceptions of the
two main characters. Apparently an adjunct to the interior
monologues, the narration seems to limit itself to the per-

ceptions and frame of reference of the character, either Stephen or Bloom. Yet this restriction, like the monologue itself, is a fiction. Joyce exploits the author's omniscient powers in several ways in the opening episodes: the excursions beyond either character's mind, the shift from one main character to another, and the imposition of the stylistic variations. (Authorial omniscience also exists throughout the early episodes in the use of external parallels to the action, mainly those from the *Odyssey*.) Thus, when he fractured and then dropped the initial style, he exploited tendencies of authorial omniscience that were an integral but muted part of his original conception of *Ulysses*.

It is tempting to speculate on why Joyce first violently distorted and then replaced the monologue method. For one thing, he probably grew tired of it. It served his initial purposes well; it provided a unique view of character and a consistent style on which he could play his variations. Stuart Gilbert, unconcerned with character, describes the method as "a bridge over which to march his eighteen episodes" (Gilbert, p. 16); we can dismiss Gilbert's implication of the style as a mere tool (and correct his numerical error) but accept the idea that the method serves as a common substructure for eleven episodes. However, the technique ultimately proved a constricting one, since Joyce obviously began to want a way of moving beyond Bloom and Stephen to present them from viewpoints other than their own.

Perhaps he also realized the limitations the monologue method would place on the resolution of his story: he would have to describe the meeting of Stephen and Bloom and the other questions posed by the conclusion—what will happen to Bloom and Molly? will Stephen stay the night? will he and Bloom meet again? will he learn what Bloom can teach him?—on a psychological level, presented through the impressions of one or more of the characters. We cannot say with certainty whether Joyce ever planned a resolution in the monologue method, but the 1920 Linati schema, which probably contained his unrevised early plans for the "Nostos" episodes, suggests that he might have. (The schema implies that, until his 1921 work on the last three episodes, he planned a less ambiguous conclusion than he eventually wrote, since it labels the "Nostos" episodes the "fusion of Bloom and Stephen.") By late 1918 he must have sensed the bind he would be led into by the monologue technique, and he began to move away from the method.

The initial style was also proving inadequate to Joyce's evolving vision of his book and its characters, his art, and mankind. To the Joyce of *Dubliners* and *A Portrait of the Artist as a Young Man*, the concept of the epiphany (as expressed in *Stephen Hero*) is fundamental:

> By an epiphany he meant a sudden spiritual manifestation, whether in the vulgarity of speech or of gesture or in a memorable phase of the mind itself. He believed it was for the man of letters to record these epiphanies with extreme care, seeing that they themselves are the most delicate and evanescent of moments.[13]

The "sudden spiritual manifestation" was capable of presenting an insight of great significance for either a character or the reader, or both, and he built *Dubliners* (his "chapter of the moral history of my country"; *Letters*, II, 134) and *A Portrait of the Artist as a Young Man* (his account of an individual history) out of such intensely significant moments. Examples are the conclusion of "Two Gallants" in *Dubliners*, in which an Irish slavey gives a gold coin to her seducer in a symbolic reenactment of the betrayal of Ireland by her conquerors, and the Christmas dinner scene in Chapter I of *A Portrait of the Artist as a Young Man*, where the young Stephen Dedalus witnesses the traumatic effect of Parnell's fall from power on his family, which in the force of its opposed emotions stands for all of Ireland.

During his writing of *Ulysses*, and beyond it, Joyce's vision expanded; individual and even national history gave

[13] *Stephen Hero*, ed. Theodore Spencer (New York: New Directions, 1944, 1963), p. 211.

way to a larger view in which any specific individual or situation recreates archetypal patterns from the past. Probably aided by his rereading of Vico's *Scienza nuova* and his immersion in Homer and Homeric criticism, he came to believe that life consists of cyclically recurring forms, always repeating themselves despite altered specific settings. The epiphanies of the earlier works now served as specific manifestations of the large historical pattern. As Stephen thinks in "Scylla and Charybdis," "Hold to the now, the here, through which all future plunges to the past" (186.19-20). The unique incident, the epiphany, retains its validity, in fact achieves a more important validity, as a means through which the larger patterns reveal themselves. Thus, Stephen on the strand recognizes the objects around him as "signatures of all things I am here to read, seaspawn and seawrack, the nearing tide, that rusty boot" (37.2-4); and when Bloom descends into a twentieth-century Hades in his visit to Glasnevin Cemetery and responds with a decisive affirmation of life ("Plenty to see and hear and feel yet. Feel live warm beings near you. Let them sleep in their maggoty beds. They are not going to get me this innings. Warm beds: warm fullblooded life"; 115.6-9), he reenacts a pattern set by many epic heroes before him.

Joyce's view of the epiphany and recurring structures led him in two directions. On the one hand, he developed a broader, more inclusive mythic system. He added details with Homeric parallels; he constructed entire late episodes in mythic rather than realistic structures. On the other hand, he also became obsessed with minute details, "the now, the here" of his book's setting and characters. He added details of Bloom's life and thoughts, and names of Dublin residents, shops, and streets. (Critics have often noted that these two concerns are reflected in the subjects of two lectures Joyce gave in Trieste in 1912, Blake and Defoe.) Eventually even the epiphany concept disappeared as Joyce developed a series of narrators—the anonymous debt collector in "Cyclops," the author of a romantic novel in "Nausicaa," a succession of English prose writers in

"Oxen of the Sun"—to communicate his book's events. As a result, the focus shifts from the individual act of apprehension to the arbitrary point of view imposed on the events by Joyce's choice of narrative method. The authorial omniscience that he suppressed in the first half of *Ulysses* becomes one of the most prominent characteristics of the second half.

The Middle Stage

The radical change in Joyce's writing—from characters to correspondences, from story to structure—did not occur suddenly, nor did he plan it in advance. Rather, as he worked on the episodes following "Scylla and Charybdis," he first elaborated and played with the monologue technique; then he replaced the method with various parodic styles. After this work he was ready (even though, again, he was not aware of it) for the major new directions of his final stage of writing: the expansive, encyclopedic concerns of the last four episodes, especially "Circe" and "Ithaca," and the elaborate revisions of the earlier episodes.

To reach a point at which he could write episodes like "Circe" and "Ithaca," he needed to pass through a fairly long transitional stage of work. This middle stage involves five episodes—"Wandering Rocks," "Sirens," "Cyclops," "Nausicaa," and "Oxen of the Sun." Curiously, the structural unit these episodes constitute has been most clearly perceived by S. L. Goldberg, who rejects all five:

> The first chapters of the book carry us forward dramatically; the last bring the temporal perspectives of the whole to a final focus; but these central chapters—from "Wandering Rocks" to "Oxen of the Sun"—seem as a group merely to elaborate rather than develop, to be organized in no way more vital than the chart Mr Gilbert prints of organs, arts, colours, symbols and techniques: the kind of organization, in fact, suggested by Joyce's own declaration of intention.
>
> (Goldberg, p. 284)

Goldberg proceeds to quote the letter Joyce sent to Carlo Linati in September 1920 to accompany the first extant *Ulysses* schema:

> It is an epic of two races (Israelite-Irish) and at the same time the cycle of the human body as well as a little story of a day (life). The character of Ulysses always fascinated me—even when a boy. . . . It [*Ulysses*] is also a sort of encyclopaedia. My intention is to transpose the myth *sub specie temporis nostri*. Each adventure (that is, every hour, every organ, every art being interconnected and interrelated in the structural scheme of the whole) should not only condition but even create its own technique. Each adventure is so to say one person although it is composed of persons—as Aquinas relates of the angelic hosts.
>
> (*Letters*, I, 146-47; cf. *Selected Letters*, pp. 270-71)

Goldberg's linking of the letter with the five episodes is very shrewd, since Joyce wrote the letter shortly after he had finished "Oxen of the Sun."

As Goldberg says, these episodes do not "develop" as did the first nine; the "novel" *Ulysses* ended with "Scylla and Charybdis." The characters do make crucial decisions in these five episodes: in "Sirens" Bloom decides to follow Blazes Boylan to the Ormond Hotel but not to 7 Eccles Street; at the end of "Oxen of the Sun" he follows Stephen. However, Joyce does not present these decisions directly; rather, the sign of the book's middle stage is his use of a series of narrative techniques that are themselves as prominent and as important as the characters.

"Wandering Rocks" and "Sirens" involve variations on the monologue method. "Wandering Rocks" extends the method to characters other than Stephen and Bloom, directly to Tom Kernan, Miss Dunne, and Master Patrick Dignam, and indirectly to Father Conmee. Besides, eighteen of the nineteen sections contain interpolated passages from one or more of the other sections to indicate simultaneous events in different parts of Dublin. For the first time in the fair copy-*Little Review* version of *Ulysses* (and in

the final version for the first time since the "Aeolus" subheads), a voice distinct from that of the characters or of the
narrator clearly announces himself through both the new
monologue subjects and the interpolations.

"Sirens" plays with the monologue technique far beyond
the relatively limited experiment of "Wandering Rocks."
After the startling overture/prelude/list of motifs, Joyce fil-
ters the initial style through a musical structure; the result
is far different from the variations in metaphor and
rhythm among the first nine episodes. The musical
metaphor dominates Bloom's interior monologue; occasionally Joyce even alters the appearance of Bloom's
thoughts on the page to fit the pattern: "Her
wavyavyeavyheavyeavyevyevy hair un comb: 'd" (277.31).[14]
More often, though, Joyce leaves Bloom's monologue intact and the narrator asserts his independence far more
defiantly than even in "Scylla and Charybdis":

> Miss Douce, engaging, Lydia Douce, bowed to suave
> solicitor, George Lidwell, gentleman, entering. Good af-
> ternoon. She gave her moist, a lady's, hand to his firm
> clasp. Afternoon. Yes, she was back. To the old
> dingdong again.
> —Your friends are inside, Mr Lidwell.
> George Lidwell, suave, solicited, held a lydiahand.
> Bloom ate liv as said before. Clean here at least. That
> chap in the Burton, gummy with gristle. No-one here:
> Goulding and I. Clean tables, flowers, mitres of napkins.
> Pat to and fro, bald Pat. Nothing to do. Best value in
> Dub. (270.42-271.9)

[14] Originally Joyce left Bloom's monologue intact. In the fair copy
Bloom's thought of Molly is simply "Hair uncombed" (MS, "Sirens," fols.
27-28). Marilyn French discusses this passage in her very interesting book
on the relationship between *Ulysses'* styles and its meanings. See *The Book
as World: James Joyce's* Ulysses (Cambridge: Harvard Univ. Press, 1976),
pp. 128-30 and *passim*. Her study, much more extensive than mine in this
chapter, comes to different conclusions, but she and I offer similar
analyses of several episodes' styles and of the broad movement of *Ulysses*
through its styles.

In "Sirens" Joyce takes advantage of several aspects of authorial omniscient powers precluded by the restraints of the initial style. For one thing, the "Sirens" narrator begins to assume the reader's familiarity with earlier episodes. The first nine episodes seem to be self-contained units, with the narrator reporting only the situation immediately at hand (Bloom's and Stephen's thoughts, of course, constantly refer to incidents in earlier episodes); but the "Sirens" narrator asserts himself as part of a larger whole.[15] For example, a sentence in the preceding quotation, "Bloom ate liv as said before," refers to an earlier passage in "Sirens" that itself recalls the first paragraph of "Calypso":

> Pat served uncovered dishes. Leopold cut liverslices. As said before he ate with relish the inner organs, nutty gizzards, fried cods' roes while Richie Goulding, Collis, Ward ate steak and kidney, steak then kidney, bite by bite of pie he ate Bloom ate they ate.
>
> (269.33-37)

The "Sirens" narrator not only appropriates earlier passages of narration; he also makes use of spoken words and phrases. For example, in "Wandering Rocks," after Tom Rochford asks Lenehan to mention his new invention to Boylan, he says to Lenehan, "Tell him I'm Boylan with impatience" (232.25-26). The "Sirens" narrator picks up this phrase and uses it as a motif for Boylan: "With patience Lenehan waited for Boylan with impatience, for jingle jaunty blazes boy" (263.25-26); "—I'm off, said Boylan with impatience" (267.9; see also 269.42-270.1, 276.23). The phrase, of course, does apply to Boylan, who is "off" to

---

[15] "Wandering Rocks" contains adumbrations of this technique. One of the linked elements is the "Elijah is coming" announcement that Bloom threw into the Liffey in "Lestrygonians" (227.6-10, 240.14-16, 249.33-36; 151.6-19, 152.28-31); references to it repeat its language. And, when the "Wandering Rocks" narrator lists Lydia Douce and Mina Kennedy among the viewers of the viceregal cavalcade, he uses the language of the upcoming "Sirens" episode (252.29-31).

Molly Bloom's bed, as does Lenehan's question to Boylan, "Got the horn or what?" which the narrator likewise appropriates as a motif for Boylan (267.15, 270.1-2, 289.34-35). Several additional phrases from other parts of *Ulysses* occur in "Sirens," not as motifs but as single recurrences. Bloom's uncertainty in "Calypso" about the name of an instrument ("Strings. Listen. A girl playing one of these instruments what do you call them: dulcimers"; 57.31-32) becomes part of the "Sirens" narration ("Through the hush of air a voice sang to them, low, not rain, not leaves in murmur, like no voice of strings of reeds or whatdoyoucallthem dulcimers . . . "; 273.40-42; the phrase "What do you call it" is used for another uncertain word, "Gossamer," at 374.40-41 and 414.35). The narrator similarly uses Stephen's "Aeolus" epithet for Admiral Nelson, "the onehandled adulterer" (148.9), as he describes Boylan's progress from the Ormond to Eccles Street (276.18-19), and he employs a phrase of Tom Kernan's, which Jack Power talks about (91.7) and Kernan uses in his brief monologue (241.4), to describe Kernan: "harking back in a retrospective sort of arrangement" (277.18-19). (The phrase can serve as one of Joyce's indirect comments on his own method in *Ulysses*. After this appearance in "Sirens," it becomes a minor motif as it recurs in different voices: in the Lamb segment of "Oxen of the Sun" [413.4-5], in Bloom's flirtation with Josie Breen during a "Circe" fantasy [444.22], and in the voices of the narrators of "Eumaeus" [651.39] and "Ithaca" [724.24].) Finally, the narrator twice appropriates dialogue from "Wandering Rocks" and uses it in "Sirens": "—So sad to look at his [the blind piano tuner's] face, Miss Douce condoled. / God's curse on bitch's bastard" (263.19-20; cf. 250.18-19, 284.14, and 286.2), and "He ambled Dollard, bulky slops, before them (hold that fellow with the: hold him now) into the saloon" (267.35-36; cf. 244.22-24).

The most startling use of this technique produces an apparent violation of character. Bloom questions the postscript to his letter to Martha Clifford, "I feel so sad today":

Too poetical that about the sad. Music did that. Music hath charms Shakespeare said. Quotations every day in the year. To be or not to be. Wisdom while you wait.

In Gerard's rosery of Fetter lane he walks, greyed-auburn. One life is all. One body. Do. But do.

Done anyhow. Postal order stamp. Postoffice lower down. Walk now. Enough. . . .

(280.23-29)

The middle paragraph is striking in this context, since it previously occurred in Stephen's thoughts in "Scylla and Charybdis" (202.9-13). It is certainly a problem in "Sirens" if it is meant to be in Bloom's mind, but more likely it represents another announcement by the narrator of his own power to make connections between elements in the book, in this case between one cuckolded man and another.[16] It is an assertion of the narrator's independence, his freedom to use any material already part of the book and to make any connections or juxtapositions he chooses.

By the end of "Sirens" Joyce had distorted his initial style about as much as possible while still retaining it, and his decision to replace it followed almost immediately; the technique, as well as Emmet's speech and Bloom's fart, is "Done" (291.13). He dropped the style very early in his work on the next episode, "Cyclops," and the decision was final: he resurrected the method only in the second half of "Nausicaa," where it joins the variety of styles with which he filled the three episodes of "Cyclops," "Nausicaa," and "Oxen of the Sun." (Joyce ended *Ulysses* with one more

---

[16] Critics have often discussed the "Fetter lane" passage. Robert M. Adams considers the presence of Stephen's thought in Bloom's mind "an arbitrary authorial intrusion, perhaps an authorial accident" (*Surface and Symbol*, p. 98). However, Adams supports his claim of an "accident" with an account of the passage's first appearance on the Buffalo page proofs (p. 99), all of which is completely wrong. Joyce added it, out of context, to the earliest extant "Sirens" draft (Buffalo MS V.A.5, p. 27v), and although it is not in the fair copy of "Sirens" (MS, fol. 31), it is in the typescript (Buffalo TS V.B.9, pp. 16-17) and in the *Little Review* (6, iv [Aug. 1919], p. 64). See Arnold Goldman's review of *Surface and Symbol* in *Essays in Criticism*, 13 (1963), pp. 288-89.

monologue, not a return to the initial style but a pure monologue with no third-person narrator.) The middle stage thus consists of Joyce's two elaborations of his original monologue style and his first three ventures beyond the monologue.

To supplant the initial style Joyce first turned to a succession of new voices: an unnamed debt collector; the writers of legal briefs, newspaper reports and features, and scientific accounts; the authoress of a romantic Victorian novel; the great prose writers in English literary history. Just as he psychologically needed to write his play *Exiles* to work out the problems of his own jealousy before he could create Leopold Bloom, a character who could accept his wife's infidelity with "more abnegation than jealousy, less envy than equanimity" (733.25-26; see Litz, p. 4), so now he turned to a series of literary and sub-literary parodies before he attempted to create new styles in the last four episodes.

Freed from the constrictions of the interior monologue, Joyce obviously delighted in the creation of these parodies. His letters, primarily to Frank Budgen, contain elaborate descriptions of his developing episodes; he summarized "Cyclops," with brief excerpts (*Letters*, I, 126); described "Nausicaa" as "written in a namby-pamby jammy marmalady drawersy (alto là!) style with effects of incense, mariolatry, masturbation, stewed cockles, painter's palette, chitchat, circumlocutions, etc. etc." (I, 135); and outlined "Oxen of the Sun" in terms of its parody sources (with examples), interlinkings with earlier episodes, and main symbols (I, 139-40). These are also the first episodes for which large groups of notesheets have survived; Joyce may have accompanied his technical changes with a new, more elaborate process of notetaking to precede his writing.[17]

---

[17] Phillip F. Herring, editor of the British Museum notesheets, believes that sheets probably did exist for earlier episodes (*Notesheets*, p. 4). It is a curious coincidence, though, that notesheets have survived only for the last seven, the most elaborate, episodes. I suspect that, although Joyce must have prepared and used isolated sheets of notes or small notebooks for the earlier episodes (such as Buffalo MS VIII.A.5, in *Notes and Early*

In "Cyclops," "Nausicaa," and "Oxen of the Sun," he plays with various "translations" of his story. Each narrator exhibits a different method of telling a story—the "I" of "Cyclops" presents a first-person account, Gerty's half of "Nausicaa" uses an indirect report of a single character's thoughts, and "Oxen of the Sun" contains a collection of different narrative styles. Like the extension of the monologues to new characters in "Wandering Rocks" and the musical form of "Sirens," each successive narration undermines the realistic substructure built up in the first nine episodes, though the substructure never entirely disappears, as the return of Bloom's monologue reminds us. We know from the momentum of the opening episodes that a continuing story is taking place, but it now proceeds through a series of semi-transparent screens that clash with the patterns and rhythms to which we have grown accustomed until now.

Two misconceptions are possible regarding these episodes as translations of Joyce's story. For one thing, he did not first write out the story lines and then redo the episodes in alien styles. The progress from the early drafts to the final versions of these episodes is one of increased complexity rather than a change of style: the story and the manner of telling it developed together. In "Cyclops," in fact, he apparently began with the parodies and then worked on the incidents in the pub and the first-person narrator. Second, translation does not mean that the style represents an impediment to our understanding of some real action, an intrusion we should get around or beneath. These episodes contain a tension (both Goldman, approvingly, and Goldberg, disapprovingly, call it a "gap" [Goldman, p. 83; Goldberg, p. 281]) between the narrated events and the method of narration. But we must remember Hugh Kenner's summary of the strange verbal juxtapositions in "Sirens":

Drafts, pp. 1-33), he did not do so to such an obsessive extent, or depend on them as greatly, as in the last seven episodes.

Things are not talked about, they happen in the prose. Appropriate exegesis does not consist in transposing the allegorical to the propositional, but in detailed apprehension of the rich concrete particularity of what has been placed before our eyes.[18]

Clive Hart has made a less abstract but similar argument about "Oxen of the Sun":

We see Stephen and Bloom as they might have been at other periods of history, and as they might have appeared to other authors. It is a mistake to try continually to "read through" the style. The present is never forgotten, but the past is there also.[19]

Each narrator in these episodes idiosyncratically reports what he sees in front of him; only two, the debt collector in "Cyclops" and the initial-style narrator in Bloom's half of "Nausicaa" (who, like the narrator of "Proteus," serves primarily as an adjunct to the interior monologue), possess any previous information about the characters. This gives the impression of yet another fresh start as the action we have already witnessed now appears through a series of vastly different, often contradictory, styles.

Because these styles, with only one exception, preclude access to Bloom's and Stephen's minds, these three episodes partake very little of the intricate web of cross-references and correspondences that dominates the first eleven and last four episodes. However, there are a few places where such cross-references do filter into the narratives. All occur in "Oxen of the Sun." Phrases from earlier episodes occasionally show through the narration (like the "Aeolus" subheads, most are planted by the voice behind the narrator) to indicate the presence of specific characters:

Then spoke young Stephen orgulous of mother Church

[18] *Dublin's Joyce* (1956; rpt. Boston: Beacon, 1962), p. 153.
[19] *James Joyce's* Ulysses (Sydney: Sydney Univ. Press, 1968), p. 69.

that would cast him out of her bosom, of law of canons, of Lilith, patron of abortions, of bigness wrought by wind of seeds of brightness or by potency of vampires mouth to mouth. . . .

(389.42-390.3; cf. 132.12-15)[20]

Sometimes, a process like that in "Sirens" occurs, as words or phrases that formed part of a character's thoughts or were spoken by another narrator now become part of the "Oxen of the Sun" narration:

It is she, Martha, thou lost one, Millicent, the young, the dear, the radiant. How serene does she now arise, a queen among the Pleiades, in the penultimate antelucan hour, shod in sandals of bright gold, coifed with a veil of what do you call it gossamer!

(414.31-35; cf. 275.35-39, 374.40-41)[21]

For the most part, though, these narrators exist as if they had no connection with the rest of the book.

We can best study Joyce's technique in the episodes of the middle stage by analyzing a specific example and comparing it to passages about a similar topic from earlier episodes. In "Oxen of the Sun," the first episode in which Bloom and Stephen actually meet, there are representations of Bloom's paternal thoughts regarding Stephen. One occurs in an imitation of Malory:

But sir Leopold was passing grave maugre his word by cause he still had pity of the terrorcausing shrieking of shrill women in their labour and as he was minded of his good lady Marion that had borne him an only manchild which on his eleventh day on live had died and no man of art could save so dark is destiny. And she was wondrous stricken of heart for that evil hap and for his bur-

---

[20] Other examples are Lenehan's "Expecting each moment to be her next" (388.6-7; cf. 338.4) and Bloom's thoughts of "his dame Mrs Moll with red slippers on" (397.28; cf. 381.11-12).

[21] Also Bloom as "the meekest man and the kindest that ever laid husbandly hand under hen" (388.12-13; cf. 315.20-25).

ial did him on a fair corselet of lamb's wool, the flower of
the flock, lest he might perish utterly and lie akeled (for
it was then about the midst of the winter) and now sir
Leopold that had of his body no manchild for an heir
looked upon him his friend's son and was shut up in sorrow for his forepassed happiness and as sad as he was
that him failed a son of such gentle courage (for all ac-
counted him of real parts) so grieved he also in no less
measure for young Stephen for that he lived riotously
with those wastrels and murdered his goods with whores.

(390.28-391.2)

Bloom has remembered his dead son Rudy several times
before this, and at one point in "Hades" he links these
thoughts to Simon Dedalus:

Noisy selfwilled man. Full of his son. He is right. Something to hand on. If little Rudy had lived. See him grow
up. Hear his voice in the house. Walking beside Molly in
an Eton suit. My son. Me in his eyes. Strange feeling it
would be. From me. . . . I could have helped him on in
life. I could. Make him independent. Learn German too.

(89.2-6, 13-14)

Later, the song that Ben Dollard sings in the Ormond bar,
"The Croppy Boy," inspires similar thoughts:

All gone. All fallen. At the siege of Ross his father, at
Gorey all his brothers fell. To Wexford, we are the boys
of Wexford, he would. Last of his name and race.
I too, last my race. Milly young student. Well, my fault
perhaps. No son. Rudy. Too late now. Or if not? If not?
If still?
He bore no hate.
Hate. Love. Those are names. Rudy. Soon I am old.

(285.1-8)

The two early passages are among the most moving in
Ulysses; their pathos derives from Joyce's startling use of
very simple words: "My son. Me in his eyes. . . . From me."

(This is Bloom's equivalent of Stephen's more intellectual definition of fatherhood: "a mystical estate, an apostolic succession, from only begetter to only begotten"; 207.21-22.) Unlike Simon Dedalus in his reaction to his wife's death, Bloom refuses to sentimentalize the major loss in his life; his mind quickly moves from Rudy to the very alive Molly and Milly—"Molly. Milly. Same thing watered down. . . . Yes, yes: a woman too. Life. Life" (89.18-21). For the reader, the passage avoids sentimentality because of Bloom's idiosyncratic plans for Rudy, including the Eton suit and the German lessons. Joyce thus allows Bloom the dignity of his sorrow while he invites us to laugh at the comedy of his unique ideas.

In the later "Sirens" passage, Joyce exhibits greater technical virtuosity, but his principle within Bloom's monologue is still one of compression. As in "Hades," Bloom's mind responds to an external stimulus. There it was Simon's conversation; here it is Ben Dollard's singing of "The Croppy Boy." The passage merges words from the song with Bloom's reactions; it presents the song as Bloom's mind processes it. At this point Dollard is singing the fifth and seventh stanzas:

> "At the siege of Ross did my father fall,
> And at Gorey my loving brothers all,
> I alone am left of my name and race,
> I will go to Wexford and take their place.
>
> "I bear no grudge against living thing. . . ."[22]

Following Dollard's singing, Bloom's thoughts about a son rise to a climax ("Too late now. Or if not? If not? If still?"), at which point Joyce merges Bloom, the father deprived of a son, and the Croppy Boy, the son about to die, in words that apply equally to both, "He bore no hate." The other men in the Ormond bar sentimentalize their own and Ireland's failures by becoming "lost in pity" while Dollard

---

[22] Weldon Thornton, *Allusions in* Ulysses: *An Annotated List* (Chapel Hill: Univ. of North Carolina Press, 1968), p. 502. Dollard apparently sings "hate" rather than "grudge" in the last quoted line.

sings the song (286.19), but Bloom again avoids such a reaction through his own kind of logic: "Instance enthusiasts. All ears. . . . Thinking strictly prohibited. Always talking shop. Fiddlefaddle about notes" (288.24, 26-27).

The "Oxen of the Sun" passage is obviously very different. Because of the early episodes, we clearly recognize the sequence of thoughts as Bloom's: the concern for women in childbirth, the transition to Rudy and Molly, the connection between one son, Rudy, and another, Stephen. The passage's last section represents a crucial point in the development of Bloom's recognition of Stephen as a son, a process that culminates with Bloom's vision of Rudy while Stephen lies prostrate at the end of "Circe."

Clearly the passage depicts only part of Bloom's mind. Since the narrator desires to represent a smooth, unbroken sequence of thoughts, he eliminates the many facts, details, and twists of reasoning that clutter Bloom's mind. The passage requires many more words to say much less than those in "Hades" and "Sirens." Clive Hart has called the sequence of narrators in "Oxen of the Sun" a technique wherein "Stephen and Bloom are revealed in a succession of different lights and their potential significance is revealed for past times as well as for the present."[23] This is an excellent approach to the episode, ultimately more fruitful than the "embryonic development" of Joyce's nine-month pattern,[24] if we include the ironic possibilities inherent in such a series of juxtapositions. The passage that attempts to depict Bloom's thoughts about Rudy and Stephen reveals the degree to which Joyce's modern story of Ulysses can be narrated in older styles and the degree to which the narration and the story are hopelessly divergent, a set of dual purposes characteristic of the middle stage of Joyce's work.

By presenting his continuing story through a succession of styles, mostly parodic, Joyce accomplishes several things.

[23] *James Joyce's* Ulysses, p. 69.
[24] See the 1921 Schema; *Letters*, I, 139-40; and A. M. Klein, "The Oxen of the Sun," *Here and Now*, 1 (1949), pp. 28-48.

On the one hand, he shows each individual style's limited ability to convey the story's complexities. In the passage from "Oxen of the Sun," the conventions of the heroic style impose onto the situation attitudes and points of view that we know are not those of the characters; for example, neither "so dark is destiny" nor "that evil hap" accurately expresses Bloom's attitude toward the forces that resulted in Rudy's death. Similarly, "a son of such gentle courage" hardly represents the qualities Bloom admires in Stephen, the "professor and author" (735.25-26) who could teach Molly Italian and earn a living by writing for the newspapers. In both cases Joyce translates Bloom's attitudes into a mental and stylistic universe very different from Bloom's own. From the point of view of the attitudes implied by the heroic style, Bloom is inevitably diminished—Rudy armed with a knowledge of German is not a son "of real parts," whatever they may be—but the style with its corresponding attitudes is itself reduced because of its inability to present more than a fragment of Leopold Bloom.

Both Bloom and the heroic style are satirized when they are violently yoked together, but there is also a positive side to the juxtaposition. To some extent, as Clive Hart notes, Bloom's story can indeed be narrated through the heroic style, since Joyce has created modern equivalents for the details of an heroic plot. Besides this, the juxtaposition has a positive value since it seems to eliminate our expectation that the story needs to be told with the interior monologue technique and its excursions into Bloom's and Stephen's minds. The parody styles can do this because, their individual limitations notwithstanding, together they reveal that Joyce's modern story is sufficiently flexible and universal to survive, and in fact to be enlarged by, a parade of different styles and narrative methods.

These techniques are indeed an "intellectualization of structure," as Goldberg charges (p. 281), but Goldberg's condemnation is justified only if we accept his claim that the life of *Ulysses* must lie in its characters and its human drama. Joyce changed his focus of interest from his charac-

ters to his styles, knowing that the first nine episodes provided support to sustain the characters as much as necessary through the successive elaborations. In the middle
stage Joyce wanted both to continue his story and to enlarge the scope of narration. As much "happens" in "Cyclops," "Nausicaa," and "Oxen of the Sun" as in most of the
early episodes. (Only after "Circe," as the book moves toward its conclusion, does "action" diminish until it practically disappears. This is a mark of Joyce's last stage of
work.) Yet the events in the middle-stage episodes occur
within styles dominated by other concerns, such as a debt
collector's attitudes toward Bloom (and everything else
around him) or the world view of Gerty MacDowell. Joyce
needed to continue the sequence of events while he began
to distance the narration from the events; only when he
achieved and then exhausted this new relationship was he
ready to dispense almost entirely with the characters' actions as his book's major reality.

The middle-stage episodes thus represent a midpoint between the compression of the early episodes and the encyclopedic expansion of the last ones. They reveal Joyce balanced between two goals, because they are products of the
period in his work on *Ulysses* when he sought an accommo-
dation between the story and the symbols (a "both/and"
approach which seems to me the most fruitful critical one
to *Ulysses*). Just as "Aeolus" (in its final form) looks like a
late episode while it remains for the most part an early one,
so the passages of "gigantism" in "Cyclops," with their
exaggerations and seemingly endless lists, and the succession of authors parodied in "Oxen of the Sun" make the
group of episodes made up of "Cyclops," "Nausicaa," and
"Oxen of the Sun" seem like the full encyclopedic ex-
travaganzas of "Circe" and "Ithaca," whereas actually they
are relatively restrained. In texture they tend to be loose
and rambling; they achieve their encyclopedic dimension
primarily in their cumulative effect. They represent Joyce's
attempt to filter his story through established forms of narration (including his own initial style), always distorted by

his instinct for parody. The fully controlled *tour de force* of "Oxen of the Sun," which he apparently wrote without major complications (though it required a thousand hours; *Letters*, II, 465) and which he later revised very little, culminates this process. It is hardly surprising that, after spending so much time and energy parodying other styles, he was finally prepared to move on to new styles of his own.

The Last Stage

Joyce did not plan the end of the middle stage in advance; it came about during his early work on "Circe." His notesheets, drafts, and revisions on the typescripts and proofs reveal a man always searching for a well-defined controlling order, but the episodes after "Oxen of the Sun" often refused to remain within the ordering design he planned for them. These episodes, especially "Circe" and "Ithaca," took him much longer to write than he expected, and he found himself elaborating them far beyond his original intentions. His work on "Circe" was crucial; he seems to have begun it as an episode similar in scope and length to the previous three, but by the time he finished it he had left the middle stage behind for new developments.

Both in new work and in revision, his last stage of work is marked by his goals of expansion and elaboration. The last four episodes exceed the others in length and range of reference, and carry to new extremes his interests in both realistic and symbolic details. His well-known revision of earlier episodes occurred almost exclusively during this stage—he added many new Homeric and other correspondences to the earlier episodes, and he "recast," "amplified," or "retouched" them to resemble the later ones more closely (*Letters*, I, 172). The schemata he prepared during this stage and offered to selected friends as guides to his book serve as emblems of his last period of work on *Ulysses*.

Joyce wrote the final episodes in pairs—"Circe" with "Eumaeus" and "Ithaca" with "Penelope"—with "Eumaeus" and "Penelope" balancing the more demanding work of the two longer and more diverse episodes. He wrote "Eumaeus" fairly quickly during the several months needed for the typing of "Circe." In depicting Bloom's exhaustion, he created the late episode that most closely resembles the middle-stage parodies, but there is a significant post-Circean difference. Whereas "Cyclops," "Nausicaa," and "Oxen of the Sun" contain externally intruded narrative styles, "Eumaeus" attempts to be an internally evolved narration, a literary equivalent of the state of Bloom's mind at 1:00 A.M. It is not a parody, even though it often becomes as wildly humorous and occasionally as tedious as the conscious parodies. Beyond these differences, "Eumaeus" progresses in about the same way as the middle-stage episodes.

"Penelope" was more complicated, but it presented far fewer difficulties than did "Ithaca," which Joyce wrote at the same time. Molly's monologue, the "indispensable countersign" (*Letters*, I, 160) to the portrait of Bloom, presents both facts and attitudes without which the enormous picture of Bloom from his own and the many extrinsic points of view would remain decidedly incomplete. As "Penelope" is a return after many literary and scientific viewpoints to a human one ("human, all too human," Joyce wrote; *Letters*, I, 160), so it presents another monologue. This one extends beyond the initial style, though, as it gives the illusion of being a pure monologue, the stream of consciousness itself, unencumbered by any objective narrative statements. Without punctuation, seemingly (but not actually) without structure at all,[25] "Penelope" provides an effective contrast to the obsessively ordered questions and answers of *Ulysses'* other ending, "Ithaca." And perhaps, as

[25] That Joyce carefully constructed the eight sentences of "Penelope," linking sentences 1 and 8, 2 and 7, 3 and 6, and 4 and 5, has been demonstrated by Diane Tolomeo, "The Final Octagon of *Ulysses*," *James Joyce Quarterly*, 10 (1973), pp. 439-54, esp. p. 450. Joyce's pattern of linked sentences resembles the design David Hayman discovered among the first six episodes.

an episode of circles, "Penelope" loops back (with variations) to the monologue method that began *Ulysses*.

Joyce could have written "Eumaeus" and "Penelope" with only slight adjustments from his work on "Cyclops," "Nausicaa," and "Oxen of the Sun." "Circe" and "Ithaca," however, represent major changes, the origin of which seems to be his mining of his earlier episodes for the "Circe" hallucinations, his attempt to include in "Circe" the people and ideas that have been a part of Bloom's and Stephen's day, either in actuality or in thought. (See, for example, the list of characters on "Circe" notesheets 20 and 21.) As he brought together more and more material from the earlier parts of the book, he also expanded the middle-stage technique of re-using material from the earlier narrators as well as from the characters' minds. By the time he finished "Circe" he had included so much previous material that, in addition to the characters' psyches, *Ulysses* itself was turned inside-out.[26]

This occurrence marked a major change in Joyce's attitude toward his work. Instead of imposing extrinsic forms of narration on his material to extend the viewpoints from which the events can be seen, he began to reorder the various arrangements that the events themselves could form. As Arnold Goldman has said, "By its fifteenth chapter, *Ulysses* has begun to provide its author enough in the way of material to become self-perpetuating" (Goldman, p. 99). The middle-stage episodes provided Joyce with enough experience away from the monologue technique to make possible the upheaval such self-perpetuation involved.

A. Walton Litz has summarized the process: "The 'reality' to be processed into art is both the imitated human action and the rich artistic world already created in the ear-

[26] "As *Ulysses* is the *Odyssey* transposed and rearranged, 'Circe' is *Ulysses* transposed and rearranged." Hugh Kenner, "Circe," in *James Joyce's Ulysses: Critical Essays*, ed. Clive Hart and David Hayman (Berkeley and Los Angeles: Univ. of California Press, 1974), p. 356.

lier and plainer episodes."[27] Joyce begins to exploit this
"world" fully in "Circe" to such an extent that *Ulysses* itself
becomes one great "character"; like the strands of thought
in Bloom's and Stephen's minds, any themes or correspondences in *Ulysses* become usable sources of new juxtapositions or cross-references. Critics have often noted
that there are numerous violations of character in "Circe";
for example, *"nebrakada femininum,"* a phrase Stephen
reads in a book in "Wandering Rocks" (242.41), appears in
one of Bloom's "Circe" hallucinations (440.2), and "Bello"
alludes to Shakespeare's "secondbest bed" (543.21), which
has previously appeared only in Stephen's episode, "Scylla
and Charybdis" (203.22-30). In "Circe" Joyce further
reorders the world of *Ulysses* by making associations and
connections that lie beyond the characters altogether and
involve only the book's styles. For example, as Zoe reads
Bloom's hand to tell his fortune, she says, "Short little finger. Henpecked husband," and "Black Liz," a hen that appeared in a passage of "Cyclops" gigantism (itself a response to one of the narrator's unspoken opinions), now
appears sexually transformed into a female rooster
(563.3-10; cf. 315.20-25). Likewise, John Wyse Nolan appears in one of Bloom's fantasies dressed in an "Irish National Forester's uniform" (547.24-25), an association based
only on the parodic newspaper account of his marriage to
Miss Fir Conifer (327.1-36; in a parody passage that Joyce
originally wrote for "Cyclops" but later deleted, Nolan appeared in the forester's uniform). In listing and discussing
some of these examples, Arnold Goldman concludes that
they are based on information "solely available to the narrator" and that "cross-referencing . . . here takes on an appearance of autonomy" (Goldman, pp. 98-99).

Two examples from "Circe," one from an hallucinatory
sequence and one from "reality," will show this autonomy:

[27] "Ithaca," in *James Joyce's* Ulysses: *Critical Essays*, ed. Hart and
Hayman, p. 386.

J. J. O'MOLLOY

(*Almost voicelessly.*) Excuse me, I am suffering from a severe chill, have recently come from a sickbed. A few wellchosen words. (*He assumes the avine head, foxy moustache and proboscidal eloquence of Seymour Bushe.*) When the angel's book comes to be opened if aught that the pensive bosom has inaugurated of soultransfigured and of soultransfiguring deserves to live I say accord the prisoner at the bar the sacred benefit of the doubt. (*A paper with something written on it is handed into court.*)

BLOOM

(*In court dress.*) Can give best references. Messrs Callan, Coleman. Mr Wisdom Hely J. P. My old chief Joe Cuffe. Mr V. B. Dillon, ex-lord mayor of Dublin. I have moved in the charmed circle of the highest . . . Queens of Dublin Society. (*Carelessly.*) I was just chatting this afternoon at the viceregal lodge to my old pals, sir Robert and lady Ball, astronomer royal, at the levee. Sir Bob, I said . . .

MRS YELVERTON BARRY

(*In lowcorsaged opal balldress and elbowlength ivory gloves, wearing a sabletrimmed brick quilted dolman, a comb of brilliants and panache of osprey in her hair.*) Arrest him constable. He wrote me an anonymous letter in prentice backhand when my husband was in the North Riding of Tipperary on the Munster circuit, signed James Lovebirch. He said that he had seen from the gods my peerless globes as I sat in a box of the *Theatre Royal* at a command performance of *La Cigale*. I deeply inflamed him, he said. He made improper overtures to me to misconduct myself at half past four p.m. on the following Thursday, Dunsink time. He offered to send me through the post a work of fiction by Monsieur Paul de Kock, entitled *The Girl with the Three Pairs of Stays*.

(465.1-32)

This passage occurs in Bloom's second major hallucination, his trial for sexual misconduct. Bloom's own "best references" include people he has known and those who have merely entered his mind throughout the day, among them Sir Robert Ball, whose book first inspired Bloom's thoughts about the meaning of "parallax" (154.5-7; Bloom owns the book, as we learn at 708.27). Mrs. Yelverton Barry's accusations also repeat several of Bloom's earlier thoughts—the ogling she mentions resembles his attempts in "Lotus Eaters" to watch a society lady (73.32ff), not to mention his enjoyment of the sight of Gerty's bloomers. At the "Wandering Rocks" bookstall, he saw a book by James Lovebirch (235.37-38), and Molly asked for a new book by Paul de Kock (64.39). The most important element of Mrs. Yelverton Barry's charge is the time, 4:30 on a Thursday, the moment he became a cuckold: "Was that just when he, she?" (370.6).

The second and third speeches thus link material from Bloom's perceptions or thoughts at various times during the day. The first speech, though, does something different. It stems from Bloom's musings about J. J. O'Molloy during "Aeolus": "Cleverest fellow at the junior bar he used to be. Decline poor chap" (125.2-3). However, both the description of O'Molloy and his words involve a pastiche of "Aeolus" itself, not of Bloom's thoughts, since they merge the three orators (Dan Dawson, Seymour Bushe, and John F. Taylor) and their speeches that are read or recalled in the newspaper office, the last two after Bloom has departed.

It appears that in "Circe" Joyce wished to maintain a certain degree of psychological verisimilitude, since most (though not all) of the fantasies and hallucinations can be assigned to either Stephen or Bloom and many of the details result from previous incidents or thoughts, but his intentions clearly go beyond this. It does not matter in the J. J. O'Molloy speech if the specific details are accessible to Bloom's mind. These hallucinations are meant to occur instantaneously (Joyce carefully indicates that Bloom's dreams of glory, all twenty pages, occur between Zoe's un-interrupted words to him, "Go on. Make a stump speech out of it" and "Talk away till you're black in the face"; 478.6, 499.9), and they serve as literary equivalents of what sudden rushes of impressions might be like in Bloom's mind.

A slightly different situation exists in the scenes of "realistic" events. For example, Zoe invites Bloom into Bella Cohen's brothel:

ZOE

(*She pats him offhandedly with velvet paws.*) Are you coming into the musicroom to see our new pianola? Come and I'll peel off.

BLOOM

(*Feeling his occiput dubiously with the unparalleled embarrass-ment of a harassed pedlar gauging the symmetry of her peeled pears.*) Somebody would be dreadfully jealous if she knew. The greeneyed monster. (*Earnestly.*) You know how difficult it is. I needn't tell you.

ZOE

(*Flattered.*) What the eye can't see the heart can't grieve for. (*She pats him.*) Come.

(500.11-23)

Here the speaker of the stage directions (who, unlike the initial-style narrator, neither represents Bloom's mind nor even accompanies his thoughts) appropriates Bloom's "Aeolus" recollection of Martin Cunningham's "spell-ingbee conundrum" (121.11-17), lifts it out of context, and uses it in a stage direction to communicate Bloom's embar-rassment.[28] Similarly, as *Ulysses* in general causes its charac-

---

[28] The speaker of the stage directions also appropriates language from earlier narrators, such as those of "Sirens" (433.33-434.1) and "Nausicaa" (521.6-7).

ters to repeat patterns with which they are not familiar, so the scenes of small talk between Bloom and Zoe contain dialogue from Swift's *Polite Conversation*,[29] a work certainly beyond the experience of either Bloom or Zoe.

These violations of character do not mean that the story of *Ulysses* is lost or that Joyce so rearranged his work that the original relationships disappear. Indeed, "Circe" presents one of the two climaxes of *Ulysses*, as Bloom ends his search for a son. The hallucinations force both Bloom and Stephen to face directly their worst anxieties and fears— for Bloom, this means Molly's adultery and his own masochistic tendencies; for Stephen, it means his mother's death and his refusal to grant her last wish. Joyce sets up the hallucinations as if they should serve to purge these fears ("Circe" has often been compared to the *Walpurgisnacht* scene of Goethe's *Faust*), but Stephen is too drunk and Bloom probably too tired for any significant revelations to take place except Bloom's final recognition while Stephen lies unconscious. The hallucinations ultimately exist for Joyce and the reader as both achieve a position quite removed from the characters.

Joyce's work on "Circe" was crucial in the development of *Ulysses* for a reason beyond the self-perpetuation of the book that it engendered. While writing it he revised and augmented the earlier episodes for the first time. He had probably begun to accumulate details for such revision as soon as he sent off the typescript of each episode for the *Little Review* publication. However, only in this last stage did he augment his earlier work to such an extent that some sections grew by as much as a third after the printer began to pull proofs for the book. It may seem surprising, given the final results, that the attitude that characterized the revising was caution. At first he added small details, usually new Homeric or other correspondences, and only very late in his work did he add huge amounts of new ma-

[29] See Mackie L. Jarrell, "Joyce's Use of Swift's *Polite Conversation* in the 'Circe' Episode of *Ulysses*," *PMLA*, 72 (1957), pp. 545-54.

terial. The "Aeolus" subheads, for example, did not enter until August 1921, and Joyce's letter to Harriet Shaw Weaver of October 7, 1921, not only summarized his revisions but indicated the work he had done as recently as the previous five or six weeks:

> *Eolus* is recast. *Hades* and the *Lotus-eaters* much amplified and the other episodes retouched a good deal. Not much change has been made in the *Telemachia* (the first three episodes of the book).
>
> *(Letters,* I, 172)

If these revisions represent one result of "Circe" 's transforming powers, "Ithaca" is the other. Like "Circe," "Ithaca" developed far beyond Joyce's expectations while he was writing it. About six months before he began to work seriously on it, he described its technique in such early-stage terms as "dialogue, pacified style, fusion" (Linati Schema); his conception of the "mathematico-astronomico-physico-mechanico-geometrico-chemico sublimation of Bloom and Stephen" *(Letters,* I, 164) apparently occurred only as he began to gather material for the episode.

"Circe" destroyed the line between the parts of *Ulysses* that belong to the characters and those that belong to the narration, and it made the entire book a vast scheme of references and correspondences that could be linked in new juxtapositions. "Ithaca" begins with this new relationship and moves on from it. Joyce described the episode's technique as "catechism (impersonal)," balancing the "catechism (personal)" of "Nestor" (1921 Schema). The linking of these two episodes reveals a structural parallel between the first and last episodes, although the parallel calls attention more to the vast differences in their techniques than to their similarities. (It also serves as a reminder of Joyce's early work on *Ulysses,* which apparently included both the beginning and the end of the book.) The questions in "Ithaca" are answered, as Clive Hart has written, by a "computer which has not been programmed to distinguish between what is important and what is not,"[30] rather than by the very human, but not especially knowledgeable, students in Stephen's class in "Nestor." This lack of "programming" results in the episode's frequent resemblance to an encyclopedia. "Cyclops" contains seemingly endless lists among the "gigantic" interpolations; "Circe" uses encyclopedic passages for the details of the hallucinations; but only in "Ithaca" do blocks of encyclopedic data become the style. For example, in "Cyclops," when the Citizen takes out his handkerchief, "I" 's narration is interrupted by a full-page description of the handkerchief, including "the legendary beauty of the cornerpieces" and "the scenes depicted on the emunctory field," all of which are then listed (331.39-332.28). In "Ithaca," when Bloom turns on the faucet, the question "Did it flow?" elicits a two-page response explaining how and why the water flows (671.1-672.38). This answer does not interrupt any action or narration, since the water is indeed flowing; in fact, like the twenty-page hallucinations in "Circe" which actually last only seconds, this long description serves as an equivalent of the type of thought that passes through Bloom's scientific mind as he turns on the water.

"Ithaca" also continues the practice of disregarding the logical limits of character. At one point, describing Bloom after he supposedly gave Bantam Lyons a tip on the Gold Cup race, the narrator/answerer echoes John F. Taylor's speech, which Bloom never heard:

> he had proceeded towards the oriental edifice of the Turkish and Warm Baths, 11 Leinster street, with the light of inspiration shining in his countenance and bearing in his arms the secret of the race, graven in the language of prediction.
>
> (676.13-17)

This process does not occur very often in "Ithaca," but it does not need to; the technique has become so much a part

---

[30] *James Joyce's* Ulysses, p. 74.

of *Ulysses* that we no longer need to be reminded that such juxtapositions can be made.

Even though the story of *Ulysses* climaxes in "Ithaca"—Bloom takes Stephen to 7 Eccles Street, Stephen decides not to stay, Bloom faces his problem with Molly and psychologically slays her suitors—"Ithaca" is far from an episode of characters. The book ends in hopeless ambiguity for the reader desiring a definite conclusion. It is true, as S. L. Goldberg says, that the episode's obsessive objectivity cannot destroy "our sense of an imperishable dignity and vitality in the two characters" (Goldberg, p. 190), since the characters we know from the first nine episodes repeatedly show through the surface. (Whether it "heightens" that sense, as Goldberg insists, is more problematical.) "Ithaca," however, seems opaque and finally remains that: the responder fills in much past history, narrates the present when necessary, but leaves the future as a question and a dot.

"Circe" 's transforming powers, though, are not lost on the computerlike voice of "Ithaca." A. Walton Litz has described the major development that occurs at the end of "Ithaca":

> It was Joyce's unique gift that he could turn the substance of ordinary life into something like myth, not only through the use of 'parallels' and allusions but through direct transformation: and the ending of 'Ithaca', like that of 'Anna Livia Plurabelle', would seem to vindicate his method. Most of *Ulysses* can be understood by the same methods one applies to *The Waste Land*, where the manipulation of a continuous parallel between contemporaneity and antiquity 'places' the contemporary action, but the ending of 'Ithaca' consists of metamorphosis rather than juxtaposition.[31]

This transformation and Molly Bloom's thoughts, which remain negative through most of her monologue but cul-

[31] "Ithaca," p. 403.

minate in her memory of Bloom's proposal, represent the
only resolutions *Ulysses* offers.

If Bloom, Molly, and Stephen achieve the status of myths
at the end of "Ithaca," this is possible because of both the
realistic grounding of the first nine episodes and the ero-
sion of that grounding in the next eight. (The conclusion
of "Ithaca" is foreshadowed, for example, in Bloom's mock
apotheosis that ends "Cyclops," the first episode to drop
the monologue style.) The myth itself is not conclusive,
though, since in several ways Joyce forces it to rest in suspension with a more ironic conclusion. As Stanley Sultan
has shown, Bloom's mythical companions in his
wanderings—"Sinbad the Sailor and Tinbad the Tailor and
Jinbad the Jailer and Whinbad the Whaler," etc. (737.17-
22)—represent the other characters of *Ulysses* elevated to
mythological status;[32] this transformation occurs on a
much more ironic level than that of Bloom, Stephen, and
Molly, and it tempers the significance we can attach to the
mythic ending as a whole. More important, of course, is the
sudden drop back to earth in Molly's "amplitudinously
curvilinear" soliloquy, the "countersign" to the end of
"Ithaca" (*Letters*, I, 164, 160). The two episodes, balanced at
the end of the book as they were in Joyce's composition
process, together represent the conclusion of the book; the
gradual expansion of all aspects of *Ulysses* since the end of
"Scylla and Charybdis"—a proliferation of possible per-
spectives and readings, all of which are valid to some
degree—makes inevitable such an ambiguous, unresolved,
"allincluding" ending.

[32] *The Argument of* Ulysses (Columbus: Ohio State Univ. Press, 1964),
pp. 413-14. This is foreshadowed in a "Cyclops" parody in which the patrons of Barney Kiernan's pub become saints who march in a procession
to the pub.

The Early Stage: "Aeolus

"**Y**OU will scarcely recognise parts of *Ulysses* I have worked so much on them," Joyce wrote to his friend Valery Larbaud in September 1921 (*Letters*, III, 49). For a reader who had followed *Ulysses* as it appeared serially in the *Little Review* from 1918 to 1920, the least recognizable episode in the published book would certainly have been "Aeolus." Joyce "recast" the episode before the final publication (*Letters*, I, 172); he radically altered its appearance to include symbolic correspondences and aspects of exaggeration and parody like those he built from the beginning into the later episodes. In "Aeolus," however, he superimposed the new form on top of the old. He revised all Bloom's early episodes through a continual process of expansion, but he chose the newspaper episode to receive the greatest burden of augmentation. The composition of the episode is a miniature model of the composition of the book as a whole; the different stages reflect Joyce's changes in aesthetic aims as he wrote *Ulysses*. His original work emphasized the novelistic story of Stephen and Bloom; later, he augmented the episode with many symbolic correspondences or elements from the schema that he prepared late in his work on *Ulysses*: references to wind and to the color red, rhetorical devices and newspaper subheads.

Joyce's work on "Aeolus," like his work on the whole of *Ulysses*, fell into three main stages. He began the episode in Zurich during the summer of 1918. On May 18, 1918, he told Harriet Shaw Weaver that the sixth episode, "Hades," was being typed (*Letters*, I, 113); presumably he had already begun work on "Aeolus" or would soon do so. Two months later, on July 29, he told Harriet Weaver, "Very soon I shall send the seventh [episode] 'Eolus' " (I, 115), and on August 25 he said, "I sent the eighth [*sic*] episode of

Ulysses (Eolus) to Mr Pound some days [ago] and hope you have it now" (I, 118). The composition of the episode from the first drafts (not extant) to the autograph fair copy (Rosenbach MS) thus occurred between mid-May and mid-August 1918. Using a typescript prepared probably not from this fair copy but from an intermediate manuscript or typescript (there are about one hundred differences between the extant fair copy and typescript), the *Little Review* published the episode in its October 1918 issue, ending the first stage of composition.[1]

The middle stage consists of the few changes and additions Joyce wrote in ink onto a copy of the original typescript (the typescript prepared for the *Little Review*) before he sent it to his French printer, Maurice Darantiere, in mid-1921. In a letter of November 24, 1920, Joyce described these changes as "chiefly verbal or phrases, rarely passages" and said that he sorted them by episode before he left Trieste in July 1920 (*Letters*, III, 31; II, 348). It is impossible to say with certainty when he planned or compiled these changes. One of them, the alteration of Murray's first name from John to Red, appears on a "Circe" notesheet (20:28), which Joyce probably compiled during the spring or early summer of 1920 (*Notesheets*, p. 526). However, other revisions probably did not occur to him until he actually added the phrases to the typescript in mid-1921. He compiled the revisions on cards or scattered sheets of paper whenever they occurred to him; he arranged them by episode in mid-1920; in mid-1921 he added the accumulated "Aeolus" phrases to the typescript and sent the augmented episode to the printer.

The third stage marks Joyce's "great revision" of the episode. He filled "Aeolus" with correspondences, adding, among other things, all the subheads and many of the wind references and rhetorical devices. This process was taking

---

[1] See the Introduction for an explanation of the various documents, and the Appendix for the problems involved in the assumption that the typescript was prepared directly from the autograph fair copy.

place while Darantiere pulled the *placards* and page proofs—from early August until October 1921. On August 30 Joyce told Harriet Shaw Weaver, "I have made a great deal of addition to the proofs so far (up to the end of *Scylla and Charybdis*)" (*Letters*, I, 171); this covers the first two sets of *placards* for "Aeolus," by which time the subheads were added. On October 7 he wrote Harriet Weaver that the episode was "recast" (I, 172), but the revision of the episode was not at an end, for he added a few more passages between then and the publication of the book in February 1922.

The table on pages 68-69 summarizes the stages of composition and the relevant documents.

The Early Form

"In the Heart of the Hibernian Metropolis," the opening words in the final version of "Aeolus," serve remarkably well to upset the expectations that *Ulysses* gradually promotes in the first six episodes. Despite its changes in style and its second beginning in the fourth episode, the book up to now has seemed unified in its balance between external description and interior monologue, and in its concentration on single characters, first Stephen Dedalus and then Leopold Bloom. "Aeolus" stands apart from the six preceding episodes, and it boldly announces this fact. However, as Joyce wrote the episode in 1918 and submitted it to the *Little Review*, no such conspicuous new direction exists; in fact, one of its prominent features is its continuity with the six previous episodes.

In many ways, the finished "Aeolus" seems like a new beginning for *Ulysses*: it is the first episode after the opening six scenes linked by a common time scheme; it represents the first extended appearance of both Bloom and Stephen in a single episode; and Dublin and the other Dubliners become increasingly prominent. (The opening head, "In the Heart of the Hibernian Metropolis," suggests both the new beginning and the new emphasis on the city and its inhabitants.) These features (except the head) exist in the fair copy-*Little Review* version, but the episode in its early form displays more continuity with what has preceded it. For example, the fair copy "Aeolus," like Bloom's first three episodes, begins with a declarative sentence in the narrator's voice, reinforcing the outward-moving development of the episodes:

"Calypso"—Bloom alone in his kitchen: "Mr Leopold Bloom ate with relish the inner organs of beasts and fowls."

(MS, "Calypso," fol. 1; cf. *Ulysses*, 55.1-2)

"Lotus Eaters"—Bloom alone in the streets of Dublin: "By lorries along Sir John Rogerson's quay Mr Bloom walked soberly, past Windmill lane, Leask's the linseed crusher, the postal telegraph office."

(MS, "Lotus Eaters," fol. 1; cf. 71.1-3)

"Hades"—Bloom within a circle of acquaintances: "Martin Cunningham, first, poked his silkhatted head into the creaking carriage and, entering deftly, seated himself."

(MS, "Hades," fol. 1; cf. 87.1-2)

"Aeolus"—Bloom within the city: "Grossbooted draymen rolled barrels dullthudding out of Prince's stores and bumped them up on the brewery float."

(MS, "Aeolus," fol. 1; cf. 116.23-24)

This progression continues until Bloom leaves in the middle of the episode to the words, "Go. ['Begone' in the final version] . . . The world is before you" (MS, "Aeolus," fol. 13).

As the four opening sentences make clear, the original "Aeolus" resembles the three preceding episodes in the careful adaptation of the narrator's voice to the episode's theme and setting. If "Calypso" is dominated in language and style by the briskness of Bloom's early-morning inquisitiveness and "Lotus Eaters" by the pervasive langour,

THE DEVELOPMENT OF "AEOLUS"

Stage	Date	Name	Description	Other Documents
Early	1918			Buffalo MS VIII.A.5—notes from Joyce's reading earlier drafts not extant
	July-Aug.	Rosenbach MS	autograph fair copy now in possession of the Philip H. and A.S.W. Rosenbach Foundation, Philadelphia	
	Aug.	typescript —Buffalo TS V.B.5	the autograph fair copy was probably made from another MS, which (with additions and corrections) also served as the typist's copy; perhaps contains a few corrections and additions by Joyce in margins	
	Oct.	*Little Review*	set from typescript, with Joyce's corrections and additions—5, vi (Oct. 1918), pp. 26-51	

Stage	Date	Name	Description	Other Documents
Middle	1920–1921	typescript—Buffalo TS V.B.5	between the lines and in the margins, Joyce revised and augmented a copy of the typescript prepared in August 1918	notes or cards not extant
Last	1921 Aug.-Sept.	*placards*—Harvard; Buffalo V.C.4	two or three different proofs pulled for each page; first set pulled from typescript; each subsequent set incorporates new additions	Buffalo MS V.A.2—notes for late revisions
	Sept.-Oct.	page proofs—Buffalo V.C.1,2; Texas	three different proofs pulled for each page; each set incorporates new additions	
	1922 Feb. 2	publication	published book includes additions written onto last page proof	

then in "Aeolus," especially at the beginning, the dominant
feature is sound, from rolling barrels to creaking doors to
snipping scissors:

> Grossbooted draymen rolled barrels dullthudding out
> of Prince's stores and bumped them up on the brewery
> float.
> —There it is, John Murray [*sic*]. Alexander Keyes.
> —Just cut it out, will you? Mr Bloom said, and I'll take
> it round to the *Telegraph* office.
> The door of Ruttledge's office creaked again.
> John Murray's long shears sliced out the advertise-
> ment from the newspaper in four clean strokes.
>
> (MS, "Aeolus," fol. 1)[2]

The statements of the omniscient narrator at the beginning, like those in "Lotus Eaters," are long, verbose, full of
many prepositional phrases. However, the style, sleepy earlier, becomes windy here, and the rhythmical repetition of
the prepositional phrases echoes the noise of the machines.
Occasionally, the noise even breaks into the narration
("Sllt. The nethermost deck of the first machine jogged
forward its flyboard with sllt the first batch of quirefolded
papers. Sllt"; MS, fol. 5), or the narrator lets Brayden's
slow rhythm replace that of the machines: "It passed state-
lily [*sic*] up the staircase, steered by an umbrella, a solemn
beardframed face" (fol. 1; when Joyce substitutes Brayden's rhythm for the machines', he echoes the subservience
of the editors and reporters to their publisher). Bloom's
mind fully reflects the noise around him, whether in the

---

[2] The opening sentence, which appears once in the fair copy and typescript, is repeated in the *Little Review* (5, vi [Oct. 1918], p. 26). It is possible
that Joyce in some way indicated the repetition to the *Little Review*. But the
printer may have set the sentence twice by mistake (Hans Walter Gabler
has suggested that this is especially possible because the first printing of
the sentence involves special type for the word "Grossbooted") and, taking
advantage of the error, Joyce may have seen the opportunity for an additional rhetorical form by reversing the order of the phrases to produce a
chiasmus. The reversed sentence appears as a handwritten addition to
Buffalo TS V.B.5, the copy Joyce sent to Darantiere in 1921.

abrupt thought, "We" (fol. 1), or in the rhythm of a string of thoughts:

> Hynes here too: account of the funeral probably. Thumping. Thump. This morning the remains of the late Mr Patrick Dignam. Machines. His machines are working away too. Like these, got out of hand: fermenting. Working away, tearing away. And that old grey rat tearing to get in.
>
> (fol. 2)

The noise of the machines, and the accompanying style of the narration and the interior monologue, end after Bloom leaves the machine room, and he enters the *Evening Telegraph* office "softly" (fol. 7; the first words he hears are "murmured softly," the repetition emphasizing the contrast with the machines).

Even in its earliest form, "Aeolus" contains two different structural patterns that are evident in the final version. On the one hand, the episode splits in half, as Bloom leaves the newspaper office halfway through and Stephen then enters. On the other hand, it consists of a long central section in the *Evening Telegraph* office, flanked by shorter sections at the beginning in the machine room and at the end in the streets of Dublin. These two patterns parallel those of *Ulysses* itself, which splits in half after "Scylla and Charybdis" as an alternative to the more obvious three-part structure. Joyce's list of the episodes in a September 1920 letter to John Quinn notes both structural divisions (*Letters*, I, 145).

Since "Aeolus" is the first episode in which Bloom and Stephen both appear, it is not surprising that the two-part structure contrasts the two men. In the newspaper office Bloom faces a larger, less familiar, and more hostile group of people than that in "Hades" (significantly, Simon Dedalus, the only holdover from "Hades," is kindest of all the men to Bloom). The only time the men in the office consider Bloom part of the group occurs after he has gone, when the professor includes him in the list of professions represented in the room. Stephen, on the other hand, finds himself for the only time in the book among people who flatter him and court his literary aspirations; his reception contrasts strongly with the one shortly to come in "Scylla and Charybdis." The group misunderstands his ambitions, as will the sympathetic individuals Almidano Artifoni and Leopold Bloom later in the day, but Myles Crawford unwittingly invites Stephen to write *Ulysses*:

> —Foot and mouth disease! the editor cried scornfully. Great nationalist meeting in Borris-in-Ossory. All balls! Bulldosing the public. Give them something with a bite in it. Put us all into it, damn its soul. Father, Son and Holy Ghost.
>
> (fol. 19)

Bloom enters and leaves alone (though a "file of capering newsboys" follows him when he leaves; fol. 14), but Stephen is "escorted" in (fol. 16) and leaves as the center of attraction in a small crowd.

There are distinct differences in the interior monologues of the two characters. Bloom's thoughts continue to reveal his interest in his surroundings and his ability to adapt himself to them:

> Mr Bloom, glancing sideways up from the cross he had made, saw the foreman's sallow face, think he has a touch of jaundice, and beyond the obedient reels feeding in a huge web of paper. Clank it. Clank it. Miles of it unreeled. What becomes of it after. O, wrap up meat, parcels: various uses, one thing or another.
>
> (fol. 4)

Through both the noise of the machines and the snubs from the men in the office, Bloom retains his equilibrium, flexibility, and curiosity, as he has done throughout the book. Stephen's thoughts, though, differ from those in his first three episodes. After his long meditations in "Proteus," and probably in response to the verbosity around him, his thoughts here are short, terse, uncomplicated. Many are direct quotations from his reading, repetitions of remarks people have made to him during the day or in the past, or echoes of his own words to others. Others are abrupt words or phrases: "Bit torn off" (fol. 16), "Dublin" (27), "Dubliners" (27), "Poor Penelope. Penelope Rich" (31). None of his thoughts here begins to approach the complexity of those in "Telemachus," "Nestor," or "Proteus."

The three-part structure contrasts Stephen and Bloom to some extent, since the opening and closing sections focus on them. Joyce presents both characters in their milieus performing their occupations. The opening section portrays Bloom doing his job (a late addition calls him "the canvasser at work"; 119.35), but primarily it shows his compatibility with his urbanized, mechanized surroundings. We watch Bloom "slipping his words deftly into the pauses of the clanking" (fol. 4), and he admires this adaptability of man to machines in others, since he recognizes the power of the machines:

> The machines clanked in threefour time. Thump, thump, thump. Now if he got paralysed there and no-one knew how to stop them they'd clank on and on the same, print it over and over and up and back. Monkeydoodle the whole thing. Want a cool head.
>
> (fols. 2-3)

In the closing section Stephen (typically on the way to a pub) creates his "vision" as a response to other aspects of Dublin: a work of art, John F. Taylor's speech; a monument in front of him, Nelson's Pillar; and two real women of his acquaintance.

In the long central section, Bloom and Stephen are adjuncts to the other Dubliners. The 1920 schema that Joyce wrote for his friend Carlo Linati described the meaning of "Wandering Rocks" as "the hostile environment" (Linati Schema), and Joyce begins to present this aspect of the city in the newspaper office. The noise of the machines is replaced by the noise of human bombast in the three set speeches, the professor's stilted language and syntax,

Myles Crawford's yelling, Lenehan's jokes, and the newsboys' screams. Like the competing newspapers, the men strive for attention by interrupting, yelling, or orating. This is the beginning of Joyce's extended presentation of the other Dubliners, a facet of the book that he will continue to develop, especially in "Wandering Rocks," "Sirens," and "Cyclops."

None of these aspects of "Aeolus" is missing from the final version, but Joyce's later elaborations obscured some of them. This process is evident, for example, in the beginning of Stephen's parable. (The words in angle brackets were not yet in the episode when Joyce faircopied it.)

—Come along, Stephen, the professor said. That is fine, isn't it. It has the prophetic vision. ⟨*Fuit Ilium!* The sack of windy Troy. Kingdoms of this world. The masters of the Mediterranean are fellaheen today.⟩

The first newsboy came pattering down the stairs ~~behind them~~ ⟨at their heels⟩ and rushed out into the street, yelling:

—Racing special!

Dublin. ⟨I have much, much to learn.⟩

They turned to the left along Abbey street.

—I have a vision too, Stephen said.

—Yes, the professor said, skipping to get into step. Crawford will follow.

Another newsboy shot past them. Yelling as he ran:

—Racing special!

⟨DEAR DIRTY DUBLIN⟩

Dubliners.

—Two Dublin vestals, Stephen said, elderly and pious, have lived ~~fiftyfive~~ ⟨fifty and fiftythree⟩ years in Fumbally's lane.

(fol. 27; 144.24-145.4)

Besides the two changes, there are only three additions to the passage—"*Fuit Ilium!*" and the words following; Stephen's brooding "I have much, much to learn"; and the subhead. Yet these additions change the movement of the passage. As Joyce originally wrote it, the professor, less oratorically than usual, invites Stephen to comment on Taylor's speech, and after a quick succession of stimuli—the speech, the newsboys, the pillar—Stephen responds with his parable. Like two opening chords in a musical piece, the words in Stephen's mind, "Dublin" and "Dubliners," announce the parable's distinct setting and theme and indicate its contrast to both Taylor's speech and his own shadowy poem.

The revisions changed the passage's emphasis. The professor's invitation to Stephen becomes much less sincere; he answers his own rhetorical question and reveals that he asked it only to hear himself speak. (The addition brings in one of the few explicit references in the book to the world of Homer.) Joyce also destroyed the symmetry of Stephen's two thoughts. The addition of "I have much, much to learn" represents one indication that Stephen is becoming aware of the need to associate himself with his Dublin environment, rather than to isolate himself. The subhead, which in context functions as a hackneyed sentimentalization of Dublin squalor, contrasts fully with Stephen's unsentimental attitude in the parable. Stephen's thought, "Dubliners," its relationship with the earlier "Dublin" cut off by both additions, now alone introduces the parable and even suggests that Joyce as omniscient author is linking the parable with the stories in *Dubliners*.

These revisions were still years in the future when Joyce first wrote the episode. Before discussing them in more detail, we need to consider another aspect of "Aeolus" that occupied Joyce from the start.

The Early Scaffolding

Although Joyce emphasized the story of *Ulysses* much more during the early writing than during the late revisions, he meticulously built elaborate parallels and correspondences into the early versions. The "scaffolding" existed from the start,[3] although the correspondences were neither so noticeable nor so necessary for an understanding of the book as they were after the late revisions. An extant notebook from early 1918 (Buffalo MS VIII.A.5; *Notes and Early Drafts*, pp. 1-33) provides important evidence about Joyce's general concerns at that time and some of the specific sources for "Aeolus."

Joyce used this notebook to record information from books he read in the Zentralbibliothek Zürich. As the notebook's editor, Phillip F. Herring, has shown, the notes come primarily from two sources: Victor Bérard's *Les Phéniciens et l'Odyssée* and W. H. Roscher's *Ausführliches Lexikon der Grieschischen und Römischen Mythologie*, with a few entries from three of Thomas Otway's plays and a seventeenth-century French translation of Aristotle's *Rhetoric*. These notes indicate some ways in which Joyce built up his system of correspondences, and they also provide rich clues for further exploration. (The following discussion is greatly indebted to Herring's efforts in locating the specific sources for Joyce's notes.)

The notebook shows, for one thing, that at a quite early stage in his work on *Ulysses* Joyce was carefully sorting out his notes by episode and storing them for future use. The division into episodes here is not as systematic as in the later notebooks and sheets—the British Museum notesheets for the last seven episodes, the 1921 notebook (Buffalo MS V.A.2), or the *Finnegans Wake* notebook edited as *Scribbledehobble*[4]—but Joyce did group the notes as he

---

[3] "These correspondences are part of Joyce's mediaevalism and are chiefly his own affair, a scaffold, a means of construction, justified by the result, and justifiable by it only." Ezra Pound, "Paris Letter" (June 1922), rpt. in *Pound/Joyce: The Letters of Ezra Pound to James Joyce*, ed. Forrest Read (New York: New Directions, 1967), p. 197. Pound greatly underestimated the importance the parallels and correspondences eventually assumed in Joyce's mind.

[4] Thomas E. Connolly, ed., *James Joyce's Scribbledehobble: The Ur-Workbook for* Finnegans Wake (Evanston: Northwestern Univ. Press, 1961). See also Buffalo *Finnegans Wake* notebook VI.C.7, in which Mme. France Raphael transcribed earlier (and presumably unused) *Ulysses* notes, all grouped according to episode.

read sections of Bérard or Roscher. There are clear references to "Lotus Eaters" (VIII.A.5, pp. 3, 15), "Hades" (p.
26), "Aeolus" (p. 15), "Lestrygonians" (p. 13), "Scylla and
Charybdis" (p. 1), "Nausicaa" (p. 19), "Oxen of the Sun" (p.
11), "Circe" (p. 16), "Eumaeus" (pp. 4, 7), "Ithaca" (p. 5),
and "Penelope" (pp. 7, 9). He always said that he had
drafted the last three episodes very early in the writing of
the book (in mid-1920 he wrote that "a great part of the
Nostos or close was written several years ago"; *Letters*, I,
143), and the notebook provides support for this conten-
tion, since it shows him taking notes for the entire book at
once, even while he was writing specific early sections.
(This should not suggest, however, that his plans for the
later episodes were very far advanced at this stage in his
work. He probably had no idea that the later episodes
would differ at all from the ones he was then writing.)

Joyce compiled at least the first few pages of the
notebook before he wrote "Lotus Eaters" in early 1918 and
the "Aeolus" notes before he wrote the manuscript of that
episode. Such notes as "LB.—all eat it—all one family ∴ "
(VIII.A.5, p. 2; see Herring's introduction to the notebook
in *Notes and Early Drafts*, pp. 3-5) and "Grey bootsole,
petticoat" (p. 3) appear in the fair copy of "Lotus Eaters,"
and one of the "Aeolus" notes, "pillar of cloud by day (Israel)" (p. 15), which occurs in the fair copy, suggests that
the "Aeolus" notes preceded the completion of the
episode's first version. His general use of the notebook was
rather curious, though. Many of the notes and phrases recorded here entered the book after the *Little Review* publication; examples are "Get wind of it (Glasnevin)" in
"Aeolus" (p. 3; 125.15-20), "P. Mooney's father bailiff
bumbailiff" in "Cyclops" (p. 1; 303.3; see "Cyclops"
notesheet 4:6), and "U. astride of a beam" in "Nausicaa" (p.
19; 378.41). Joyce apparently used a few notes for the original versions of the episodes and then regularly returned to
the notebook for his revisions and augmentations of 1920
and 1921. (He raided the notebook when he compiled the
notesheets for the last seven episodes; over 50 of the notes
reappear on the sheets, bunched mainly on "Cyclops" 7,

"Nausicaa" 6, and especially "Circe" 3:100-21.)[5] Despite all this, there are surprisingly few specific uses of these notes in the book. Many furnished broad ideas that he later reworked in the idiom of the individual episodes (for example, "Eumaios pigherd good" and "Melanthus goatherd— bad"; p. 4), and some provided specific information which he probably intended to use but never did ("7 notes = isles"; p. 16). Herring suggests that "like a patient scholar he researched his subjects thoroughly, if sometimes credulously, making notes that suggested hitherto unforeseen possibilities for his art, trusting to genius for transforming trivia into the sublime" (*Notes and Early Drafts*, p. 4). As he transformed this notebook into his art, Joyce used some notes directly, reworked others, but rejected even more.

Most of the notes for "Aeolus" are grouped together in a series of jottings from Victor Bérard's chapter on the Aeolian islands in *Les Phéniciens et l'Odyssée* (see Figure 1):

$$Aoelus \text{ [sic]} = \left. \begin{array}{l} \text{conical} \\ \text{high} \end{array} \right\} \text{ isle}$$

brazen walls (solidified lava)
fer spéculaire
pumice isle erupted before ?boiling from depths.
Stromboli with a lifebelt of floating pumice
∧ smokefumes index of winds
Lipari—alum mines (7 isles)
Lipari, then Stromboli capitol.
pillar of cloud by day (Israel)
    by night (press nightshift)
flame
cisterns
figs—malmsey
incest
6 sons—6 daughters
7 notes = isles

             (VIII.A.5, pp. 15-16)

---

[5] Phillip F. Herring has indicated these borrowings in his notes to the individual British Museum notesheets.

Joyce's notes from Victor Bérard (Buffalo notebook VIII.A.5). Reproduced courtesy of the Society of Authors and the Lockwood Memorial Library, State University of New York at Buffalo. (Figure 1)

A few others occur elsewhere in the notebook:

> pressgang (p. 1)
> Get wind of it (Glasnevin) (p. 3)
> *Antisthenes*—placed P. above Helen (p. 8)
> philosophical essay ρτψ of Ods (p. 8)

Finally, several notes on diction and rhetoric probably apply to "Aeolus":

heroic	1 to 1	par a par
dactyl	‖ — ǀ ∪ ∪ ‖	narrative
spondee	‖ — ǀ — ‖	solemn
iamb	‖ ∪ ǀ — ‖	conversat
trochee	‖ — ∪ ‖	dance
pean	‖ — ǀ ∪ ∪ ∪ $^{3-2}$‖	
	∪ ∪ ∪ ǀ—	

prose (numerous) — rhythm
          verse — measure
anabole?
antistrophe?
Periode diction
—qui de soi a un commencement et une fin est de grandeur à être vue tout d'un coup sans donner de peine

~~Simple~~ compound period: perfect, complete
  (members) pronouncable in 1 breath
Comp. period
  antithesis in clauses to sustain length
  of equal limbs = parisose
    equal ends
          = paromoeose
     " starts?
(isocolic
isocolon)
parison the good is geason and short is his abode
        the bad bides long and easy to be found

paromœon O Tite, tute, Tati, tibi tanta tyranne tulisti
Paromology I grant he is resolute—but to his undoing

Object—to make folk learn easy
  ∴ foreign words; proper names ?tabu
  Metaphor prefer to comparison
  Comparison makes folk wait and tells you
  only what smthg is like.
  Good diction tria
  metaphor, antithesis, energy

(VIII.A.5, pp. 23-25)

These three groups of notes provide important clues to Joyce's method of building up his episode. Most of the notes from Bérard pertain to a physical description of the Aeolian islands, particularly Stromboli, which Bérard derives from the French Navy's *Nautical Instructions*, Lazzaro Spallanzani's *Travels in the Two Sicilies* (1792), and his own visit to the islands. Joyce used notes like "brazen walls (solidified lava)" or *"Aoelus [sic] = high"* (a summary of Bérard's etymological account of the name) to create an analogy in the Dublin pressroom for Aeolus' island as described by Bérard. Stuart Gilbert discusses these analogies using ideas certainly supplied by Joyce himself:

> The brazen walls of the palace of Aeolus have, perhaps, their counterpart in the tramlines, "rows of cast steel", which encircle the office. . . . A buoyant debris, vomited by the printing machines, like pumice from a volcano, litters the offices—"strewn packing paper", "limp galleypages", light "tissues" which, "rustling up" in every draught, "floated softly in the air blue scrawls and under the table came to earth".

(Gilbert, pp. 185-86)[6]

---

[6] Gilbert never mentions Bérard in his chapter on "Aeolus," although he does name him elsewhere in his book. Yet the quotation from Thévenot, and everything else on pp. 184-86, comes directly from Bérard.

No doubt Joyce planned analogies like these for the other notes, such as "7 notes = isles," but later changed his mind.

A note like "pillar of cloud by day (Israel)" shows a different process at work. Joyce read two passages in Bérard:

> Elle [Stromboli] atteint presque mille mètres d'altitude et, de son cratère, monte une colonne de fumée durant le jour, une lueur de feux intermittents durant la nuit.
>
> (II, 184)
>
> Des Sept Iles, Stromboli est, sinon la plus haute, du moins la plus lointainement visible: vers sa pointe de 940 mètres, vers son panache de fumée durant le jour, vers sa lampe de feu durant la nuit. . . .
>
> (II, 198)

He translated "colonne de fumée" and "panache de fumée" into another everpresent guide, from Exodus 13:22: "He took not away the pillar of the cloud by day, nor the pillar of fire by night, from before the people." Apparently Joyce originally planned an ironic parallel between the dependable "pillar of the cloud by day" and that capricious guide, the daily newspaper, since he included an analogy for Bérard's (and Exodus') nocturnal fire in "press nightshift." But he ultimately incorporated the "pillar of the cloud" into his version of John F. Taylor's speech (143.11-12; Taylor did not actually use the phrase in his speech),[7] and he dropped the "nightshift" entirely. (The phrase "pillar of the cloud by day" recurs twice in *Ulysses*; 210.25, 727.20.)

Although generally dismissed as a Homeric scholar, Victor Bérard was a major influence on *Ulysses*. Led to *Les Phéniciens et l'Odyssée* by Joyce, Stuart Gilbert emphasizes two aspects of Bérard's account that must have been extremely attractive to Joyce: the arguments that the *Odyssey* is a fictional transformation of the Mediterranean voyages

---

[7] A pamphlet containing Taylor's original peroration is reprinted in Robert Scholes and Richard M. Kain, eds., *The Workshop of Daedalus: James Joyce and the Raw Materials for* A Portrait of the Artist as a Young Man (Evanston: Northwestern Univ. Press, 1965), pp. 155-57.

of Phoenician sailors and that the place names in the *Odyssey*, as well as the Greek language and culture, have a Semitic origin. These interpretations surely appealed strongly to the creator of Leopold Bloom, the modern Odysseus, but Bérard offered Joyce even more important support. Following the nineteenth century archeologists (as well as Strabo, a geographer of the first century B.C.), Bérard insists on the geographic verisimilitude of the *Odyssey*. For example, he writes of the Aeolian islands, "Il faut seulement prendre au pied de la lettre ses épithètes dites poétiques, et tout aussitôt nous apercevons, derrière les vers du poète, la Haute Pierre Montante, enclose d'une muraille circulaire de laves métalliques, et flottant sur une ceinture de ponces" (II, 192). And most important of all, as Michael Seidel has recently demonstrated, Bérard provided Joyce with a theory of epic geography and movement, a southeast-northwest pattern, from centers of known lands to borders of the unknown, that characterizes Odysseus' movements in the Mediterranean and Bloom's wanderings in Dublin.[8]

Bérard's presence in *Ulysses* is much more pervasive than the notebook would indicate. Joyce's notes are specific details from Bérard's descriptions of the islands, and they lead to individual correspondences such as those Stuart Gilbert discusses, but Joyce found other things in Bérard equally important to him. It is possible that the notes in notebook VIII.A.5 resulted from Joyce's second, or even later, reading of *Les Phéniciens et l'Odyssée*, rather than from his first encounter with Bérard's idiosyncratic account.

Joyce employed Bérard's geographical analysis of Homer in a startling way: just as he superimposed Homer's world onto his own, he superimposed Bérard's map of the Tyrrhenian Sea onto Dublin. When Bloom comes to the

---

[8] *Epic Geography: James Joyce's* Ulysses (Princeton: Princeton Univ. Press, 1976). The following pages in my discussion consider Bérard's precise influence on a single episode of *Ulysses*; Joyce's general use of Bérard for the geography and movement of *Ulysses* as Seidel presents it is a logical, consistent extension of his specific use in "Aeolus."

newspaper offices from Glasnevin Cemetery and Stephen arrives there from Sandymount strand, they duplicate the routes to the Aeolian islands of, respectively, Odysseus from Cyclops' cave and the Phoenician sailors from the Straits of Messina (Bérard, II, 115, 199, and see my Maps 1 and 2).[9] When Odysseus first leaves Aeolus' island for Ithaca, he moves south before going east, and Bloom too goes south to find Keyes in Dillon's auction rooms in Bachelor's Walk (129.16-18). Joyce added several other parallels in the late revisions. First, a subhead gives Brayden an identifiable home, "William Brayden, Esquire, of Oaklands, Sandymount" (117.9-10), which means that he comes from the same direction as Stephen did; and when Joyce changed "a stately figure entered from Prince's street" (MS, fol. 1) to "a stately figure entered between the newsboards of the *Weekly Freeman and National Press* and the *Freeman's Journal and National Press*" (117.15-17), he included the part of the voyage from the Mediterranean through the narrow Straits of Messina. Then, the tramlines that Joyce added to the beginning of the episode all go south or southeast when they leave Nelson's Pillar (116.3-7); Bérard says of Odysseus' original departure from the island, "Ulysse s'embarque. Aiolos . . . lui procure un bon vent de la partie Nord, une brise du Nord-Ouest" (II, 195). Like Odysseus and his men, the tram cars return to their point of embarkation to face an unhappy situation, a short circuit. Thus, moving through Dublin, Joyce's characters (and the machines) trace the paths of Homer's men, as interpreted by Bérard.

Joyce uses another feature of Bérard's geography. There are two analogues to Aeolus' volcanic island in the episode, the upstairs newspaper offices and Nelson's Pillar. (The monument was prominent in the fair copy because of Stephen's parable, but when, in the late revisions, Joyce

[9] See Seidel's discussion of Bloom's and Stephen's movements (*Epic Geography*, pp. 164-65). If Stephen goes directly from the pub on Abbey Street to the National Library, he traces the path of sailors from the Aeolian islands through the Straits of Messina, hence by Scylla and Charybdis.

added it along with the tramlines to the beginning and end of the episode, he increased its significance as an Aeolian island.) Here, too, Joyce follows Bérard, who emphasizes that the capitol of the Aeolian archipelago frequently shifted back and forth between Stromboli and Lipari (II, 196); curiously enough, these two islands are situated in the same position relative to each other as are Nelson's Pillar and the Prince's Street newspaper offices.

As if to acknowledge indirectly his use of Bérard's geography, Joyce included a similar act of superimposition among the happenings in the newspaper office.[10] Myles Crawford recounts Ignatius Gallaher's brilliant method of cabling to New York the escape route of the Invincibles following the Phoenix Park murders; Gallaher superimposed a map of Dublin onto a newspaper advertisement:

> Take page four, advertisement for Bransome's coffee, let us say. . . . B is parkgate. . . . T is viceregal lodge. C is where murder took place. K is Knockmaroon gate. . . . F to P is the route Skin-the-goat drove the car for an alibi. Inchicore, Roundtown, Windy Arbour, Palmerston Park, Ranelagh. F. A. B. P. Got that? X is Davy's publichouse in upper Leeson street. . . . X is Burke's publichouse, see? . . . Gave it to them on a hot plate, . . . the whole bloody history.
>
> (136.30-137.16)

Gallaher successfully transmitted his message across the space of the Atlantic Ocean; Joyce, the superior artist, uses the method to recreate a map across both time and space, and moving far beyond Gallaher, to indicate an entire conception of epic geography and movement.

Joyce augmented his basic analogy between the newspaper offices and the island of the winds with several details from Bérard. According to Bérard, the smoke from the Aeolian volcanoes was considered a predictor of good or bad weather for sailing (II, 193). Joyce recorded this fact as

---

[10] Peter Garrett suggested the following extension of Joyce's use of Bérard.

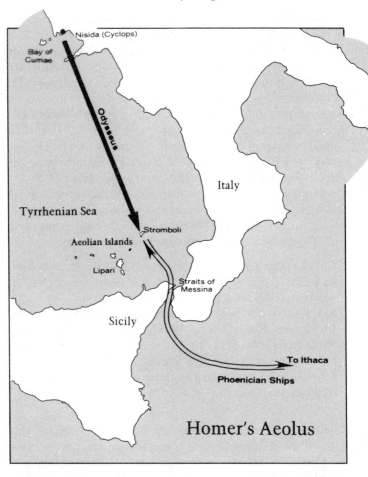

Victor Bérard's map of the Homeric Aeolian islands (Map 1)

"smokefumes index of winds" (VIII.A.5, p. 15). So "Aeolus" is filled with predictions, from Bloom's belief about Nannetti ("Soon be calling him my lord mayor"; 119.20), to MacHugh's forecast of Bloom's success ("He'll get that advertisement"; 129.26), to Myles Crawford's prediction of the World War ("Sent his heir over to make the king an Austrian fieldmarshal now. Going to be trouble

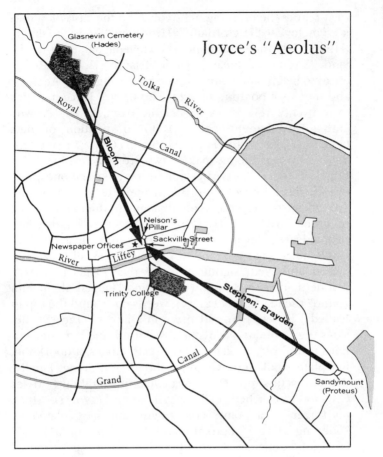

Joyce's "Aeolus": Dublin: June 16, 1904 (Map 2)

there one day"; 132.34-35. This is a late addition, perhaps
intended to replace a prediction of the war that Joyce deleted from "Cyclops" before the fair copy of that episode).
He may also be commenting ironically on newspapers
when Crawford praises them not for forecasting events but
for quick response after the fact: "The Old Woman of
Prince's street was there first" (137.23-24).

There are other parallels. Although Aeolus' home in
Homer is usually considered to be a "floating island," Bé-

rard refines the meaning of "Aeolus" on the basis of Semitic etymology to "High Island" (II, 192) or "Pointing Island" (II, 190). On the other hand, the Hellenic name for the island, "Strongyle," means "Round Island" (II, 190). References to height and roundness occur throughout "Aeolus," and there are pointing fingers everywhere. Joyce includes over twenty references to height, from "glossy crown" (118.29) to haughtiness (141.16) to mention of hats (121.18, 130.25, 146.7) and mountains (125.5, 131.12-13, 143.13). When Bloom makes "two crossed keys" with his fingers (120.21), he creates a mountain like the one Joyce drew in his notebook, and the printer's term, "round the top in leaded" (120.26), is an analogue to the island's "wall of bronze" (Bérard, II, 187). On the other hand, when people leave, they go "round," Bloom to the *Evening Telegraph* office (116.29) and to Bachelor's Walk (129.16), Simon and Ned, significantly, to the "Oval" (130.6-7). Nannetti "turned round" (120.6) and "looked about him round" the machines (121.32); words go "round the top in leaded"; Keyes is "round there in Dillon's" (129.18). Besides the frequent use of the word itself, the episode contains round objects like barrels, reels, circles, a doorknob, hot plate, hook and eye, globe, hoop, and dome. Finally, the characters point or gesticulate throughout: Myles Crawford "stretched forth an arm amply" (129.21), "stuck his finger on a point" (136.28-29), and gesticulated by "pointing sternly" (130.26) and "holding out a hand" (131.36). Lenehan "extended his hands in protest" (134.15), MacHugh "raised an outspanned hand to his spectacles" (141.22), and Bloom talked to Hynes, "pointing backward" (119.28). All these examples appear in the fair copy of the episode.

Nelson's Pillar combines the Semitic "high, pointing" island and Hellenic "round" island. Bérard points out that there are two ways of viewing Stromboli, since it appears high from the sea and round from the top or from the slopes (hence, according to Bérard, the different Semitic and Hellenic names; II, 184, 190), and he asserts that "le poète odysséen nous en décrit très exactement l'élévation et la rondeur tout ensemble" (II, 192). Stephen's parable includes this double mode of perception. Inside the pillar the two "Dublin vestals" climb a round "winding staircase" (145.26), but they also react to the pillar's height: "They had no idea it was that high" (145.30). As the "onehandled adulterer" (148.9), the statue is also a "pointing island"; at least, its hand is outstretched, and it "tickled the old ones too" (150.14). Commentators on the parable have pointed out both the analogy with Bérard's etymology and also the likelihood that Stephen's subtitle for his creation, "The Parable of the Plums" (a late addition), is a pun on *periplum*, an account of a voyage around an island and a word Bérard frequently uses when he talks about the Odyssean poet's source.[11]

Bérard discusses the importance of a guard on each island, who watched the sea from the rocks to protect the villagers from invading pirates, especially at night (II, 191-92); Gumley is "minding stones for the corporation" as a "night watchman" (136.19), and a newspaper, the *Skibereen Eagle*, is called "our watchful friend" (139.7; a late addition). Furthermore, the Aeolian islands, despite their rocky terrain, produced enough goods to be self-sufficient (II, 201); in Dublin, "sufficient for the day is the newspaper thereof" (139.9).

Bérard spends a great deal of time seeking factual bases for the myth of Aeolus as "lord of the winds" and for his island as "island of the winds." Joyce incorporates several of Bérard's explanations in the episode. The smoke rising from the volcano can serve the sailors by predicting the weather around the islands (II, 193); no danger exists when the winds come from the north, but there is great danger when they are from the south (II, 204). Joyce uses the volcano's smoke, the sailors' ship, and the storm ac-

---

[11] Irene Orgel Briskin, "Some New Light on 'The Parable of the Plums,'" *James Joyce Quarterly*, 3 (1966), esp. pp. 248-51; J. G. Keogh, "*Ulysses*' 'Parable of the Plums' as Parable and Periplum," *James Joyce Quarterly*, 7 (1970), pp. 377-78.

companying the southerly wind in the poem which
Stephen "revises" from Douglas Hyde:

> Hyde:
> And my love came behind me—
> He came from the South;
> His breast to my bosom,
> His mouth to my mouth.[12]

> Stephen:
> On swift sail flaming
> From storm and south
> He comes, pale phantom,
> Mouth to my mouth.
>
>> (MS, "Aeolus," fol. 16; Joyce later revised
>> "phantom" to "vampire," 132.14)

In another conjecture, Bérard suggests that Aeolus became
"lord of the winds" by successfully predicting the weather
from the volcano's fumes (II, 193), and the analogy with a
city's leading newspaper is obvious.

A final use of Bérard exists in Joyce's equivalent for the
incestuous marriage of Aeolus' sons and daughters. The
1921 schema simply lists "journalism" as the correspondence, suggesting the movement of journalists from one
newspaper to another either in Bloom's general opinion
about them (125.18-24) or in Myles Crawford's specific account of Ignatius Gallaher's career (137.25-29; Gallaher, in
Crawford's idiom, "was all their daddies," like Aeolus). Gilbert applies the correspondence to the journalists' craft itself; he calls it "an illicit union, of aspiration and com-
promise, of literature and opportunism" (Gilbert, p. 187).
In discussing Aeolus' family, Bérard states that Aeolus
himself ruled one of the Seven Islands and that his six sons,
each married to a sister, ruled the others (II, 201). Joyce's
analogy for this seems to be the paired newspapers, joined
either in a single building or under one management or

---

[12] Weldon Thornton, *Allusions in* Ulysses: *An Annotated List* (Chapel
Hill: Univ. of North Carolina Press, 1968), entry 48.3. Thornton credits
Joseph Prescott with the identification.

editorship: "the *Weekly Freeman and National Press* and the
Freeman's Journal and National Press" (117.16-17), "the *Irish
Catholic* and *Dublin Penny Journal*" (146.13-14; both phrases
are late additions), and the *Freeman's Journal* and *Evening
Telegraph*, housed in the same building and "closely as-
sociated" with one another (*JJ*, p. 297; Gilbert, p. 177).

In Bérard's unorthodox view of Homer, Joyce obviously
found an extremely compatible group of ideas, and he
built a significant number of Homeric-Bérardian correspondences into "Aeolus" from the start. But he went to
other sources for information about the Homeric myth.
Phillip Herring has demonstrated Joyce's familiarity with
W. H. Roscher's six-volume encyclopedia of ancient myth,
the *Ausführliches Lexikon der Griesischen und Römischen
Mythologie* (*Notes and Early Drafts*, pp. 7-8). Herring suggests that this compendium of information on the classical world probably supplied Joyce with the many character correspondences he sought and used in *Ulysses*. Buffalo
notebook VIII.A.5 contains entries from Roscher's accounts of Penelope, Hades, Alcmene, Anticleia, and
Eriphyle, but there are no notes from Roscher's section on
Aeolus. If Joyce did read Roscher on Aeolus, he would
have seen the more orthodox equivalents of some of Bérard's idiosyncratic conjectures.

Even if he did not read Roscher's account of Aeolus, the
account of Penelope perhaps gave him a clue for the newspaper episode. As Herring reveals, the notes
"*Antisthenes*—placed P. above Helen" and "philosophical
essay ρτψ of Ods" come from Roscher, and they may have
supplied Joyce with the information for one of Professor
MacHugh's responses to Stephen's parable. Roscher says,

Ihre [Penelope's] Tugenden wurden überdies gefeiert
in besonderen Lobschriften, so angeblich von *Isokrates*
. . .; wahrscheinlich lief auch *Antisthenes'* verlorene
Schrift περὶ Ἑλένης καὶ Πηνελόπης . . . auf eine Ver-
herrlichung der treuen Gattin des Odysseus hinaus, die
bisweilen sogar wegen ihrer Schönheit über Helena

gestellt wird . . . , während seine Abhandlung περὶ
᾿Οδυσσέως καὶ Πηνελόπης καὶ τοῦ κυνός . . . eine
rhetorisch-philosophische Wiedergabe der einschlägi-
gen Bücher der *Odyssee* (ρτψ) gewesen sein mag.[13]

MacHugh's words are very similar to the first part of this
account:

—You remind me of Antisthenes, . . . a disciple of
Gorgias, the sophist. It is said of him that none could tell
if he were bitterer against others or against himself. He
was the son of a noble and a bondwoman. And he wrote
a book in which he took away the palm of beauty from
Argive Helen and handed it to poor Penelope.

(148.30-149.4)

Joyce had to go beyond Roscher for the information on
Antisthenes' background; if he looked up the "rhetorical-
philosophical rendering" of the three books of the *Odyssey*
that recount Odysseus' return to Penelope in the source
listed by Roscher (Mullach's *Fragmenta Philosophorum
Graecorum*), he must have discovered a curious fact that
suggests Antisthenes as one of the unacknowledged patrons of the "Aeolus" episode. Alone among critics of
Homer, Antisthenes discussed πολύτροπος (polytropos)—
the word used to describe Odysseus in the first line of the
Odyssey, usually translated as "of many turns" (i.e., widely
experienced) or "of many sides" (i.e., wily)—in a way that
seems to mean "of many tropes."[14]

Tropes were on Joyce's mind during his early work on
"Aeolus," as notebook VIII.A.5 clearly indicates. Of the
ninety-five rhetorical devices Stuart Gilbert lists for the

[13] W. H. Roscher, ed. *Ausführliches Lexikon der Griesischen und Römischen
Mythologie* (Leipzig: Teubner, 1884-1937), III, col. 1907.

[14] "*Polytropos*, he [Antisthenes] argues, does not refer to character or
ethics at all. It simply denotes Odysseus's skill in adapting his figures of
speech ('tropes') to his hearers at any particular time." W. B. Stanford, *The
Ulysses Theme: A Study in the Adaptability of a Traditional Hero*, 2nd ed. (Ann
Arbor: Univ. of Michigan Press, 1963, 1968), p. 99.

episode, sixty-four were included by the time of the fair copy. As A. Walton Litz notes, the thirty-one late additions "provide the margin that makes rhetorical experimentation such an obvious characteristic" of the episode (Litz, p. 50), since Joyce's late desire for all-inclusiveness increased his audacity in the examples of rhetorical devices; nevertheless, he filled the episode with devices from the start. The notebook confirms the suspicion that Joyce went to rhetoric books to learn about the terms and devices.

In notebook VIII.A.5, Joyce copied from Book III, Sections 8, 9, and 10 of Aristotle's *Rhetoric*, using a seventeenth-century French translation by François Cassandre (see *Notes and Early Drafts*, p. 9). He was perhaps searching in the Zurich library for information on periodic diction to improve the "polished periods" (139.23) of Seymour Bushe and John F. Taylor, and he went to Aristotle (as he did for the three types of speeches in the episode; see Gilbert, pp. 187-88). He first copied in French and then switched to English. At one point in section 9 Aristotle discusses a periodic sentence in which the parts are antithetical and names some specific devices:

> Quant aux autres manieres de figurer les Periodes, le tout consiste, Ou à faire que le Periode soit composée de membres égaux, ce qui s'appelle *Parisose*: Ou bien par le moyen de la *Paromœose*, de faire que les extremitez de châque membre se ressemblent pour le terminaison. Or ceci arrive en deux façons, car il faut de necessité ou que cette Ressemblance se rencontre au commencement de châque membre, ou seulement à la fin; Si c'est au commencement, toûjours il faudra que les mots entiers se ressemblent; & Si c'est à la fin, ce sera assez que la ressemblance se trouve dans les dernieres syllabes; ou qu'un Nom soit mis en divers Cas, ou que le même mot soit repeté.[15]

[15] Aristotle, *La Rhétorique d'Aristote*, trans. François Cassandre (1654; Amsterdam: J. Covens and C. Mortier, 1733), pp. 413-14. See pp. 402-25 *passim*.

Wanting English examples of parisosis and paromoeon, Joyce went to a reference source, probably the O.E.D. (*Notes and Early Drafts*, p. 9). Reading along after "paromoeon," he noticed that the next word is also a rhetorical device, "paromology," and he copied down an example of it. He then returned to Aristotle, read on into section 10 about clever words and phrases, and took a few more notes.

He crossed out the examples of parison and paromology in the notebook, and after the *Little Review* publication of "Aeolus" he added a parison to John F. Taylor's speech ("Israel is weak and few are her children: Egypt is an host and terrible are her arms"; 143.2-3), and a paromology to J. J. O'Molloy's dialogue ("—Seems to be, J. J. O'Molloy said, taking out a cigarette case ⟨in murmuring meditation, but it is not always as it seems⟩"; 130.16-17; the bracketed words are the addition. Gilbert cites this sentence as an example of epanalepsis; pp. 195-96). None of the three rhetorical terms appears in Stuart Gilbert's list of devices, which suggests that when he made these notes Joyce was involved in a different hunting game from the one that resulted in the inclusion of nearly a hundred devices in "Aeolus." For the latter endeavor, he probably used a standard nineteenth-century prosody book that included a list of devices, and he certainly showed either this book, or his own list culled from it, to Gilbert for the exegesis of the episode. (See Gilbert's preface to the 1952 edition of *James Joyce's* Ulysses, pp. viii-ix.)

Given Joyce's detailed reading of Bérard, Roscher, and Aristotle in early 1918, it is amazing that his use of them in the first version of "Aeolus" remains buried so far under a realistic surface. Clearly, research of this kind was an essential part of his initial preparation for the episodes of *Ulysses*, but it is equally clear that at the beginning he did not want such "scaffolding" to show. We must turn to the various stages of revision to see this private background become public.

The Early Revisions

Unfortunately, we cannot explore Joyce's earliest work on "Aeolus," because no documents prior to the autograph fair copy have survived. However, we can see some of Joyce's concerns before the *Little Review* published the episode (hence, the end of the first stage of composition) in a few revisions on the fair copy itself and in some differences between the fair copy and the typescript from which the *Little Review* version was printed.[16] There are about one hundred changes; most involve single words or short phrases. The few complete sentences that were added occur in dialogue or in Bloom's interior monologue: "He ran that workaday worker tack for all it was worth" (MS, "Aeolus," fol. 2; TS V.B.5, pp. 1-2; cf. 118.31-32), in which Bloom's mind echoes the rhythm of the machines; and "Shema Israel Adonai Elohenu. No, that's the other" (MS, fol. 7; TS, p. 3), which augments the original "Adonai." The changes or additions serve the novelistic aspect of the episode, increasing the precision of wording, the vividness of expression as a reflection of the episode's setting, and the details of characterization. To increase precision, Joyce altered many lifeless words and expressions into memorable ones:

> He took out his handkerchief to dab his nose. ~~Almond?~~ ⟨Citronlemon?⟩ Ah, the soap I put there.
>
> (MS, fol. 7; TS, p. 4)

> —Look at the young ~~arab~~ ⟨guttersnipe⟩ behind, Lenehan said, and you'll kick.
>
> (fol. 14; cf. TS, p. 7)

> —The point is did he forget it, J. J. O'Molloy said quietly. Saving princes is a ~~bad~~ ⟨thankyou⟩ job.
>
> (fol. 17; TS, pp. 8-9)

---

[16] These differences point up the problematical position of the Rosenbach Manuscript in the textual transmission of *Ulysses*. See the Appendix for further discussion.

Onomatopoeic words include the description of the machines as "clanking" (MS, fol. 2; TS, p. 1) and the alteration of "His machineries are working away too" to "pegging away" (fol. 2; p. 1). The sharpening of characterization primarily involves Myles Crawford. He is given a straw hat (fols. 14, 19, 29; pp. 7, 10, 15), and a pet expression, "That'll be all right," which replaces "That's all right" and "That'll go in all right" (fols. 12, 27; pp. 6, 14; Joyce later restored both original phrases). Joyce builds up the general impression of Crawford as a raving bird through such additions as "scarlet face" (fol. 29; p. 15; red, as the color of the episode, figures prominently in the late revisions). In the late revisions, Joyce identified the bird when Bloom calls the newsmen "Weathercocks" (125.20), appropriate for the Bérardian predictor of the winds. (The *Little Review* printer, perhaps recognizing the editor's birdlike qualities, at one point misprinted his name as "Crowford"; *LR*, 5, vi [Oct. 1918], p. 41.)

Some of the changes serve the function of "rhetoric." Although the famous list of rhetorical devices was not yet a part of the episode, rhetoric itself was integral, and several changes, often simply the addition or deletion of articles or connectives, heighten the artificial, rhetorical aspect of much of the dialogue or narration. A single "but" increases the artificiality of Dan Dawson's style: "Or again if we ⟨but⟩ climb the towering mountain peaks" (MS, fol. 9; TS, p. 5). In "Pyrrhus ⟨, misled by an oracle,⟩ made a last attempt to retrieve the fortunes of Greece" (fol. 17; p. 9), Joyce heightens the lecture-like speech of Professor MacHugh. He further "polishes" Seymour Bushe's "period": "that eternal symbol of wisdom and of ~~admonition~~ ⟨prophecy⟩ which, if aught that the ⟨imagination or the⟩ hand of sculptor has wrought in marble . . ." (fol. 23; p. 12).[17] The

---

[17] Joyce heard Bushe's speech in 1899 and included a phrase from it in his 1904 Pola notebook: "which, if anything that the hand of man has wrought of noble and inspiring and beautiful deserves to live deserves to live" (*Workshop of Daedalus*, p. 90). Joyce had already altered Bushe's words when he wrote the fair copy of "Aeolus," and his subsequent addi-

description of O'Molloy's gestures while he quotes Bushe becomes more rhetorical when it loses two articles: "His slim hand with a wave graced ~~the~~ echo and ~~the~~ fall" (fol. 23; p. 12). Finally, Lenehan, the other "rhetorician" of the episode, says "expectorated" rather than the original "expected" in his long adjectival account of Moses' career (fol. 26; p. 14).

The last significant aspect of early revision occurs in Stephen's parable, "A Pisgah Sight of Palestine." Although the parable underwent practically no revision after the *Little Review* publication, Joyce augmented it significantly between the fair copy and the typescript. These revisions fall into several categories. Some tighten Stephen's account by changing general statements into specifics, primarily by adding Dublin information. Thus, the two women "buy one and fourpenceworth of brawn and four slices of panloaf" originally "in an eatinghouse in Marlborough street" but then "at the north city diningrooms in Marlborough street from Miss Kate Collins, proprietress" (MS, fol. 28; TS, p. 15). "Rathmines church" becomes "Rathmines' blue dome" (fol. 30; p. 16), and Stephen adds the Dublin expression "to take off the thirst of the brawn" as the reason for the purchase of the plums (fol. 28; p. 15). Other changes increase the rhetorical nature of Stephen's talk: "fiftyfive years" becomes "fifty and fiftythree years" (fol. 27; p. 14); "twentyfour ripe plums" becomes "fourand twenty [*sic*]" (fol. 28; p. 15); and the women carry umbrellas "for fear it may ⟨come on to⟩ rain" (fol. 28; p. 15). Finally, Joyce reveals a typical concern for precise detail. The "tin letterbox moneybox," like real Dublin mailboxes, is now "red" (fol. 28; p. 15; this addition shows Joyce's early interest in the episode's symbolic color); Florence Mac-Cabe's weekly drink changes from "stout" to "double X" (fol. 28; p. 15); and for no apparent reason, the economic level of the venture is lowered, as the women's total savings

---

tions made Bushe's speech even more of a "polished period" than it was originally.

drop a shilling from "four and tenpence" to "three and tenpence" and the coppers drop from "two and seven" to "one and seven" (fol. 28; p. 15). Joyce made one deletion from the parable: the women originally look down from the pillar on "Rathmines church, Saint Michael and John's, Adam and Eve's," but the typist, presumably following Joyce's instructions, crossed out the middle church (fols. 30-31; p. 16).

These revisions brought "Aeolus" to the version published in the *Little Review*. Some of the changes serve the interest of the correspondences in the episode, such as the use of "prophecy" in Bushe's speech or the few additions of "red." Most do not, although from this point on in the development of the episode, the balance between the novel and the schema begins to shift in favor of the latter.

The Middle Stage

When Joyce wrote to John Quinn on November 24, 1920, and demanded that all his insertions to the episodes already published in the *Little Review* be included in any projected book publication of *Ulysses*, he described the new passages as "chiefly verbal or phrases, rarely passages" and named the four episodes having the greatest number of additions. "Aeolus" was not among these (*Letters*, III, 31). Joyce was still several months away from his "recasting" of the episode (I, 172) and the middle-stage revisions, which appear as handwritten additions to the typescript he sent to his printer Maurice Darantiere in June or July 1921, do not differ radically from those between the fair copy, typescript, and *Little Review* texts, except that the thirty-five changes are equally divided between the novelistic and symbolistic aspects of the episode. By the time Joyce compiled these revisions (probably beginning in 1920 and lasting until mid-1921), the expansive, symbolistic aspects had assumed a much greater importance in his conception of *Ulysses* than they had had before, but they had not yet come to dominate that conception.

The additions to Bloom's interior monologue reveal

both Joyce's growing concern with symbols and correspondences and his continued interest in precise phrasing and minute delineation of character. Joyce provides Bloom with responses to the machines' power, "Smash a man to atoms if they got him caught. Rule the world today" (TS, p. 1; 118.22-23); to the smell in the printing works, "Lukewarm glue in Thom's next door when I was there" (p. 4; 123.4-5); and to J. J. O'Molloy, "A mighthavebeen" (p. 5; 125.13). On the other hand, Bloom contributes a trope and several allusions to wind: "More Irish than the Irish" (p. 2; 119.11-12), "Bladderbags" (p. 4; 124.9), "Windfall when he kicks out" (p. 4; 124.17), "What's in the wind, I wonder" (p. 5; 125.4), and "Wonder is that young Dedalus ~~standing~~ ⟨the moving spirit⟩" (p. 15; 147.3; Joyce must have enjoyed this revision especially, since, without changing the meaning, he created motion out of stasis). In all, there are eighteen new novelistic phrases and sixteen symbolistic additions. These changes do not cause the episode to seem overwhelmed by the schema, although they do show that Joyce had begun to add allusions to wind and examples of rhetoric where they seemed appropriate. His limited revisions from the schema during his middle stage of work paved the way for the dramatic recasting in the last stage.

In discussing the revisions of "Aeolus," A. Walton Litz quotes a paragraph that he feels epitomizes Joyce's overhauling of the episode (Litz, p. 51). The paragraph is a fascinating example of the gradual accretion of symbolistic elements. Litz provides both the *Little Review* and final versions:

Practice dwindling. Losing heart. Used to get good retainers from D. and T. Fitzgerald. Believe he does some literary work for the *Express* with Gabriel Conroy. Well-read fellow. Myles Crawford began on the *Independent*. Funny the way they veer about. Go for one another baldheaded in the papers and then hail fellow well met the next moment.

(*LR*, p. 32)

Practice dwindling. A mighthavebeen. Losing heart.
Gambling. Debts of honour. Reaping the whirlwind.
Used to get good retainers from D. and T. Fitzgerald.
Their wigs to show their grey matter. Brains on their
sleeve like the statue in Glasnevin. Believe he does some
literary work for the *Express* with Gabriel Conroy. Well-
read fellow. Myles Crawford began on the *Independent*.
Funny the way those newspaper men veer about when
they get wind of a new opening. Weathercocks. Hot and
cold in the same breath. Wouldn't know which to believe.
One story good till you hear the next. Go for one
another baldheaded in the papers and then all blows
over. Hailfellow well met the next moment.

(125.13-24)

We will be following the growth of this passage through the
different stages of revision. An indication of Joyce's aims in
his additions to the typescript is the fact that, given all the
eventual augmentation, only "A mighthavebeen," a non-
windy phrase, entered at the middle stage.

One other document belongs to this stage of composition: the first of Joyce's two schemata for *Ulysses*. He prepared the outline for Carlo Linati and sent it to him with a
letter on September 21, 1920 (*Selected Letters*, pp. 270-71).
The entries for "Aeolus" include the following information:

Time—12-1
Colour—Red
Persons—Aeolus, Sons, Telemachus, Mentor, Ulysses(2)
Technic—Simbouleutike [deliberative oratory], Di-
kanike [forensic oratory], Epideictic [public oratory],
Tropes
Science, Art—Rhetoric
Sense (Meaning)—The Mockery of Victory
Organ—Lungs
Symbol—Machines: Wind: Hunger: Kite: Failed Des-
tinies: Press: Mutability

(Linati Schema)

How important was this schema to Joyce? The fair copy includes the entries for the time, the technic, the sense (as in various failures near the goal), and the symbols. In his additions to the typescript, Joyce was filling in the categories of tropes, rhetoric, lungs, wind, and redness. But some of the schema entries present problems. The symbolic meaning of MacHugh's hunger is not clear (is it a contrast with the feasts in Aeolus' castle?), nor are some of the "persons." The journalists may represent Aeolus' sons, and perhaps either John F. Taylor or MacHugh, each a conscience of Ireland, is Mentor, but who is the second Ulysses? When Joyce wrote the schema, these correspondences must have been like the entries of rhetoric, tropes, lungs, wind, and redness: ideas and plans in his mind rather than actual parts of the written episode. He compiled the schema after he had written the middle-stage episodes ("Cyclops," "Nausicaa," and "Oxen of the Sun") that leave behind the early novelistic concerns and the interior monologue technique for new directions of parody and exaggeration. But the revised "Aeolus" typescript shows that even though a major change in aesthetic direction had occurred in Joyce's new work, it was only beginning to appear in his revisions to the early episodes.

The Last Stage

Joyce's final work on "Aeolus" involved a great deal of addition and reworking in an extremely short period. The last revisions occurred in several stages between early August and the end of September 1921. (Darantiere pulled the first set of *placards* on August 11 or 12 and the last page proofs on October 3; Joyce's work probably preceded those dates by no more than a few weeks.) The recasting of the episode took place during the second and third weeks of August 1921, when he received the first set of *placards*. This was almost two months before he told Harriet Shaw Weaver of his reworking of "Aeolus" (Oct. 7, 1921; *Letters*, I, 172) and just before he wrote her, "I have made a great deal of addition to the proofs so far (up to the end of *Scylla and Charybdis*)" (Aug. 30, 1921; *Letters*, I, 171).

Darantiere's men prepared the episode seven different times. In the following discussion I will refer to the various proofs by letter symbols; the letters refer to the typescript or set of proofs onto which Joyce wrote his revisions:

> A—typescript; Buffalo TS V.B.5
> B—first *placards, ca.* Aug. 11-13, 1921; Harvard
> C—second *placards, ca.* Aug. 23-25; Harvard
> D—third *placards, ca.* Sept. 12-14; Harvard
> E—first page proofs, *ca.* Sept. 18-20; Buffalo V.C.1
> F—second page proofs, *ca.* Sept. 23-25; Buffalo V.C.1
> G—third page proofs, *ca.* Oct. 2-4; Texas

The late revisions involve only a very few novelistic aspects of the episode. Two additions to Stephen's monologue intensify the possibility that a new humility and receptiveness to experience distinguish the Stephen of *Ulysses* from that of *A Portrait of the Artist as a Young Man*; these are "I have much, much to learn" (144.31), Stephen's response to the Dublin around him, and "Dare it" (145.10), an addition at the beginning of Stephen's parable that suggests a break in his protective self-irony. Additions like these, though, are extremely rare compared to the increase in the schematic aspects of the episode.

A general pattern emerges in Joyce's revisions. He began by developing an initial impulse only to a limited extent; then in subsequent revisions he expanded and expanded. (It should be remembered, though, that some passages in the episode remain intact from earliest to last stage with no changes at all.) The broad categories of these changes follow the entries in the Linati schema: rhetoric (both tropes and subheads), allusions to wind, machines, lungs, and redness. No set of proofs is augmented in only one of these categories; Joyce increased all of them all the time.

The stages of Joyce's accretion process can be seen in every passage that underwent significant expansion. He augmented Bloom's thoughts about J. J. O'Molloy and ca-

pricious newsmen on each of the first five sets of proofs.
(All of the bracketed passages are additions; superscripts
indicate the typescript or proof onto which the addition is
written.)

> Practice dwindling. ⟨A mighthavebeen.ᴬ⟩ Losing
> heart. ⟨Gambling. Debts of honour.ᶜ⟩ ⟨Reaping the
> whirlwind.ᴰ⟩ Used to get good retainers from D. and T.
> Fitzgerald. ⟨Their wigs to show their grey matter. Brains
> on their sleeve like the statue in Glasnevin.ᴮ⟩ Believe he
> does some literary work for the *Express* with Gabriel
> Conroy. Wellread fellow. Myles Crawford began on the
> *Independent*. Funny the way ~~they~~ ⟨those newspaper
> menᴮ⟩ veer about ⟨when they get wind of a new
> openingᴮ⟩. ⟨Weathercocks.ᴱ⟩ ⟨Hot and cold in the same
> breath. Wouldn't know which to believe. One story good
> till you hear the next.ᴰ⟩ Go for one another baldheaded
> in the papers and then ~~hail~~ ⟨all blows over. Hailᴮ⟩ fellow
> well met the next moment.
>
> $$(125.13-24)^{18}$$

Wind references appear as additions to B, D, and E. The
addition to B, "get wind of a new opening," coupled with
that to C about Glasnevin, comes from an entry in the
Zurich notebook (VIII.A.5, p. 3). At every step, when
Joyce received a set of proofs he added and elaborated
(and corrected printer's mistakes in the previous set of additions). He had determined the general plan for the paragraph, but he decided the specific degree to which he
would carry the elaboration only as he finished each successive stage.

This process occurs in other passages—in Bloom's
monologues, in dialogue, and in the set speeches:

---

[18] The printers misread Joyce's symbols for his additions and substi-
tuted "those newspaper men" for "Their wigs to show the [*sic*] grey matter. Brains on their sleeve like the statue in Glasnevin" on C. Joyce had to
repeat the additions on C, substituting "their" for "the," and the words
appear correctly on D. Also, the printers mistakenly set "Hail fellow" as
one word on C, and the error persisted through all the proofs and all published editions.

Strange he never saw his real country. Ireland my country. Member for College green. He ~~ran~~ ⟨boomed^F⟩ that workaday worker tack for all it was worth. ⟨It's the ads and side features sell a ~~paper~~ weekly not the stale news^B⟩ ⟨in the official gazette^E⟩. ⟨Queen Anne is dead.^B⟩ ⟨Published by authority in the year one thousand and. Demesne situate in the townland of Rosenallis, barony of Tinnahinch. To all whom it may concern schedule pursuant to statute showing return of number of mules and jennets exported from Ballina.^F⟩ ⟨Nature notes.^B⟩ ⟨Cartoons.^D⟩ ⟨Phil Blake's weekly Pat and Bull story.^G⟩ ⟨Uncle Toby's page for tiny tots. Country bumpkin's queries. Dear Mr Editor, what is a good cure for flatulence?^B⟩ ⟨I'd like that part. Learn a lot teaching others.^F⟩ ⟨The personal note. M. A. P. Mainly all pictures. Shapely bathers on golden strand. World's biggest balloon. Double marriage of sisters celebrated. Two bridegrooms laughing heartily at each other.^C⟩ ⟨Cuprani too, printer. More Irish than the Irish.^A⟩

(118.30-119.12)[19]

—⟨You take my breath away.^B⟩ Is it not ⟨perchance^C⟩ a French compliment? Mr O'Madden Burke asked. ⟨'Tis the hour^A⟩ ⟨, methinks,^B⟩ ⟨when the winejug^A⟩ ⟨, metaphorically speaking,^C⟩ ⟨is most grateful^A⟩ ⟨in Ye ancient hostelry^B⟩.

(143.36-39)

—As ~~it were~~ ⟨'twere^B⟩, *in the peerless panorama* ⟨of Ireland's portfolio, ^B⟩ ⟨unmatched, ^A⟩ ⟨despite their wellpraised prototypes in other^B⟩ ⟨vaunted^D⟩ ⟨prize regions,^B⟩ ⟨for very beauty, ^A⟩ *of bosky grove and undulating plain and luscious pastureland* ⟨of vernal green^C⟩, *steeped in the transcendent*

---

[19] Joyce changed "paper" to "weekly" on B. He added "of sisters" to the addition he wrote onto C, but the printers omitted it on D. He rewrote it onto D, and it first appears on E. "Tinnahinch" was erroneously printed as "Tinnchinch" on G, the final page proofs. Joyce noted the error, but instead of changing the "c" to "a," the printers added the "a," and the name appears incorrectly as "Tinnachinch" in all published editions.

translucent glow of our mild mysterious Irish twilight. . . .

$$(125.33-38)^{20}$$

Every category of revision follows this process, including the rhetorical devices and the subheads. As we have seen, Joyce filled the episode with rhetorical devices from the start, but included in the thirty-one new examples are the startling, unique phrases that make Gilbert's list seem like a dominant part of the episode. Among the new devices are Lenehan's "Clamn dever" (137.36; his remark remains the unexciting "Clever idea" until Joyce changed it on D); his palindromes, "Madam, I'm Adam. And Able was I ere I saw Elba" (137.22); and his quips, "Muchibus thankibus" (140.25), "I feel a strong weakness" (134.24), and "O, for a fresh of breath air!" (135.11). The new forms entered at every stage of revision, as Joyce thought of more and more examples to include. Joyce added five examples to A, eight to B, eleven to C, four to D, and three to E.

The subheads, the most noticeable single group of additions to "Aeolus," follow a similar pattern. Joyce added them to the first *placards* (B) as part of the large single wave of recasting (see Figure 2), but he revised some and introduced others on the many proofs. There are sixty-three subheads in the final text; he wrote slightly over half of them in their final form directly on B. He included many of the others in their basic form on B but augmented or changed them later; a few exist in their final location in the additions to B, but he entirely rewrote them; still others he added to later proofs. After they first appeared on the proofs Joyce dropped only one subhead entirely: on the third page, "His Little Joke" originally existed between "—Well, he is one of our saviours also" and "A meek smile accompanied him . . ." (118.9-10). Joyce probably deleted this head when he added "The Crozier and the Pen" (118.1) on the next set of proofs to avoid crowding the first pages of the episode with subheads.

---

[20] The printers transposed "prize regions" and "other" on C. Joyce corrected the error on C, and the phrase appears correctly on D.

The "great revision" of "Aeolus" (the first *placard* of the episode's opening, corrected and augmented by Joyce). Reproduced courtesy of the Society of Authors and by permission of the Houghton Library, Harvard University. (Figure 2)

The accompanying list shows the subheads as Joyce originally added them to the first *placards* (left column) and the heads as they appear in the published book (right column).

The Heart of the Metropolis	In the Heart of the Hibernian Metropolis
	The Wearer of the Crown
Old Woman of Prince's Street	Gentlemen of the Press
One of Our Saviours	William Brayden, Esquire, of Oaklands, Sandymount
	The Crozier and the Pen
His Little Joke	(deleted)
With Unfeigned Regret it is We Announce the Dissolution of a Most Respected Citizen	With Unfeigned Regret It Is We Announce the Dissolution of a Most Respected Dublin Burgess
How a Great Modern Daily is Turned Out	How A Great Daily Organ Is Turned Out
The Canvasser at Work	We See the Canvasser at Work
House of Key(e)s	House of Key(e)s
Orthographical	Orthographical
Noted Churchman a Contributor	Noted Churchman an Occasional Contributor
A Dayfather	A Dayfather
	And It Was the Feast of the Passover
That Soap Again	Only Once More that Soap
Erin, the Gem of the Sea	Erin, Green Gem of the Silver Sea
To the Point	Short But to the Point
Sad	Sad
His Native Doric	His Native Doric
What Wetherup Said	What Wetherup Said
Memorable Battles Recalled	Memorable Battles Recalled
Harp Eolian	O, Harp Eolian
Spot the Winner	Spot the Winner
They Collide	A Collision Ensues
Exit Bloom	Exit Bloom
A Street Procession	A Street Cortège
The Calumet of Peace	The Calumet of Peace
The Grandeur that was Rome	The Grandeur that was Rome
? ? ?	? ? ?
Shindy in Restaurant	Shindy in Wellknown Restaurant
Lost Causes	Lost Causes/Noble Marquess Mentioned
Kyrie eleison!	Kyrie Eleison!

Lenehan's Limerick

"You can do it!"
The Great Gallaher
A Distant Voice
Clever, very
Rhymes and Reasons
Sufficient for the Day . . .

A Polished Period
A Man of High Morale
Impromptu
From the Fathers
Ominous—for him!
Let us Hope
Dear Dirty Dublin

Return of Bloom
Interview with the Editor

Raising the Wind

Those Slightly Rambunctious
Females
Dames Donate Dublin's Cits

Sophist Smites Haughty Helen
on Proboscis. Spartans Gnash Molars. Ithacans Vow Pen is Champ

Hello There, Central!
What?—and Likewise—Where?
Virilian [*sic*], Says Pedagogue.
Sophomore Plumps for Old Man
Moses
Horatio Now is Cynosure

Diminished Digits Prove Too
Titillating for Frisky Frumps.
Anne Sighs, Flo Wangles—Yet Can
You Blame Them?

Lenehan's Limerick
Omnium Gatherum
You Can Do It!
The Great Gallaher
A Distant Voice
Clever, Very
Rhymes and Reasons
Sufficient for the Day . . .
Links with Bygone Days of Yore
Italia, Magistra Artium
A Polished Period
A Man of High Morale
Impromptu
From the Fathers
Ominous—For Him!
Let Us Hope
Dear Dirty Dublin
Life on the Raw

Return of Bloom
Interview with the Editor
K. M. A.
K. M. R. I. A.

Raising the Wind
Some Column!—That's What
Waddler One Said

Those Slightly Rambunctious
Females
Dames Donate Dublin's Cits/
Speedpills Velocitous Aeroliths,
Belief
Sophist Wallops Haughty Helen
Square on Proboscis. Spartans
Gnash Molars. Ithacans Vow Pen is
Champ

Hello There, Central!
What?—and Likewise—Where?
Virgilian, Says Pedagogue.
Sophomore Plumps for Old Man
Moses
Horatio is Cynosure This Fair
June Day
Diminished Digits Prove Too
Titillating for Frisky Frumps.
Anne Wimbles, Flo Wangles—Yet
Can You Blame Them?

Several patterns exist in the development of these heads. For one thing, Joyce was apparently less certain of what he was doing at the beginning and at the end of the episode than he was in the middle. The first eight subheads in the final version (and thirteen out of the first sixteen) were either changed or completely rewritten after they first appeared, or they were added after B. Similarly, seven of the last twelve were altered or added later. Only a few of the heads in between underwent any type of revision except Joyce's correction of the ubiquitous printer's errors. There are two possible explanations for this. First, the historical aspect of the subheads is most prominent at the beginning and end, and Joyce probably needed more time to perfect these than he did for the less conspicuous heads in the middle. Second, the lifeless quality of some of the beginning subheads—a phrase merely lifted from the text, "One of Our Saviours," or a tag line, "Old Woman of Prince's Street"—suggests that Joyce may not yet have warmed up to the project of creating these heads when he began to write them. On the successive proofs, Joyce made some of the original subheads much livelier by changing the grammatical structure or by adding single words or phrases, usually adjectival. Like all the revisions, then, the heads entered in stages and underwent a regular process of revision.

Stuart Gilbert discusses the subheads (which he calls captions) as a preparation for later stylistic developments in *Ulysses*:

It will be noted that the style of the captions is gradually modified in the course of the episode; the first are comparatively dignified, or classically allusive, in the Victorian tradition; later captions reproduce, in all its vulgarity, the slickness of the modern press. This historico-literary technique, here inaugurated, is a preparation for the employment of the same method, but on the grand scale, a stylistic *tour de force*, in a later episode, the *Oxen of the Sun*.

(Gilbert, p. 179n)

This is an orthodox view, the one Joyce wished to convey, and it is true to the book as it finally came to exist. In the actual writing, however, the *tour de force* came first and the preparation for it fifteen months later.

The great collection of additions to the first *placards* included Nelson's Pillar and the tramlines at the beginning and end of the episode. (Joyce added the "vermilion mail-cars" and their accompanying subhead [116.15-21] to C, the second *placard*.) The pillar and tramlines increase the emphasis on machines, placing the trams as well as the newspaper presses at the "heart" of Dublin. There is thus a contrast with "Hades," the organ of which is the heart. Bloom makes a connection like this when he analyzes the human heart as a machine in "Hades" (105.36-38), and in "Aeolus" his thoughts bring together Dignam's remains, the wording of the newspaper account of the funeral, the noise of the machines (118.21-22). The tramlines serve as an analogy to the "walls of bronze" of Aeolus' castle (Gilbert, p. 185), and they seem to correspond to Aeolus' children. Joyce originally included only twelve destinations for the trams ("Sandymount Tower" came later), which is the number of Aeolus' sons and daughters.[21] (Joyce noted "6 sons—6 daughters" in notebook VIII.A.5, p. 16, and in "Aeolus" Bloom thinks of another family of twelve, "the twelve brothers, Jacob's sons"; 122.24-25.) These analogies come as much from Bérard as from Homer; they are a sign that Bérard's influence on Joyce never waned.

Some of Joyce's late revisions were filtered through other documents. He obviously returned to notebook VIII.A.5 for entries like "6 sons—6 daughters" and "Get wind of it (Glasnevin)." A more important notebook at this time, though, was the one containing entries for thirteen episodes (notes similar to those on the British Museum notesheets for the last seven episodes). This notebook, Buffalo MS V.A.2, contains only a few notes for "Aeolus":

[21] Joyce added a thirteenth tramline perhaps to suggest the tower as the home of Christ and Judas, perhaps to link it with the man in the mackintosh, the mysterious thirteenth mourner at Paddy Dignam's funeral (111.9-13).

wind on stomach, divine afflatus, blarney, caricature, Irish Catholic, messenger of Sacred Heart, Donegal tweed, parked [illegible word] Solon——belief, Velocitous, bambino Jakes M'Carthy, Dubl. Gazette, circulation establ. 1763 replies to correspondents

(V.A.2, p. 27)

Joyce handled these notes like those on the British Museum notesheets: he crossed out the words he used (though no pattern to his use of colors is immediately apparent) and, conversely, used no words in "Aeolus" that he did not delete.[22] The notes are very specific; Herring concludes that Joyce used this notebook for "verbal insertions" or "finishing touches" to the episodes he was reviewing in proof (*Notes and Early Drafts*, pp. 39, 41). He seems to have known exactly where he would use most of the notes. For example, "parked" went into the following paragraph, the rest of which was intact when the third *placard* (D) was pulled:

> Under the porch of the general post office shoeblacks called and polished. I̶n̶ ⟨Parked in⟩ North Prince's street His Majesty's vermilion mailcars, bearing on their sides the royal initials, E. R., received loudly flung sacks of letters, postcards, lettercards, parcels, insured and paid, for local, provincial, British and overseas delivery.

(116.16-21)

Likewise, "caricature" refers to the alteration of "swiftly" to "in swift caricature" (130.1), and "belief, Velocitous" signals the addition "Speedpills Velocitous Aeroliths, Belief" to a subhead that, through the pulling of E, read only "Dames Donate Dublin's Cits" (148.12-14). Joyce must have had these specific revisions in mind when he noted these words and phrases; the notes probably served to remind him to make the changes.

He added all eleven notes from notebook V.A.2 which

---

[22] "Solon," one of the deleted notes that does not appear in "Aeolus," is in a *Finnegans Wake* notebook (Buffalo MS VI.C.7, p. 137), where Joyce again listed it under the category "Aeolus."

appear in "Aeolus" to the third *placards* or the page proofs. Since most of the additions to the episode were entered on the first two sets of *placards*, it is significant that this notebook contains revisions that followed the initial recasting. The proofs in question date from mid-September 1921, so Joyce probably compiled the "Aeolus" notes at just about that time. This concurs with the conclusion of most other scholars who have studied this notebook that Joyce compiled and used notebook V.A.2 in the very last stages of addition and revision. (For a summary of the evidence, see *Notes and Early Drafts*, pp. 38, 41.)

The late revisions reveal a certain amount of cross-exchange between "Aeolus" and later episodes that Joyce had already written, although not as much as might be expected. The subheads as preparation for "Oxen of the Sun" are the main examples of this, but there are more minute ones. For example, "Davy Stephens" (116.30), whom Joyce added to "Aeolus" on C, speaks to Bloom in one of the "Circe" hallucinations, where his words contain one of the V.A.2 entries that did not get into "Aeolus": "*Messenger of the Sacred Heart* and *Evening Telegraph* with Saint Patrick's Day Supplement. Containing the new addresses of all the cuckolds in Dublin" (469.15-17). Stephens, however, and some of the details about him, did move from "Circe" back to "Aeolus." Likewise, the references in "Aeolus" to the specific Dublin newspapers, "the *Weekly Freeman and National Press* and the *Freeman's Journal and National Press*" (117.15-17) and "the offices of the *Irish Catholic* and *Dublin Penny Journal*" (146.13-14), both late additions, occur distorted in "Circe" as Myles Crawford says, "Hello. *Freeman's Urinal* and *Weekly Arsewiper* here" (458.19).

One final document is relevant to Joyce's late revisions: the second of his schemata for the book. Joyce first gave this schema to Valery Larbaud in November 1921 for Larbaud's December 7 lecture on *Ulysses* (*Letters*, III, 53-54), and a few of Joyce's friends saw it during the 1920s. Stuart Gilbert published it, minus the list of correspondences, in

1930. Joyce's 1921 plan contains less information than the earlier one, although it is clearly an outline of an existing episode:

Scene—The Newspaper
Hour—12 noon
Organ—lungs
Art—rhetoric
Colour—red
Symbol—editor
Technic—enthymemic
Correspondences—Crawford – Eolus: Incest – journalism: Floating Island – press

(1921 Schema)

This schema is a bare outline, lacking obscure symbols like "hunger" and, significantly, lacking such an explicit statement of "meaning" as the earlier "mockery of victory." Yet the outline is truly indicative of the work Joyce had done on the episode since his previous schema.

Joyce's late revisions to "Aeolus" changed the shape of the episode, and as a result they altered the entire first half of *Ulysses*. The subheads foreshadow not only the succession of parody styles in "Oxen of the Sun," as Gilbert suggests, but all the voices—distinct both from the characters and from the narrators of the early episodes—who tell the story in the second half of the book. The heads fragment an episode that otherwise flows quite smoothly; they slow down an episode that otherwise moves at a pace similar to the other early episodes and cause "Aeolus" to resemble the slower last half of *Ulysses*. The final version of "Aeolus" looks like a late episode and prepares us for the elaborations to come, but compared to "Cyclops" or "Ithaca," for example, its recasting was very restrained. Only the subheads and the tramlines change the episode's look and feel; the other additions, such as the allusions to wind, redness, and machines, are no different from Joyce's late revisions to the surrounding episodes, "Lotus Eaters,"

"Hades," or "Lestrygonians." He changed "Aeolus" sufficiently for it to foreshadow later developments, but no more. He was careful that his early work would not be obscured beyond recognition by his late revisions, and that all his stages of work on "Aeolus"—early, middle, and late—would be visible. In its final form, "Aeolus" serves as a microcosm of Joyce's work on *Ulysses*.

The Middle Stage: "Cyclops"

T HE summer following Joyce's completion of "Sirens" was a crucial period in the development of *Ulysses*. In "Wandering Rocks" and "Sirens," the first two episodes in Joyce's middle stage of work, he employed the interior monologue technique of the opening nine episodes, but he stretched and distorted it to such an extent that its collapse was inevitable. "Cyclops" followed with a technique radically different from the interior monologue, a combination of a first-person naturalistic description of the scene in Barney Kiernan's pub, narrated by an unnamed debt collector, and a series of elaborate extensions and exaggerations of incidents in the pub. In his 1921 schema Joyce called the technique "gigantism": the gigantic verbal escapades correspond to the physical giant Polyphemus, and both the narrator and the speakers of the interpolated passages, like the one-eyed giant, conspicuously lack the two-eyed vision of their subject, Leopold Bloom. He is unique among the men in the pub; surrounded by bigots, he makes a plea for tolerance based on "love . . . I mean the opposite of hatred" (333.14).

Joyce's early drafts of "Cyclops" have survived, and they provide a unique glimpse into the book *Ulysses* eventually became. He began the episode without a clear idea of the technique he would use; he even planned briefly to continue the monologue method. The drafts reveal him working to create the first new technique for *Ulysses*, a process that resulted in the middle-stage episodes "Cyclops," "Nausicaa," and "Oxen of the Sun," and eventually led to the culminating work of the last four episodes.

Chronology

Because the early drafts of "Cyclops" are extant, we can carefully document Joyce's attempts to construct the episode. He probably began his work in June 1919, almost immediately after he sent the typescript of "Sirens" to Ezra Pound for submission to the *Little Review*. On June 19, Joyce wrote to Frank Budgen that "Cyclops" was "being lovingly moulded in the way you know," and in the letter he described and quoted a section from the episode:

> The Fenian is accompanied by a wolfhound who speaks (or curses) in Irish. He unburdens his soul about the Saxo-Angles in the best Fenian style and with colossal vituperativeness alluding to their standard industry. The epic proceeds explanatorily 'He spoke of the English, a noble race, rulers of the waves, who sit on thrones of alabaster, silent as the deathless gods.'
>
> (*Letters*, I, 126)

In the episode's final published form, Garryowen's poem and the Citizen's tribute to the English "thrones" are widely separated (312.25-32, 325.24-26), but they originally formed part of one scene. They occur together near the beginning of what is probably Joyce's first draft of the episode, copybook V.A.8 at Buffalo.[1] (See the accompanying table for a list of the "Cyclops" documents.) Joyce must have begun copybook V.A.8, and hence the episode, shortly before June 19, 1919.[2]

[1] Two scholars have recently offered editions of Buffalo MS V.A.8: Phillip F. Herring (*Notes and Early Drafts*, pp. 119-87), who includes the other Buffalo and Cornell "Cyclops" documents discussed in this chapter, and Myron Schwartzman, "The V.A.8 Copybook: An Early Draft of the 'Cyclops' Chapter of *Ulysses* with Notes on Its Development," *James Joyce Quarterly*, 12 (1974/75), pp. 64-122. Schwartzman reproduces four pages from the copybook.

[2] Phillip Herring is less certain that V.A.8 is the first draft of "Cyclops." Joyce's letter to Budgen, Herring suggests, may refer to an earlier draft that Joyce copied into V.A.8. Either sequence is conjectural, but Herring and I agree that the least problematical explanation is that Joyce completed the first couple of scenes of copybook V.A.8 before both the June 19 letter to Budgen and the list of characters at Cornell (see below), and the remaining scenes after that date. See *Notes and Early Drafts*, pp. 127-28.

The copybook contains eight fragmentary scenes which Joyce, sometime after writing them, numbered 1 to 8 in blue. These fragments seem to divide into two groups of four scenes each. The first four scenes progress roughly from the beginning to the end of the episode; the second group develops new incidents for the middle. Joyce wrote scenes 1-4 in ink and 5-8 in pencil. After he began the first scene, but no later than his work on the fourth, he compiled a list of characters for "Cyclops." He did this on the back of a June 23 letter from Henry Davray;[3] he probably received the letter around June 28 and compiled the list within the next few days. By the end of June, this sequence suggests, Joyce was still working on the first few scenes in the copybook.

He needed a list of characters' names even after he began to write his scenes. In the naturalistic parts of the first few scenes, he does not name most of the patrons of Barney Kiernan's pub; instead, he provides their dialogue and replaces their names with such symbols as "——," "α," or "Ƶ." On the other hand, many of the characters in the list appear in the fourth scene and after, so Joyce probably had compiled the list by the time he was working on fragment 4. His method of composition (developing a list of characters' names after writing several scenes) is not as strange as it might initially appear, since the first four scenes consist mainly of parody passages, including those beginning "In Inisfail the fair there lies a land, the land of holy Michan" (now 293.38; cf. V.A.8, p.1r)[4] and "When, lo,

---

[3] The letter is at Cornell. Robert E. Scholes, comp., *The Cornell Joyce Collection: A Catalogue* (Ithaca: Cornell Univ. Press, 1961), item 390. Joyce's list of characters is item 55.

[4] The Buffalo documents are catalogued by Peter Spielberg in *James Joyce's Manuscripts and Letters at the University of Buffalo: A Catalogue* (Buffalo: Univ. of Buffalo, 1962). The "Cyclops" section (pp. 36-39) unfortunately contains numerous errors; most important, copybook V.A.8 clearly precedes draft V.A.6. All transcriptions from the "Cyclops" documents are my own. I have numbered the pages and leaves as follows: (1) V.A.8. This is a 24-leaf notebook. The numbering would present no problem if Joyce had not omitted 16 in his own numbering of the leaves. To facilitate

there came about them all a great brightness" (345.22; cf. p. 20r). Very early in his work on "Cyclops," Joyce apparently decided to drop the monologue technique, which he had already distorted practically beyond recognition in "Sirens." He lacked a clear idea of the technique that would replace it, but, contrary to what we might expect, his initial impulse was in the direction of the parody passages rather than in that of the first-person naturalistic narrator.

The notesheets for this episode, now at the British Museum and edited in 1972 by Phillip F. Herring, appear prominently in copybook V.A.8 and lend support to the assumption that it indeed contains the first draft. Many of the notes that Joyce crossed out in red appear in the copybook; significantly, the vast majority of them occur as additions or revisions. He seems to have written out the scenes without great use of his notes (which he then depended on heavily for revisions and additions), but many notes appear to have been written with their place in the text already in mind. This practice raises the question of whether Joyce compiled the notesheets before he began to write the episode or after he completed the first scenes in their original version. A note at 3:19-20, "Weiss' sister-in-law: death of infant, putting on an inside vest," refers to a conversation between Joyce and his Zurich friend Ottocaro Weiss that Richard Ellmann discusses among the events of the summer of 1919 (*JJ*, p. 478).[5] This would place the compilation of at least some of the sheets very near or even after the writing of the first draft; certainly most notes predate the draft, but some postdate it.

---

comparison with Phillip F. Herring's edition of the "Cyclops" documents in *Joyce's Notes and Early Drafts for* Ulysses, I have followed Herring's practice and numbered the pages as Joyce numbered them. (2) V.A.6. This document consists of two large foolscap sheets, each folded in half to produce four sides. I have numbered the pages of Spielberg's sheet "b" as 1r, 1v, 2r, and 2v, and of his sheet "a" as 3r, 3v, 4r, and 4v. For a discussion of the cataloguing of the Buffalo "Cyclops" drafts, see my article, " 'Cyclops' in Progress, 1919," *James Joyce Quarterly*, 12 (1974/75), pp. 157-58.

[5] Unless I indicate otherwise, all notesheet numbers in this chapter refer to "Cyclops" notesheets.

As Joyce used a passage or scene from one draft in his writing of the next, he followed his procedure with the notesheets and crossed it out with a colored pencil. Almost all the pages in the first-draft copybook contain at least one red diagonal line or "X" through the body of the writing, and some marginal additions are crossed out in blue. Joyce must have done this as he used each passage in a subsequent draft.

Very shortly after he completed MS V.A.8 and at least part of a copybook that continued it,[6] Joyce wrote a second draft of the last four V.A.8 scenes. This second version (Buffalo MS V.A.6) can be grouped with V.A.8 in one period of development.

The next available stage after these two drafts is the autograph fair copy that John Quinn bought from Joyce and that now belongs to the Philip H. and A.S.W. Rosenbach Foundation in Philadelphia. The transitional documents have not survived. A period of about six weeks is involved (early July to mid-August), during which Joyce developed the narrative voice for the episode, arranged the scenes he had written, and created new ones. A single sheet of paper (Buffalo MS V.A.7) provides a clue to his activities at this time. This document contains two separate elements: a list of events for "Cyclops" and a short passage (now 329.25-29). The list and the passage were not written together, since Joyce wrote the passage around one of the words from the list. The passage parodies clauses 4-8 of the Apostles' Creed:

> suffered under rump and dozen, ~~his~~ ⟨was⟩ backside flayed and ~~reddened~~ ⟨curried⟩ ~~till he~~ yelled like hell —.: he arose again the third day from the bed, ~~ascended~~ ⟨steered⟩ into haven, sitteth on his beam till further orders when he shall come to drudge

---

[6] Joyce used at least one other copybook (now lost) that continued the extant first draft. Copybook V.A.8 ends in the middle of a scene, and the complete scene exists in a second version (Buffalo MS V.A.6). Also, on p. 23r of V.A.8, Joyce told himself to see page 28, which presumably refers to a second "Cyclops" copybook that continued the pagination of V.A.8.

THE DEVELOPMENT OF "CYCLOPS"

Date	Name	Description	Other Documents
1919 June	Buffalo MS V.A.8	24-leaf copybook; contains early drafts of eight scenes	British Museum notesheets—Add. MS 49975
	Buffalo MS V.A.6	two large sheets; contains next draft of last four scenes of V.A.8	Cornell 55—list of characters for "Cyclops"
June or July	Buffalo MS V.A.7 (passage)	single sheet; contains an addition to a paragraph in V.A. 6	Buffalo MS V.A.7 (list)—list of incidents for second half of episode
Aug.-Sept.	Rosenbach MS	autograph fair copy now in possession of the Philip H. and A.S.W. Rosenbach Foundation, Philadelphia	intermediate drafts not extant
Sept.-Oct.	typescript—Buffalo TSS V.B.10.a,b	prepared from Rosenbach MS; contains a few corrections and additions by Joyce in margins	
Nov.-March 1920	Little Review	set from typescript, with Joyce's corrections and additions —6, vii (Nov.1919), pp. 38-54	

Date	Name	Description	Other Documents
1921 ca. Aug.- Sept.	typescript— Buffalo TS V.B.10.a	—6, viii (Dec. 1919), pp. 50-60 —6, ix (Jan. 1920), pp. 53-61 —6, x (Mar. 1920), pp. 54-60 Joyce added many new passages in the margins of a copy of the typescript prepared in September-October 1919	
Oct.	placards— Harvard, Princeton	three or four different proofs pulled for each page; first set pulled from typescript; each subsequent set incorporates new additions	Buffalo MS V.A.2—notes for late revisions and draft of addition to "Cyclops"
Oct.	page proofs— Buffalo V.C.1, Texas, Princeton	three to five different proofs pulled for each page; each set incorporates new additions	Buffalo MS V.A.9—next draft of same addition
1922 Feb. 2	publication	published book includes additions written onto last page proof	

This passage seems to be an expansion of the second list entry, "Whipping," a discussion of which exists in both the V.A.8 and V.A.6 drafts. Joyce wrote it specifically as an addition to a paragraph in draft V.A.6 that parodies the first three clauses of the Apostles' Creed.

The V.A.7 list contains several events for the episode in an order approximating that of the final version:

Religion—Saints (Isle of)   (337.39-40)
Whipping   (328.42ff)
Arrival Lenehan v John Nolan   (324.27)
Alaki   (334.11)
Exit of Bloom   (333.18)
Virag Discussion   (337.37)
Arrival Martin   (337.14)
Saints   (339.13ff?)
Return Bloom   (341.5)
Discussion Jews   (342.14)
Finale   (343.29ff)

The events in the list all occur in the second half of the episode; there may have been a parallel list, now lost, for the first half. Unlike the "rump and dozen" passage, which Joyce definitely wrote after both the V.A.8 and V.A.6 drafts, the list may have been compiled either before or after the two drafts. If before, then Joyce composed the fragmentary scenes in the drafts with an approximate order for them in his mind. On the other hand, entries such as "Whipping," "Alaki," "Discussion Jews," and "Finale" may refer to parts of the draft already in existence, and the list may represent Joyce's method of arranging his fragments in a workable order. Because of the disunity of the V.A.8 and V.A.6 drafts, the latter possibility seems more likely.

The autograph fair copy of "Cyclops" dates from August and September 1919, and the typescript was prepared from this fair copy.[7] On October 28 Joyce told Harriet

[7] There is no doubt that the "Cyclops" typescript, unlike those for several other episodes whose relationship to the Rosenbach MS is prob-

Shaw Weaver that he had forwarded the typescript to Pound a few days before he left Zurich for Trieste, that is, before October 15 (*Letters*, II, 455). The *Little Review* began its publication of "Cyclops" in November 1919 and continued it in three more issues (December 1919, January 1920, March 1920). This publication marks the end of the first major stage of the episode's development.

On November 24, 1920, Joyce wrote to John Quinn and discussed the work he had done on the *Little Review* episodes since their original publication. "Cyclops" was one of the four episodes he mentioned as having received the greatest number of additions:

> I began *Ulysses* in 1914 and shall finish it, I suppose, in 1921. This is, I think, the twentieth address at which I have written it—and the coldest. The complete notes fill a small valise, but in the course of continual changings very often it was not possible to sort them for the final time before the publication of certain instalments. The insertions (chiefly verbal or phrases, rarely passages) must be put in for the book publication. Before leaving Trieste I did this sorting for all episodes up to and including *Circe*. The episodes which have the heaviest burden of addenda are *Lotus-eaters*, *Lestrygonians*, *Nausikaa* and *Cyclops*.
>
> (*Letters*, III, 30-31)

Joyce was not misleading Quinn when he described the additions as "chiefly verbal or phrases, rarely passages." As he did with each of the first fourteen episodes, he took a copy of the typescript he had sent to Pound for the *Little Review* and wrote his new corrections and additions in the margins. The typescript, complete with additions, was sent

---

lematical, was prepared directly from the fair copy at the Rosenbach Foundation. One kind of evidence (there are many) involves the X's that appear on fols. 21, 30, 37, 44, and 48 of the "Cyclops" fair copy. These must have been written by the typist to indicate stopping points, since they correspond to the beginnings of pp. 13, 18, 22, 26, and 28 of Buffalo TS V.B.10.a.

to Maurice Darantiere in September 1921, after which the printer pulled three or four sets of *placards* for each page (between September 30 and October 18) and three to five sets of page proofs (between October 10 and November 7).[8] Joyce revised and augmented the episode when he received each set of proofs. The later development of "Cyclops" reveals as well as any episode in the book the accuracy of Paul Valéry's remark, which A. Walton Litz has applied to all of *Ulysses*, that "a work of art is never finished, but only abandoned" (Litz, p. 7).

The First Draft

"I am boring through a mountain from two sides. The question is, how to meet in the middle," Joyce said about writing *Finnegans Wake*. The statement has been applied to the whole of *Ulysses* (Litz, p. 7), and it accurately describes Joyce's composition of "Cyclops."

In the early drafting of the episode, the sides of the mountain are as much exaggerated parody as the specific beginning and end of the episode, and the problem of meeting in the middle involves the development of a narrative between the parodies. Given the episode's final form—the complete break with the stream of consciousness technique in the double focus provided by the first-person narrator and the succession of "gigantic" parodies—we might conjecture that Joyce began with the opinionated, bigoted narrator and then gradually developed the series of parodies as a complement to, and a check on, the authority of the naturalistic description. But the opposite was the case: Joyce created the parodies first, the barroom scene came soon after, and the narrative voice developed last.

Joyce's delay in developing a narrative voice for the episode is not surprising, since "Cyclops" constitutes the

[8] Joyce's corrected *placards* are at Harvard; the corrected page proofs are at Buffalo (V.C.1) and Texas.

first total break with the original techniques. Joyce seems to have decided to drop the interior monologue method very early in his work on the episode. The first draft copybook is almost entirely free of the technique, but one passage occurs as an addition to the second paragraph and a few appear on the back of the first page. (At the beginning of the copybook, Joyce used the backs of the leaves, that is, the left-hand pages, for additions and revisions only.) There are three passages in the initial style, one of external description and two of Bloom's thoughts:

> Bloom went by Mary's lane and saw the sordid row of old clothes' shops, the old hucksterwomen seated by ~~the~~ baskets of battered hats, amid the dangling legs of ~~legless~~ trousers, ~~culprits~~ ~~limp~~ ⟨limp⟩ coats ~~hung by the neck~~ ⟨manless⟩

> Like culprits. Be taken to the prison from whence you came and there be hanged by the neck till you are ~~bought~~ ⟨sold⟩ and may the Lord. ⟨Emmet. Martyrs. They want to be? My life for Ireland. Romance. Girl in a window watching. Wipe away a tear. ?Hung up for scarecrows. Quite the ?coiling effect. Of⟩ ⟨course— Where was it battle of Fontenoy they charged. Remember Limerick.⟩ Hard times those were in Holles street when Molly tried that game. Nothing in it: blind rut. Chiefly women, of course. Devils to please. Come back tomorrow. Ta, ta.

> Gunnard & plaice those are. Speckled backs. One after another hook in their gills. Can't be hunger drives them. Probably curiosity. Curiosity killed the fish

> (V.A.8, pp. 1r, 1v, 2r)

All three passages are fragmentary; Joyce wrote the last as an addition to a parody passage ("Who comes through Inn's quay ward . . .") and the first two around a Verlaine poem ("La lune blanche," poem VI from *La bonne chanson*) that he had copied in the middle of the first verso page.

The passages do not connect directly to the draft he was writing on the right-hand pages, but, since they concern Bloom's activities and thoughts from the end of "Sirens" to the beginning of "Cyclops," he could have worked them into the opening pages of "Cyclops." He decided against this but did incorporate parts of the first and second passages into the barroom discussions (297.36-38, 330.14-16), and "gunnard" and "plaice" from the third fragment lead the list of fish who "sport" in "murmuring waters" in the first of the episode's many lists (293.40-41). In his late revisions, he worked another phrase of the second fragment into "Sirens" (286.5); and the words after the addition are similar to many of Bloom's thoughts in the second half of "Nausicaa." If Joyce originally planned the monologue technique as a contrast to the parody passages, he must have changed his mind very early in his work on the episode, since the technique does not occur anywhere else in the copybook. His earliest work on "Cyclops" in mid-June 1919 may thus represent the precise chronological point at which he stopped writing one kind of book, basically concerned with Stephen and Bloom, and began to write another, in which a succession of parody styles, and eventually a group of schematic correspondences, began to take over.

Having decided to drop the monologue technique, Joyce confronted the problem of developing an alternative. Several of his initial problems are evident in the following passage from scene 3 that links the parody description of the Keogh-Bennett fight (318.29-319.19) and the discussion about Irish sports that originally followed it (now 316.40-317.33; see Figure 3):

> —I wouldn't like to see that,——said. And those but-
> ting matches they have in California, going for each
> heads down like a bull at a gate.
> —And bullfighting, Mr B——[*sic*], and cockfighting all
> those sports are terribly inhuman and hare hunting
> —Well, yes, of course . . .

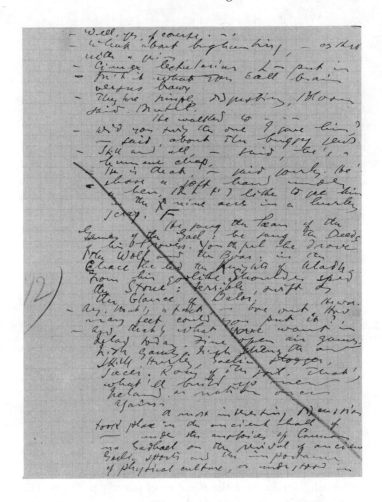

The "Cyclops" copybook (Buffalo MS V.A.8). Reproduced courtesy of the Society of Authors and the Lockwood Memorial Library, State University of New York at Buffalo. (Figure 3)

—What about bughunting,——asked with a grin.

—*Cimex lectularius*, L—— put in

—Isn't it what you call brain versus brawn

—They are simply disgusting, Bloom said. Brutal.
He walked to . . .

—Did you twig the one I gave him?——said, about
the buggy jews?

—Still and all,——said, he's a humane chap.

—He is that,——said sourly. He'd shove a soft hand
under a hen. But I'd like to see him in the nine acres in a
hurley scrap.

⟨Gara klooklooklook. Black Liz is our hen. She lays
eggs for us. When she lays her egg she is so glad. Gara
klooklooklook. Then comes good uncle Leo. She [*sic*]
puts his hand under black Liz and takes her fresh egg.
Gara klooklooklook.⟩

He sang the Pæan of the Games of the Gael: he sang
the Deeds of his Prowess. Youthful he drove the Wolf
and the Boar: in the Chace he led the Knights of Uladh.
From his godlike Shoulder sped the Stone: terrible, swift
as the Glance of Balor.

—Ay, that's a fact,——bore out. ⟨He was.⟩ How
many feet could you put it?

—And that's what ~~you~~ ⟨we⟩ want in Ireland today.
Fine open air games. Irish games. Irish strength and
skills. Hurley, Gaelic ~~slogger,~~ soccer. Racy of the soil.
That's what'll build up men Ireland a nation once again.

(V.A.8, pp. 11r, 11v, 12r)

In this passage, first of all, we can see Joyce seizing opportunities to increase the number of parody passages. He
adds the "Gara klooklooklook" passage as a response to
"He'd shove a soft hand under a hen." The interpolation
interrupts the continuity between the previous "nine acres
in a hurley scrap" and the next paragraph, but he did not
resolve the problem until he moved the hen passage to
another context and entirely revised the sports discussion.

Second, the paragraph introducing the discussion of ath-

letics ("He sang the Pæan of the Games of the Gael") reveals that the relationship between some of the parodies
and the realistic scene differs from that in the final text. In
the text, only the combination of first-person narration and
parodic exaggeration provides the double, two-eyed vision
that is lacking in all the characters except Bloom. The two
parts of the episode balance one another and implicitly
comment on each other, but they keep their distance, since
neither the nameless "I" nor the succession of parody narrators reveals an awareness of any other viewpoint. In the
final version the parodies halt the narration, but, like the
hallucinations in "Circe," most of them exist outside time,
and the narration usually resumes exactly where it left off.
This is not always the relationship in the first draft. There,
some of the parodies are indeed exaggerated accounts of
the realistic scene, but others, like the "Pæan" paragraph,
serve as the means of narration. In revising, Joyce either
eliminated such passages entirely or rewrote them in the
idiom of the anonymous narrator:

> The young chieftain O'Bergan, comely in his youth,
> quaffed the divine nectar of Iveagh. (V.A.8, p. 4r, elimi-
> nated in revision)[9]

> X perused the Missive of the Avenger, Rambold [*sic*]
> the Hand of the Law. No Man of Guilt may scape him.
> Dread is his Ire.
> —O, Christ MacKeon, says he, will you listen to this.
> (V.A.8, p. 5r; cf. 303.17-18: "—O, Christ M'Keown, says
> Joe, reading one of the letters. Listen to this, will you?")

> There entered the noble John Wyse O'Nolan, re-
> splendent in verdant and silver garb. ~~He wore the~~ Grand
> High Chief Ranger, he, of the National Foresters of Ire-
> land. He doffed low his whiteplumed helm and——.

[9] A similar phrase, "the young chief of the O'Bergan's" (300.1), is not a
reworking of the quoted passage. It exists in the copybook (V.A.8, p. 3r)
as in the final version.

(V.A.8, p. 8v; cf. 324.27-28: "So anyhow in came John
Wyse Nolan and Lenehan with him with a face on him as
long as a late breakfast." Nolan is a National Forester in
his marriage to Miss Fir Conifer, 327.3, and his gesture
with his hat occurs in one of Bloom's "Circe" hallucinations, 547.25-26.)

The original passages provide a mock-heroic frame for
the barroom dialogue that follows each of them. They do
not serve to complement, to contrast, or to comment, as do
the "gigantic" passages that are juxtaposed with the realistic incidents; rather, as gratuitously inappropriate descriptions of the incidents, they merely satirize the Dubliners in
the pub.[10] The "gigantic" passages possess a great variety
of styles and tones, even in their early copybook versions,
but these mock-heroic descriptions are all alike. They contain one voice, one not very promising for the episode's development. (A sign of their uniformity exists in Joyce's systematic revision of the first letter of each noun to a capital
letter.) These passages represent one of Joyce's early attempts at a narrative voice for the episode, but he eliminated them, probably very quickly, when he conceived of
"the Nameless One" as the narrator.

Like these early narrative passages, Joyce's original
opening for the episode establishes an easy mock-heroic attitude toward the events to follow. The first scene in the
copybook begins with a parody description of St. Michan's
parish in Dublin, that is, Barney Kiernan's section of the
city:

> In ~~green Erin of the west~~ ⟨Inisfail the fair⟩ there lies a
> land, the land of holy Michan. There rises a watchtower
> beheld from afar. There sleep the dead as they ~~slept in
> life~~ ⟨in life slept⟩, warriors and princes of high renown.
> There wave the lofty trees of sycamore; the eucalyptus,
> giver of good shade, is not absent: and in their shadow sit

[10] Hugh Kenner, "Homer's Sticks and Stones," *James Joyce Quarterly*, 6
(1969), p. 288, discusses the mock-heroic narrative passages in "Cyclops"
as parodies of the Butcher and Lang translation of the *Odyssey*.

the maidens of that land, the daughters of princes. They ⟨sing and⟩ sport with silvery fishes, caught in silken nets; their fair white fingers toss the gems of the ⟨fishful⟩ sea, ruby and purple of Tyre. And men come from afar, heroes, the sons of kings, to woo them for they are beautiful and all of noble stem.

(V.A.8, p. 1r)

This passage exists in expanded form in the final version, but it is delayed until the second page. Joyce gives the first word to his narrator (whose first word, characteristically, is "I") and diminishes the passage's function of placing the undisclosed setting in an immediate ironic framework. (An opposite process occurred in "Oxen of the Sun." The episode originally began, "Some man that wayfaring was stood by housedoor at night's oncoming" [Buffalo MS V.A.13; now 385.3-4], the first description of the episode's "action." Joyce delayed this passage until the episode's third page to achieve a grandiose linguistic framework parallel to the mock-heroic one he had eliminated in "Cyclops.")

The original version of the sports discussion also reveals his habit of composing his material in blocks with only arbitrary attempts at transition or connection. This practice is basic to the entire copybook: the eight scenes constitute large blocks, and Joyce gives no indication of how he planned to connect them, if he even knew at the time. (He apparently drafted "Scylla and Charybdis" in a similar manner; a copybook, which was lost in transit between Paris and Buffalo, contained "fragmentary conversations, which appear altered in the final version.")[11] Throughout the copybook, when Joyce wants to change direction within a scene, he tends to rely on incomplete transitional phrases like "He walked to. . . ."

Two aspects of the characters' dialogue are significant. Although many phrases and expressions are often quite

[11] John J. Slocum and Herbert Cahoon, *A Bibliography of James Joyce: 1882-1941* (London: Hart-Davis, 1953), item 5.b.iii, p. 140.

distinctive and memorable, they could be spoken by any of several characters. For example, we could not name the character who mentions the butting matches in California or the praiser of Bloom as a humane chap. On the other hand, some of the dialogue is highly appropriate to specific speakers. The man concerned about "terribly inhuman" sports could only be Bloom, and the tag-end phrase, "and hare hunting," stylistically identifies the speech as his. "*Cimex lectularius*" (i.e., bed-bug) is precisely Lenehan's kind of quip that both hits and misses the mark at the same time. (Joyce retained a part of the discussion about bugs at 323.29-30.)

Finally, the passage makes clear that from the start Joyce planned the Citizen, as yet unnamed (he soon became "Cusack"), as a religious and nationalistic bigot, and that Bloom was always intended to be his victim. This is the basic Homeric parallel in the episode. Other passages, though, reveal that Joyce had not worked out many of the episode's details when he began to write. The final pogrom exists in the first draft's fourth scene, but it does not result (as it does in the final version) from Lenehan's false report of Bloom's Gold Cup winnings (335.10-20). Here it apparently stems from Bloom's alleged participation in the fraudulent "royal Hungarian privileged lottery" (see 313.21-26, 345.8, and notesheets 5:3 and 6:12). In the first-draft scene outside the pub, Cusack ridicules Bloom with tickets from the Gold Cup race, but he seems to use them because of his own losses on the race, rather than because of Bloom's supposed winnings:

> Martin and Jack Power did their level best to keep him quiet but Bloom had his rag out. all [*sic*] the ragamuffins ~~of~~ ⟨and⟩ guttersnipes of the place were jeering round the car and says one of the fishgirls
> —Ay, mister. Look at your hat, mister!
> What was it but Cusack had stuck two of the bloody betting tickets in the front of Bloom's topper and what was on it but: W.C. 13. ~~And~~ Terry, the curate, and Alf Bergan were doubled up laughing:

—O mister! Look at what's on your hat, mister.

Arra sure Bloom didn't know what was up till Jack stood up and took off the tickets and all the sluts began to yell

—Eh, mister, give us a speech!

(V.A.8, pp. 14r, 15r; cf. 341.8-342.22)

Bloom's list of Jews follows his audience's request. By this point in his writing, the end of the first group of four scenes, Joyce had begun to use the name Cusack and to develop the narrative voice, both of which seem to have occurred to him at about this time.

Besides the problems of internal plot occurrences, the copybook implies that Joyce was uncertain about the episode's connections with the rest of the book. Bloom's rationale for going to Barney Kiernan's existed from the start, although Joyce does not mention it in draft V.A.8: Bloom has agreed to meet Martin Cunningham there to arrange for the payment of Paddy Dignam's insurance (313.4-9). The preparation for this in "Sirens" (280.29-30) occurs in the fair copy of that episode (fol. 31); hence, it existed before Joyce began to write "Cyclops." However, he originally planned explicit links with other episodes that do not exist in the published versions. In the copybook, the patrons of the pub include Stephen Dedalus, Professor MacHugh, and O'Madden Burke. Along with Lenehan, J. J. O'Molloy, and Ned Lambert, who characteristically remain in the pub through all the revisions, they constitute the central group of characters in "Aeolus." As a further parallel, Myles Crawford, chauvinistic editor, is replaced by Cusack, chauvinistic citizen. The original close links between the two episodes are not surprising, since both deal more explicitly with political and social themes than do any other episodes.[12] The reunion of the characters, though

---

[12] A further link between "Aeolus" and "Cyclops" is Joyce's use of newspapers from around June 16, 1904, for many of the incidents in "Cyclops." "Joyce's Aeolian wind flew far more strongly through 'Cyclops' than scholars have previously indicated," according to Phillip Herring, who has revealed the importance of these newspapers (*Notes and Early Drafts*, p. 146).

thematically understandable, would be highly improbable in the light of the intervening "Scylla and Charybdis," "Wandering Rocks," and "Sirens" episodes; this, besides the more important decision to eliminate Stephen from the episode, probably induced Joyce to drop several of them.

   The characterization itself exhibits several curiosities in the first draft. As with some of the speeches in the discussion about athletics, Joyce wrote out much dialogue apparently without knowing which character was talking. He named some characters from the start—Alf Bergan, J. J. O'Molloy, Bob Doran, John Wyse Nolan—but the identity of others developed only later. It is possible, but unlikely, that Joyce knew who was to be in the pub but did not indicate the names in the draft. On the back of a letter that Henry Davray of the *Anglo-French Review* wrote to Joyce on June 23, 1919—in other words, several days after that date and at least ten days after writing to Budgen about "Cyclops"—Joyce composed a list of characters for the episode. He probably did this to fill in the gaps in characterization in the existing draft. The list reads

J. J. O'Molloy	Richie Goulding
Lenehan	Alf Bergan
Stephen Dedalus	Citizen Cusack
Ned Lambert	Martin Cunningham
Bloom	Mr Power
Corny Kelleher	Leary, the Dog
Denis Breen	Sir Fred. Falkiner
Mrs Breen (b. Powell)	Seymour Bushe[13]

Joyce must have composed this list after he began to draft the episode in the copybook (since his letter to Budgen written ten days earlier quotes the end of the first scene) and before he finished the fourth scene (since Cusack and other listed names begin to appear there). The list omits MacHugh and Burke, who appear with Stephen in the sixth scene, and John Wyse Nolan and Bob Doran,

[13] At Cornell, item 55. Reproduced courtesy of the Cornell University Library.

who are named as early as the second. It significantly does not imply the existence of a narrator who is himself a prominent character in the episode.

The list includes some characters who are not really present. Denis and Mrs. Breen, in the first as well as the final version, merely walk by the pub as Alf Bergan enters (298.30-299.9), and Corny Kelleher is named by Dignam during the séance (302.1-2). Likewise, Sir Frederick Falkiner is a subject for discussion and of a parody segment (322.14-323.28). Joyce's plans for Richie Goulding and Seymour Bushe remain mysteries, though he may have transferred Bushe to "Oxen of the Sun" (410.27-28; see "Oxen" notesheet 9:61) along with other rejected "Cyclops" items as varied in importance as Stephen Dedalus and Lenehan's *"cimex lectularius"* (notesheet 4:122 is repeated at "Oxen" 8:36, but Joyce ultimately discarded the phrase entirely). If Joyce ever intended to call the dog "Leary," the drafts give no indication of it. The dog is named "Garryowen" throughout. (For more discussion of this list, see *Notes and Early Drafts*, pp. 129-30.)

Joyce's method of characterization results in the transfer of much dialogue intact from draft to draft while the speakers change. For example, the French are considered as "never worth a roasted fart to Ireland" by an unnamed speaker in V.A.8, by Ned Lambert in V.A.6, and by the Citizen in the final version (330.20-22); " 'Tis a custom more honoured in the breach than in the observance" is first O'Madden Burke's and then John Wyse Nolan's awful pun (329.8-10); and the description of Mrs. Riordan's nephew as "drunk as a boiled owl" passes from Lambert's mouth to the narrator's (306.6). In an episode in which Odysseus is "Noman," in which Bloom is not named in the last several pages (in the draft, he is named throughout), and in which the narrator is anonymous, Joyce's juggling act with his characters is almost thematically appropriate.

Finally, the drafts reveal false starts and uncertainties in Joyce's early plans for his major characters. "Stephen no longer interests me to the same extent [as Bloom]. He has a shape that can't be changed," Joyce told Frank Budgen (Budgen, p. 105), but Stephen's shape was still flexible enough for Joyce to decide to remove him from an episode in which he would appear in an extremely bad light. The following passage appears in the second draft (it is somewhat less complete in the first draft):

> —Well, says JJ, if you grant the jew human impulses why can't he love his country too. I mean, logically, why not?
>
> —Why not? says young Dedalus, when he is quite sure which country it is.
>
> . Old MacHugh began laughing and says he, settling his specs:
>
> —That's Gallic, says he. Paris did that for you, says he.
>
> Bit of a shaper that fellow, son of Si Dedalus. He was in Paris in the quartier latin and he came back an atheist. He'll never be as good a man as his father anyhow.
>
> (V.A.6, fols. 2r, 2v)

The central statement of bigotry, "when he is quite sure which country it is," occurs in the published book, but, in a complete turnabout, it is spoken by J. J. O'Molloy, and Joyce transfers O'Molloy's original attempt to restrain the anti-Semitism to John Wyse Nolan (337.22-25). The notesheets signal Stephen as the original speaker (5:76-77), and they indicate other intended plot developments: "S.D. tempted to drink" (5:58), "Lie: S.D. receives 5 £" (5:67), "S.D. for sake of addressing letter 'Paris'" (2:14), and "SD forgets to pay" (7:23). Joyce probably decided to eliminate Stephen sometime after draft V.A.6 as he structured the episode to focus more coherently on Bloom. Stephen's presence, besides deflecting attention from Bloom, would either necessitate another series of near-meetings with Bloom like those in "Aeolus" or bring about the actual meeting too long before the climactic "Circe" episode. Stephen's disappearance from "Cyclops" probably coincided with Joyce's early formulations of "Oxen of the Sun," in which the meeting does finally occur. Joyce transferred much of the notesheet material relating to Stephen to the "Oxen of the Sun" and "Eumaeus" notesheets and to the episodes themselves; as Phillip Herring has described Joyce's processes of composition, "particular ideas moved continually upstream like salmon, briefly stopping off at way stations only to rest" (*Notesheets*, p. 523).

To judge from the evidence in the copybook, Joyce's early plans for Bloom in "Cyclops" were also unclear. The fourth scene details the Citizen's attack on him and his mock apotheosis, and he participates briefly in the discussion about sports in the third scene. Much of the talk in the pub centers on him, especially the long discussion about him and Molly in the sixth scene, a great deal of which Joyce revised into a single paragraph in the narrator's voice (305.40-306.12). Although the copybook version clearly contains the basic Homeric analogy of the hero entering and barely escaping from the cave of the one-eyed giant, Joyce apparently had not yet worked out Bloom's actions in the pub in detail. In the final version, for example, Bloom stands out as the sole representative of decency and good will in the episode when he asserts,

> —But it's no use. . . . Force, hatred, history, all that. That's not life for men and women, insult and hatred. And everybody knows that it's the very opposite of that that is really life.
> —What? says Alf.
> —Love, says Bloom. I mean the opposite of hatred.
> (333.9-14)

But, as far as his actions in the pub are concerned, Bloom intensifies the animosity against him by his inability to remain silent during any of the discussions:

> —Anyhow, says Joe. Field and Nannetti are going over tonight to London to ask about it on the floor of the House of Commons.
> —Are you sure, says Bloom, the councillor is going? I wanted to see him, as it happens.

—Well, he's going off by the mailboat, says Joe, to-night.

—That's too bad, says Bloom. I wanted particularly. Perhaps only Mr Field is going. I couldn't phone. No. You're sure?

(315.26-34)

—Ruling passion strong in death, says Joe, as someone said.

—That can be explained by science, says Bloom. It's only a natural phenomenon, don't you see, because on account of the . . .

And then he starts with his jawbreakers about phenomenon and science and this phenomenon and the other phenomenon.

(304.33-38)

In the copybook, Bloom's argumentativeness hardly exists. He expresses antipathy toward brutal sports, elicit-ing the reluctant compliment from one speaker that "he's a humane chap," but the man who appeals to science to ex-plain the "ruling passion" is not Bloom, since the discussion apparently occurs while Bloom is not in the pub. (Joyce be-gins the parody passage, "XY tendered medical evidence" [V.A.8, p. 7r], as if he does not know who will offer the ex-planation.) Furthermore, in the final version, Joyce care-fully times Bloom's entrance to coincide with the Dublin-ers' reading of the hangman's letters; in the draft, he does not exploit the atmospheric possibilities at all. It appears that he began to work with the broad parallels between Odysseus in Polyphemus' cave and Bloom in Barney Kier-nan's pub; then he developed the parodies and some major segments of the action, such as the ending; but he did not work out many of the plot details until later. The list of incidents he compiled after the first draft (Buffalo MS V.A.7; see above, p. 122) documents his subsequent at-tempt to develop the episode's story.

In trying to defend the completed "Sirens" episode to

Harriet Shaw Weaver, Joyce wrote, "The elements needed will only fuse after a prolonged existence together" (July 20, 1919; *Letters*, I, 128). This process also applies to his early work on the episodes. His uncertainties and false starts in the first draft of "Cyclops" reveal that even as he began the later, more elaborate episodes of the middle stage, he first had to struggle with the details of story, characterization, internal organization, and continuity with the rest of the book. These concerns reflect the middle stage's transitional nature, since Joyce wanted to preserve a novelistic substructure in his new nonrepresentational styles. To deal with these problems and to allow the elements to "fuse," he resorted to an elaborate combination of lists, charts, and notesheets, and to extensive revisions over a period of several years.

The "Cyclops" Notesheets

As Joyce began the long process of transforming the first draft of "Cyclops" into the finished episode, he turned to his curious notesheets. The revision process started almost immediately after he wrote the opening pages of the first-draft copybook and, as with the later revisions, his corrections and additions appear first on the notesheets. He depended on these notes even for revisions of single words—the entry "battle" ("Cyclops" 3:22) signals a correction in the sentence "It was a memorable contest" (V.A.8, p. 10r; cf. 318.29). Yet, despite the notes' precise meanings for Joyce, the sheets themselves are extremely chaotic. Phillip F. Herring sums up the opinion of critics who have used the notesheets when he observes, "It is curious that Joyce's admittedly 'desperate need for principles of order and authority' is not reflected in an orderly set of notes; what order there was derived from his mind" (*Notesheets*, p. 4; Herring quotes Litz, p. 24).

The notes have been a part of the critical heritage of *Ulysses* almost since the book's publication. Valery Larbaud in 1922, Silvio Benco in 1930, and, in greater detail, Frank

Budgen in 1934 mentioned Joyce's notetaking process. Later, A. Walton Litz used the notesheets to study Joyce's making of *Ulysses*, and Phillip F. Herring edited them.[14] Herring places the notesheets at the second stage in an elaborate process of composition, following a "primitive draft or rough notes (chicken or egg)" and preceding "more rough drafts" (*Notesheets*, p. 8). Herring argues further that most of the notes were used for "expanding a draft," rather than for the later revision process of "augmenting episodes in print" (p. 528). In "Cyclops" this is definitely true, if expanding a draft includes correction and substitution, as well as enlargement.

Joyce relied on his notes for single words, short phrases, and entire passages. A note such as "fishful sea" (7:19) refers to a single word to be added to the phrase "their fine white fingers toss the gems of the sea" (V.A.8, p. 1r); Joyce even noted parts of words, as in "Bung" (6:41), which signals a marginal addition to the names of "the noble twin brothers Iveagh and Ardilaun" (V.A.8, p. 3r; cf. 299.31-32). There are brief phrases like "hearty plaudits" (7:58), which Joyce added in copybook V.A.8 to "in response to repeated requests ⟨and hearty plaudits⟩ from all parts of the house" (p. 13r; cf. 317.18-20). Usually the word or phrase in the notesheet serves as a key word for a longer phrase or passage, as in "Heblon" (1:37), which probably stands for "It's like what that chap writes under the name of Heblon," a contribution to the discussion of pseudonymous writers (V.A.8, p. 21v; cf. 334.39-41). Joyce dropped the phrase but transferred the name to Bloom's mind in "Ithaca" (685.29).[15] Besides actual additions, some

[14] Valery Larbaud, "James Joyce," *La Nouvelle Revue Française*, 18 (Apr. 1922), pp. 407-08, trans. anonymously as "The 'Ulysses' of James Joyce," *Criterion*, 1 (Oct. 1922), p. 102; Silvio Benco, "James Joyce in Trieste," *The Bookman* (New York), 72 (Dec. 1930), p. 380; Budgen, pp. 171-74; Litz, pp. 7-43; *Notesheets, passim*. Litz quotes Larbaud, Benco, and Budgen.

[15] More elaborate examples of notesheet entries serving as shorthand keys for large passages occur in the notes Joyce deleted in blue and added to "Cyclops" after the serial publication. An example is "red Jim MacDermot" (9:4), which probably served to remind Joyce of the long addi-

notes refer to corrections for words or phrases in the first draft: "Inisfail the fair" (8:68) replaces "green Erin of the west" (V.A.8, p. 1r; 293.38); "change the venue" (1:50) becomes a more colorful appeal than the original "Come on" as Hynes attempts to get Cusack away from the pub before Bloom returns (V.A.6, fol. 2r). Joyce dropped this usage, but the phrase appears twice later in the book. These different functions for the notes are all illustrated by the note "who comes? it is" (4:22), which stands for a passage to replace the original introduction to Bloom in the episode, "O'Bloom went ~~by~~ ⟨on⟩ through Inn's quay ward, the parish of saint Michan. ~~He~~ mov~~ed~~⟨ing⟩, ⟨the son of Rudolph⟩ a noble hero, . . ." (V.A.8, p. 1r). Above these words and in the margin Joyce made several changes, based on notes at 4:39, 5:21-22, and 5:26:

> Who comes through Inn's quay ward, the parish of saint Michan. ⟨It is O'Bloom, the son of Rudolph ⟨⟨the son of Leopold Peter, son of Peter Rudolph⟩⟩ he of the ~~intrepid~~ heart ⟨⟨impervious to all fear⟩⟩ ⟩
>
> (V.A.8, p. 1r)

Joyce eventually replaced Bloom's Hungarian genealogy with an Irish one, removed him from the mundane "Inn's quay ward," added appropriate clothing, and repeated an adjective that Joe Hynes has just applied to Bloom:

> Who comes through Michan's land, bedight in sable armour? O'Bloom, the son of Rory: it is he. Impervious to fear is Rory's son: he of the prudent soul.
>
> (297.39-41)

In this passage, the later revisions obscure Joyce's original use of his notes. This is a frequent occurrence, and it

---

tion from "Red Jim MacDermott" (296.39) through "Jeremiah O'Donovan Rossa" (297.20). He wrote all but fourteen of the names in the list as additions on the second of the three sets of *placards*; Sylvia Beach reproduced this page in *Shakespeare and Company* (New York: Harcourt, Brace, 1959), p. [59]. He added the remaining names to the final page proofs. A red-deleted note acting the same way is "Conifer family" (9:2).

contributes to the chaotic appearance of the notesheets if we compare them only to the final text.

Joyce used the "Cyclops" notes in an extremely precise way, both in his transfer of material from the sheets to the drafts and in his system of indicating his use of the notes. "A few lines to let you know I am here again with MSS and pencils (red, green and blue) and cases of books and trunks and all the rest of my impedimenta," he wrote to Harriet Shaw Weaver on October 7, 1921, during the final stages of composition (*Letters*, I, 172), and to most students of the notesheets his use of his pencils has often seemed as flippant as the tone of his letter. However, the conclusion of most critics that Joyce's colors simply reflect his different runs through the sheets (Litz, pp. 11-12; *Notesheets*, p. 8) is strongly supported by the "Cyclops" notesheets and, I suspect, by those for "Nausicaa" and "Oxen of the Sun" as well. Beginning with "Circe," the comfortable pattern seems to break down, and Joyce's use of his pencils becomes more complicated. In "Cyclops" the pattern is consistent: Joyce crossed out notes in red each time he revised or augmented the early drafts through the fair copy-*Little Review* stage, and also during one large transfer of notes from the "Cyclops" sheets to those for "Oxen of the Sun." He deleted notes in blue for four different purposes: post-*Little Review* additions to "Cyclops," late additions to earlier episodes, transfer of notes to the "Eumaeus" sheets, and use in the last four episodes. About 400 of the 450 notes deleted in red or blue conform to these patterns.[16]

Joyce's use of the "Cyclops" notesheets clearly reflects his "desperate need for principles of order and authority." He depended on the notesheets for every stage of revision, beginning with the earliest additions and substitutions, and he carefully, even obsessively, indicated his use of each note. Many of the words, phrases, or passages that resulted from the notes dropped out of the episode; Joyce

---

[16] I have discussed Joyce's use of his "Cyclops" notesheets in much greater detail in " 'Cyclops' in Progress, 1919," *James Joyce Quarterly*, 12 (1974/75). See especially pp. 144-49.

did this not so much in the "last" revisions, as Litz says (p. 11), as in the revisions prior to his completion of the autograph fair copy. "Each episode was repeatedly 'dipped' into the storehouse of material contained in Joyce's notes and supplemented by his memory," Herring states (*Notesheets*, p. 6). The drafts indicate how early this process began, and they reveal the intimate relationship between the notesheets and Joyce's developing book in a way that the final text alone cannot make clear.

The Early Revisions

The first few months in the development of "Cyclops" mark an important transitional period in the growth of *Ulysses*, when Joyce decided to replace his initial style with parodic distortions of everyday occurrences. These months were indeed a transition, as he slowly developed new techniques through much rewriting and a series of false starts and unsuccessful passages. Despite the expansive nature of the new techniques, as Joyce eventually perfected them, his early, exploratory "Cyclops" work reveals many movements in the direction of exactness and compression.[17] The revisions did not become predominantly expansive until well after the beginning of the middle stage in his writing of *Ulysses*, the stage that evolved from his efforts on "Cyclops" during the summer of 1919. Initially, he reworked and molded his material to find a proper form; the "predetermined pattern" (Litz, p. 9) toward which he worked during the later stages of composition developed after he began to write the intermediate episodes like "Cyclops."

Joyce certainly expanded the "Cyclops" drafts through the augmentation of existing scenes and the addition of entirely new ones, but in his first attempt to create an episode

[17] Joyce's early "Cyclops" work confirms Robert Edward Hurley's discovery from the "Proteus" drafts: there are many exceptions to the generally held belief that Joyce's revisions were exclusively expansive in nature. "The 'Proteus' Episode of James Joyce's *Ulysses*," Diss. Columbia 1963, p. 27.

without the interior monologue, he also did much alteration and a significant amount of deletion. This pattern
applies to the revisions before the autograph fair copy;
after the fair copy and the serial publication, the expansion
process took over. Much of the material he first included in
"Cyclops" does not exist in the published versions, and
specific scenes that do survive are sometimes longer and
more elaborate in the drafts than in the published texts.

An example of excision of material occurs in the newspaper account of the African chief's visit to England (now
334.11-29). The draft versions correspond quite closely to
the fair copy-*Little Review* text; the final version is longer,
since Joyce added several passages after the *Little Review*
publication. The fair copy, typescript, and serialized version all end with the words "surnamed Forty Warts" (MS,
"Cyclops," fol. 47; TS V.B.10.a, p. 27; *LR*, 6, ix, p. 58; cf.
334.28-29), but in the drafts the report continues:

> ⟨An outstanding feature of⟩ ~~T~~⟨t⟩he ceremony was
> ~~brought to a close by~~ a musical setting of the versicle *I am
> black but comely* excellently rendered by the royal musi-
> cians ~~with~~ ⟨upon⟩ ⟨their⟩ ⟨curious⟩ native instruments,
> alligator carapaces strung with the ⟨elongated⟩ guts of
> vanquished Zulu warriors and the ⟨perforated⟩
> thighbones of early christian missionaries, the effect of
> these latter being ~~quite~~ ⟨remarkably⟩ similar to the dul-
> cet ~~(plaintive)~~ ⟨melancholy⟩ tones of the Italian ~~ocarina~~
> ⟨*ocarina*⟩.
>
> (V.A.8, pp. 21r, 22r; V.A.6, fol. 1r)

Joyce added phrases to the entire account in both
copybook V.A.8 and draft V.A.6, but he apparently decided to eliminate the ending before he faircopied the
scene. Perhaps he felt that the exaggeration was becoming
excessive; if so, the excision reveals that his aims in 1919
had not yet reached the encyclopedic dimensions of 1921,
when he expanded everything. In fact, between the *Little
Review* and the final publication, Joyce added a passage
after "Forty Warts":

after which he visited the chief factory of Cottonopolis
and signed his mark in the visitors' book, subsequently
executing an old Abeakutic wardance, in the course of
which he swallowed several knives and forks, amid
hilarious applause from the girl hands.

(334.29-33)

The new passage focuses on the Alaki, rather than on the
ceremony, but had Joyce returned to his drafts in 1921 he
might have reinstated the original passage, since it is hardly
out of line with the late revisions.

Joyce also shortened sections of the barroom discussion,
especially those in which the Dubliners discuss the European nations. His prophetic instincts notwithstanding, he
eliminated a forecast of the World War:

—I tell you what it is, says ⟨O'Madden Burke⟩,
there's a war coming ⟨on⟩ for the English ⟨Sassenachs⟩
and the Germans will give them a hell of a gate of going.
⟨What they ⟨⟨the imperial yeomanry⟩⟩ got from the
B⟨⟨b⟩⟩oers is only what you might call an ⟨⟨a⟩⟩ hors
d'oeuvre.⟩

(V.A.8, p. 19v; V.A.6, fol. 2r)[18]

As both of these passages indicate, Joyce changed many
individual words in the drafts and altered phrases for
specific effects. He also added words and passages
throughout copybook V.A.8 and, less frequently, draft
V.A.6, using lines and superscripts to indicate additions between the lines, in the margins, or on the left-hand page
opposite the original text. However, at some point in the
revising process, he dropped entire sections and drastically
shortened others.

We can best study Joyce's revisions of "Cyclops" prior to
the autograph fair copy through a hindsight analysis of the
types of changes that produced a specific section in the

[18] Joyce restored his prediction in a late addition to "Aeolus," where
Myles Crawford says, "Sent his heir over to make the king an Austrian
fieldmarshal now. Going to be trouble there one day" (132.34-35).

final text. Unfortunately such a study is hindered by the absence of intermediate drafts between the V.A.8-V.A.6 and fair copy-*Little Review* versions. Both a parody and a narrative-dialogue segment need to be investigated, since Joyce treated each type of passage differently. A segment of narration and dialogue that underwent extensive, yet typical, changes is the discussion following the reading of Rumbold's letter (now 303.37-306.23). The letter itself is the same in the draft as in the final version except that, in the draft, "Rumbold" seems to be "Rambold," "Toad Smith" is "J. Smith" (Joyce's revision brings in his personal name for one of his Zurich enemies; the entire letter memorializes these demons; *JJ*, p. 472), and the names of the prisons are different.

For the ensuing discussion, Joyce brought together passages from various scenes in the draft. The attitudes toward the hangman—he is a "barbarous bloody barbarian," he has a "dirty scrawl," he is a "barber from the black country"—all exist in the draft, but, significantly, Bloom does not enter Kiernan's at this time to offer the authority of scientific evidence against the weight of unsupported rumor; this is "tendered" by the unnamed "XY" (V.A.8, p. 7r). Furthermore, Joyce had not yet developed his narrator, and therefore some of the facts and opinions that "I" provides in the final text are offered by other characters in the draft, as a comparison between the draft and the fair copy reveals (the final text contains elaborations beyond either the draft or the fair copy):

> Alf stuck them all back in his pocket.
> —They're all barbers from the black country. One chap sent in a mourning card with a black border on it. Five guineas is the fee but they make a good bit ⟨extra⟩ cutting up the rope in bits and selling it. Do you not believe me? That's a fact. They do, faith.
>
> (V.A.8, p. 6r)

> And Alf was telling us there was one chap sent in a mourning card with a black border round it.

—There [*sic*] all barbers, says he, from the black country that would hang their own fathers for five quid down
⟨and travelling expenses⟩.

And he was telling us they chop up the rope after and
sell the bits for a few bob each.

(MS, "Cyclops," fol. 16)

The fair copy version is not particularly exciting, though it
is an improvement over Alf Bergan's lifeless dialogue.
Joyce utilized the potentials of his narrator, however, when
he enlarged the third paragraph during the late revisions:

And he was telling us there's two fellows waiting below
to pull his heels down when he gets the drop and choke
him properly and then they chop up the rope after and
sell the bits for a few bob a skull.

(304.11-14)

Joyce made one significant deletion from the discussion:
Garryowen's poem (312.25-32) originally appeared here
twice (once supposedly in Gaelic and once in a translation
by Cusack), and it was part of the realistic scene rather than
a parody passage. He also interpolated an incident into the
section, the narrator's remarks about Bloom in the City
Arms hotel. In the draft, the discussion of Bloom's troubles
constitutes the entire sixth scene, and all the pub patrons
participate. Joyce revised it drastically. The passage is too
long to quote in its entirety here, but a comparison of the
V.A.8 and V.A.6 versions (see *Notes and Early Drafts*, pp.
170f., 181ff.) with the autograph fair copy (fols. 18-19) and
final text (305.33-306.16) easily reveals the reworking. For
example, in draft V.A.6 Ned Lambert mentions a rumor
about Mrs. Riordan ("Dante" in *A Portrait of the Artist as a
Young Man*):

—I'll tell you a bloody good one Gaffney told me, says
Ned. There was an old one ⟨stopping⟩ in the hotel, a
Mrs Riordan that had some money of her own ⟨and no
chick or child ⟨⟨belonged to her⟩⟩ only a nephew of hers
and a bloody mangy terrier she had⟩ and Bloom of

course got the soft side of her doing the molly coddle. Playing bezique with her every night and wouldn't eat meat of a Friday because she was an old bitch that was thumping her craw.

—Suppose he thought he'd get some of the wampum in her will, says Joe.

—What else? says Ned. The whitehaired boy. Same as he ~~made~~ ⟨sucked⟩ up to his mother-in-law.

(V.A.6, fol. 2v)

By the time Joyce faircopied "Cyclops" he had revised this rumor into a typical bit of derogatory information savored by "I," the narrator:

Time they were stopping up in the *City Arms* Pisser Burke told me there was an old one there with a cracked nephew and Bloom trying to get the soft side of her ⟨doing the molly coddle⟩ playing bezique to ~~get~~ ⟨come in for⟩ a bit of the wampum in her will and ⟨not eating meat of a Friday because the old one was always thumping her craw and⟩ taking the lout out for a walk.

(MS, "Cyclops," fol. 19)

In general, the improvements in this passage are tremendous. He transformed a long, diffuse discussion into a concise bit of narration without sacrificing the main point of the incident, the attitude of the Dubliners toward Bloom and their eagerness to seize on malicious or derogatory gossip. Joyce carefully picked the details to be retained as he often conflated the two main subjects of the original discussion (Bloom's and Molly's sexual life and the incident with Mrs. Riordan) into a single event. Of course, he also eliminated much information about Bloom; some of it he used elsewhere in "Cyclops" (at 315.12-16, 335.30-37, 338.15-17), and some he transferred to other episodes. For example, in the draft the men in the pub speculate about the possibility of Bloom and Molly's divorcing; in the final version, divorce is an option entertained and then rejected by Bloom alone (733.33). Bloom's alleged strategy with

Molly's mother, on the other hand, dropped out entirely (see 761.37-39 and 778.23-24 for the narrative inconsistency), although Bloom considers the method to be a useful one (695.17-18). Rumors about Bloom's impotence, which appear in the draft discussion, occur throughout the finished episode. And, in dropping Stephen from the episode, Joyce caused him neither to hear nor to participate in this unflattering discussion concerning both his aunt and the man he is destined to meet within eight hours.

True to form, he retained minor touches from the passage, often scattering them throughout the episode. He dropped a parodic eulogy to Molly when he transferred the City Arms incident to the voice of the narrator, but he used a revised version of it when the Dubliners question Bloom about Molly's upcoming tour (319.37-41). His elimination of some material and his transfer of other passages show him balanced between the two aesthetic goals, the waning one of compression and the growing one of expansion. He reduced the specific incident to a form only one-third its original size, but he worked much of the material into other parts of the episode and the book.

It is unfortunate that the drafts between V.A.6 and the fair copy have not survived to indicate the specific ways in which he accomplished the revisions. We can conjecture, though, that they coincided with his solidified conception of his "snarling Thersites" of a narrator; once the narrator evolved, Joyce reconstructed many passages in his voice and then submitted each one to the same types of local alteration and augmentation displayed in the early versions in the notebook.

Typically, revision of the passage continued after the fair copy-*Little Review* stage. Although he had compressed the incident to such a great extent before the fair copy, he changed direction in the late revisions and added a postscript to the incident. After bringing up the rumors about Mrs. Riordan, both the men in the pub (in the drafts) and the narrator (in the fair copy) talk about her nephew, who arrived home drunk one day, allegedly with Bloom's encouragement. The fair copy version ends with the narrator's account of the women (Mrs. Riordan, Molly, and Mrs. O'Dowd of the City Arms hotel) screaming at Bloom, but in the final version the narrator has more to say:

> And sure, more be token, the lout I'm told was in Power's after, the blender's, round in Cope street going home footless in a cab five times in the week after drinking his way through all the samples in the bloody establishment.
>
> (306.12-15)

This sequence of revision does not generally apply to the parody passages. Many of them appear in the draft in a form strikingly like the fair copy-*Little Review* version. Here, for example, is the copybook version of the Keogh-Bennett fight, with the revisions and additions silently incorporated; the brackets contain all variations between the draft and the fair copy text (fols. 31-32):

> It was a ~~memorable~~ ⟨historic⟩ battle. Handicapped as he was by lack of poundage Dublin's pet lamb made up for it by superlative skill in ringcraft. The final ~~round~~ ⟨bout of fireworks⟩ was a gruelling for both champions. Bennett had tapped some lively claret in the previous ~~bout of fireworks~~ ⟨mixup⟩ and Myler came on looking groggy. The soldier got to business, leading off with a powerful left jab to which Myler retaliated by shooting out a stiff one to Bennett's face. The latter ducked but the Dubliner lifted him with a left hook, the punch being a fine one. The men came to ~~grips~~ ⟨handigrips⟩ and the bout ended with Bennett on the ~~ropes and~~ ⟨ropes,⟩ Myler punishing him. The Englishman was ~~well~~ ⟨liberally⟩ drenched with water and when the ~~whistle~~ ⟨bell⟩ went came on gamey and full of pluck. It was a fight to a finish ⟨and the best man for it⟩. The ~~men~~ ⟨two⟩ fought like tigers ~~and the excitement was terrific~~ ⟨and excitement ran fever high⟩. After a ~~rapid exchange of blows~~ ⟨brisk exchange of courtesies⟩ during which a ~~clever~~ ⟨smart⟩

upper cut of the military man brought blood freely from his opponent's mouth the lamb suddenly landed a terrific left to Bennett's stomach ⟨,⟩ ~~which floored~~ ⟨flooring⟩ him flat. It was a knockout clean ~~&~~ ⟨and⟩ clever. Amid tense ~~excitement~~ ⟨expectation⟩ the ~~Shropshire boy~~ ⟨Portobello bruiser⟩ was counted out and Myler ~~declared the winner~~ ⟨declared victor⟩ ~~amid~~ ⟨to⟩ the frenzied ~~plaudits~~ ⟨cheers⟩ of the public who broke through the ringropes and fairly mobbed him with delight.

(V.A.8, pp. 10r, 11r)

Naturally, Joyce revised some of the parodies much more fully than this one, and even this description was changed significantly after the original publication (cf. 318.29-319.19). In general, though, he did not revise the parodies as greatly as the dialogue passages.[19]

The early revisions of "Cyclops" show that we must use caution in generalizing about the writing of *Ulysses*. Herring's conclusion, for example, that "each episode was expanded along preconceived stylistic and thematic lines, though always in the direction of the more complex, the more parodic and ironic, and, sometimes, the more fantastic" (*Notesheets*, p. 6) is certainly true for Joyce's transforming of the fair copy-*Little Review* version into the final text, but it is not the case in his early attempts to develop a style and form for the episode. Likewise, Litz's sound assessment of Joyce's revisions in one passage of "Cyclops"—"the original version provides a general outline of the situation, and establishes the realistic foundations; then, by a process of elaboration or accretion, this original outline is filled in

---

[19] Several of the post-*Little Review* typescript additions to the Keogh-Bennett fight description appear first on "Circe" notesheet 19 (19:1 and 19:70-75), a sheet that contains post-*Little Review* additions for several episodes. Although Joyce expanded all the parodies after the serial publication, some to great lengths, he added only one entirely new passage, the description of the Citizen's handkerchief (331.39-332.28). This is another indication of the parodies' dominant role in Joyce's early work on "Cyclops."

and amplified" (Litz, p. 29)—applies to all post-*Little Review* revisions and to most of the fair copy parody passages, but in the realistic sections Joyce's revisions often show him working to develop an outline rather than elaborating one already in existence. His first few months of work on "Cyclops" made final the break with the original interior monologue technique and set a pattern of nonrepresentational parody for this episode and the next two in *Ulysses'* middle stage. His early revisions of the episode created a successful structure that confirmed the new direction, leading him through the middle stage and into the final one.

The Form of "Cyclops"

The shape Joyce created for "Cyclops" in the summer of 1919 pointed the direction for the middle stage. "Cyclops" introduces into *Ulysses* several new features that recur in both "Nausicaa" and "Oxen of the Sun": a narrative method heavily dominated by parody in which Bloom is seen exclusively from the outside (the second half of "Nausicaa" is, of course, the one exception to this); a combination of narrative viewpoints within individual episodes; and a narration whose main business seems to be something other than the continuing story of Leopold Bloom. Joyce had established these qualities by the time he completed the fair copy of "Cyclops" in August-September 1919; he perfected them (and also imposed later concerns on them) when he augmented the episode in 1921.

He apparently began his "Cyclops" work with the "gigantic" parody passages, but he developed a sophisticated conception of them and their possible uses only after he had worked on the episode for several months. Most likely this happened at about the same time as the voice of "I" developed, since the parodies' functions are integrally related to the narrative voice.

At first the parodies were dominated by one type of source: the stilted, artificial language of a Victorian rendering of an heroic tale. Hugh Kenner has suggested Butcher and Lang's translation of the *Odyssey* as the general butt of the parodies.[20] Joyce originally used these parodies consistently and rather simplistically as passages of narration. Their irony cut two ways: the glorification of the mundane events in the pub satirized the events, and the language used for the narration mocked the source's absurdly false style. Throughout the early drafts, the parody passages function in this way, offering little promise for the episode.

By the time he completed the autograph fair copy of "Cyclops," Joyce had evolved a much more sophisticated conception of these passages. He did not eliminate the type of parody based on Butcher and Lang, but retained several passages, especially toward the beginning of the episode, to serve one of two purposes. As an introduction or conclusion to a realistic scene, a parody passage frames the scene. One occurs as an introduction as Alf Bergan enters the pub. As often happens in such passages, the parodic words are immediately "translated" into the narrator's voice.

> And lo, as they quaffed their cup of joy, a godlike messenger came swiftly in, radiant as the eye of heaven, a comely youth, and behind him there passed an elder of noble gait and countenance, bearing the sacred scrolls of law, and with him his lady wife, a dame of peerless lineage, fairest of her race.
> Little Alf Bergan popped in round the door and hid behind Barney's snug, squeezed up with the laughing.
>
> (298.30-36)

An example of a parody passage ending a scene is the sentence closing the section about Paddy Dignam. Speaking of Bob Doran, the Butcher-and-Lang voice says, "And mournful and with a heavy heart he bewept the extinction of that beam of heaven" (303.10-11). The finished "Cyclops" seems to be constructed in discrete units of activity—for example, most of the characters enter the pub in pairs and at regularly spaced intervals—and the framing of scenes with parody passages contributes to this effect.

The other use for these parody passages is slightly dif-

[20] "Homer's Sticks and Stones," p. 288.

ferent in that the passage appears within a scene and is not translated back into the narrator's voice. This happens, for example, as Terry Ryan serves drinks and Alf Bergan pays him (299.30-300.12). Here the action continues, but it is narrated in a different idiom, in which the double irony functions. Joyce employs the Butcher-and-Lang type of parody far less frequently in the fair copy and later versions than in the early drafts; as a result, it does not become an easy, repetitive technique as it does in the drafts.

Besides the development of the narrative voice, Joyce's major discovery in his early versions of "Cyclops" was of the possible uses of other types of parody. Originally the episode opened with the parody passage "In Inisfail the fair" (now 293.38), but when Joyce decided to focus initially on the narrator, he delayed that "gigantic" passage and introduced a new one before it, the reproduction of the contract between Moses Herzog and Michael E. Geraghty (292.37-293.16). This passage functions differently from the way the heroic parodies do: it is gratuitous, having no relevance to any action; technically, it is not even a parody since, as Arnold Goldman has pointed out, it is the contract itself (Goldman, p. 92). The question the passage raises is not one of elevation or belittlement; rather, it involves movement toward or away from the thing described (as the narrative moves closer to the document, the actual words become clearer). Hence, the passage opens the basic Cyclopean question of perspective: the "I"-narrator's point of view is interrupted temporarily by a new one, before the original returns.

The "gigantic" contract is the first exaggerated passage in the episode, but the Butcher-and-Lang type of parody is more prominent in the first part. A major division occurs at the account of the hanging of an Irish revolutionary (306.24-310.38). This parodic report of a great historical event is the longest "gigantic" passage in the episode (and Joyce doubled its length after the *Little Review* publication; see below, pp. 160-65); it breaks the rhythm of the episode as it becomes entirely involved in its own elaborations. After the hanging passage, the heroic parody style practically disappears,[21] and the "gigantism" of the rest of the episode consists mainly of extensive elaborations of incidents, words, or thoughts, all interrupting the narrative to move off in their own single-minded concerns.

The parodies in the other middle-stage episodes function in a similar way. In both "Nausicaa" and "Oxen of the Sun," the passages of parody are also the means of narration, so there is no question of balancing these with a "realistic" narrator. However, Joyce allows no parody passage to stand alone. Half of "Nausicaa" is an uninterrupted parody of a sentimental Victorian novel, but this is checked by the extended single return to *Ulysses'* initial style. And he arranges the "Oxen of the Sun" parodies in a chronological sequence that makes each one a tentative statement bound by the conventions of its own linguistic and ethical universe. Thus, as he dropped the interior monologue for parody, he introduced a relativity in the point of view that is much stronger than the variations among the initial-style episodes. The story continues, but Joyce makes us more and more aware that each individual way of telling it is tentative, partial, and incomplete. At the same time, our interest begins to shift from the story to the telling and to the relationships among the different methods of narration.

Parody comprises only half of the new direction Joyce introduced in "Cyclops"; the episode's narrator represents an equally important development. Each of the middle-stage episodes seems to be a self-contained unit. "Sirens" introduces this trend, opening with the word "Begin" and closing with "Done." The subsequent episodes appear to go about their own business: allowing an opinionated barfly to express his biases, capturing the mind of a young Dublin woman, recreating the development of English prose style. Unlike that of the first nine episodes, the business at hand seems to be not immediately the story of Bloom and Stephen. "Wandering Rocks" focuses on many characters and pays no more attention to Bloom or Stephen than to several others; the overture to "Sirens" clearly announces a set of concerns independent from the story; and from the

[21] It recurs in a few places, as at 319.37-320.3, 324.32-40, 341.28-40.

start the "Cyclops" narrator seems involved with his own business, which only accidentally includes and then becomes dominated by Leopold Bloom. The "Cyclops" narrator does not mention Bloom for six pages, and he does so only when Joe Hynes mentions him as the acquaintance who "gave me the wheeze" about acquiring some cash (297.35).

So both in narration and in the use of parody, the continuing story of *Ulysses* is told through indirection. This is quite a turnabout from the direct interior monologue technique of the opening nine episodes (although in those episodes Joyce left many details for the reader to infer or discover. He told Frank Budgen, "I want the reader to understand always through suggestion rather than direct statement"; Budgen, p. 21). It is probably only the grounding of the first nine episodes that sustains our sense of the story through the narrative manipulations of the second half, though there is little question that in the middle stage Joyce wanted the story to be sustained. As he wrote "Cyclops" he had not moved radically away from a novel about Bloom and Stephen to a collection of symbols like the ones he offered in the 1921 schema. Rather, he was filtering his story through a succession of new narrative devices, and his success in this began the process that resulted in a new book.

The Later Revisions

As with "Aeolus" and the other episodes that were published in the *Little Review*, Joyce revised "Cyclops" in two major stages. First, he added phrases and passages to a copy of the typescript used for the serial publication; in the summer of 1921, Maurice Darantiere prepared the first set of proofs from this augmented typescript. Then, after Joyce began to receive the proofs for the episode, he added many new phrases and passages, including some extremely long ones.

"Cyclops" was one of the episodes Joyce amended most heavily as he augmented the original typescripts (*Letters*,

III, 31). Yet even though there are many additions (nearly 160), no consistent set of concerns is evident. As in the typescript revisions to "Aeolus," Joyce was still interested in details of story and characterization even as his attraction to surface complexities and schematic correspondences was growing. Thus, in one paragraph, Joyce added an allusion to Cyclops' eye, "Not as much as would blind your eye," but he also included a longer emendation which serves only to sharpen the characterization of the narrator: "Do you know what I'm telling you? It'd be an act of God to take a hold of a fellow the like of that and throw him in the bloody sea" (338.22-23, 18-20). Like these examples, well over half of the changes and additions are in the narration and dialogue, rather than in the "gigantic" passages.

Joyce prepared his schema for Carlo Linati at about the time he was accumulating these typescript additions, but the entries bear little resemblance to the additions:

Time—5-6
Colour—Green
Persons—Prometheus, No one (I), Ulysses, Galatea
Technic—Alternating asymmetry
Science, Art—Surgery
Sense (Meaning)—The Egocidal Terror
Organ—(1) Muscles, (2) Bones
Symbol—Nation: State: Religion: Dynasty: Idealism:
  Exaggeration: Fanaticism: Collectivity
(Linati Schema)

Some revisions can be traced to entries on this schema, such as the color—"Thomas Osborne Davis' ~~immortal~~ ⟨evergreen⟩ verses" (TS V.B.10.a, p. 17; 317.21) and "⟨Do you see any green in the white of my eye?⟩" (p. 20; 322.8-9)—and the second organ—"the bloody mongrel after it with his lugs back for all he was bloody well worth ⟨to tear him limb from limb⟩" (p. 33; 345.18-20). Yet, although this schema corresponds in time to the first set of revisions, it does not describe the episode Joyce was actually working on.[22]

---

[22] Phillip Herring discusses the *Ulysses* schemata, especially the "Cyclops" entries, in *Notes and Early Drafts*, pp. 121-24.

In "Cyclops," as in "Aeolus," he was quite restrained when he augmented the typescript; he had not yet arrived at a goal of encyclopedism. This is especially evident in the episode's lists, most of which Joyce greatly lengthened before the final publication. For example, the fair copy contains only twenty-one of the eighty-four "saints and martyrs, virgins and confessors" who form the procession that arrives to bless Barney Kiernan's (339.12-41). Joyce augmented the list on the typescript, but only by five names. The other fifty-eight came later.

The revisions to the typescript do not reveal a consistently clear direction. Joyce was building and expanding the episode, both in narration and in parody passages, but his restraint shows that he did not really know to what extent he wanted to augment the episode. That certainty arrived only when a desire for encyclopedism merged with the existing opportunities for Cyclopean gigantism.

Between the original work on "Cyclops" in summer 1919 and the pulling of the episode's first proofs in October 1921, he began to write a new kind of book. Over a month before he started receiving the "Cyclops" proofs, he added the subheads and tramlines to "Aeolus"; during the same period he was filling the early episodes with minute Homeric parallels and other symbolic correspondences. With his new goals of expansion and encyclopedism, "Cyclops" was a natural place for many new additions, since its technique already involved exaggerated passages and numerous lists. Thus, unlike those for "Aeolus," the late revisions to "Cyclops" involved not a change of direction, but rather an extension of original tendencies far beyond the boundaries Joyce initially planned for them.

The lists naturally invited additions, and Joyce took advantage of all opportunities. For instance, he greatly increased the names of animals and plants in "Inisfail the fair" (293.38-295.10) and added the entire list of guests at the wedding of Miss Fir Conifer and Jean Wyse de Neaulan (327.4-16). Usually he increased these lists a few items at a time, adding some elements to each set of proofs.

A good example is the list of "saints and martyrs." In the fair copy the list was fairly short:

> And after came all saints and martyrs, virgins and con-
> fessors: S. Isidore Arator and S. James the Less and S.
> Phocas of Sinope and S. Julian Hospitator and S. Felix
> de Cantalice and S. Stephen Protomartyr and S. John
> Nepomenuc and S. Thomas Aquinas and S. Ives of Brit-
> tany and S. Herman-Joseph and the saints Gevasius [*sic*],
> Servasius and Bonifacius and S. Bride and the saints
> Rose of Lima and of Viterbo and S. Martha of Bethany
> and S. Mary of Egypt and S. Barbara and S. Scholastica
> and S. Ursula with eleven thousand virgins.
>
> (MS, "Cyclops," fols. 52-53)

To reach the final version, Joyce added new names at every stage. In the following quotation from the final version, superscript letters indicate the proof on which Joyce added the bracketed phrase: A represents the typescript (Buffalo TS V.B.10.a); B, C, D, and E, the four placards (at Harvard); and F, the first (and final) page proofs (at Texas).

> And after came all saints and martyrs, virgins and con-
> fessors: ⟨S. Cyr and[D]⟩ S. Isidore a⟨A[D]⟩rator and S. James
> the Less and S. Phocas of Sinope and S. Julian Hos-
> pitator and S. Felix de Cantalice ⟨and S. Simon Stylites[E]⟩
> and S. Stephen Protomartyr ⟨and S. John of God[D]⟩ ⟨and
> S. Ferreol and S. Leugarde and S. Theodotus and S.
> Vulmar and S. Richard and S. Vincent de Paul[E]⟩ ⟨and S.
> Martin of ~~Tours~~ Todi[D]⟩⟨and S. Martin of Tours[E]⟩⟨and
> S. Alfred and S. Joseph[D]⟩⟨and S. Denis and S. Corne-
> lius[F]⟩⟨and S. Leopold and S. Bernard and S. Terence
> and ~~Saint~~ ⟨⟨S.[F]⟩⟩ Edward and S. Owen ~~of Garry~~
> Caniculus and S. Anonymous and S. Eponymous and S.
> Pseudonymous and S. Homonymous[D]⟩⟨and S.
> Paronymous[E]⟩ ⟨and S. Synonymous[D]⟩ ⟨and S. Laurence
> O'Toole and S. James of Dingle and Compostella and S.
> Columcille and S. Columba[B]⟩⟨and S. Celestine and S.
> Colman and S. Kevin and S. Brendan and S. Frigidian

and S. Senan and S. Fachtna and S. Columbanus and S. Gall and S. Fursey and S. Fintan and S. Fiacre^F⟩ and S. John ~~Nepomenue~~ ⟨Nepomuc^A⟩ and S. Thomas Aquinas and S. Ives of Brittany ⟨and S. Michan^B⟩ and S. Herman-Joseph ⟨and the three patrons of holy youth S. Aloysius Gonzaga and S. Stanislaus Kostka and S. John Berchmans^C⟩ and the saints Ge⟨r^C⟩vasius, Servasius and Bonifacius and S. Bride ⟨and S. Kieran^A⟩ ⟨and S. Canice^D⟩ ⟨of Kilkenny and S. Jarlath of Tuam and S. Finbar⟨⟨r^F⟩⟩ and S. Pappin of Ballymun^A⟩ ⟨and Brother ~~Sebastian^B~~⟩ ⟨Aloysius Pacificus and Brother Louis Bellicosus^D⟩ and the saints Rose of Lima and of Viterbo and S. Martha of Bethany and S. Mary of Egypt ⟨and S. Lucy^D⟩ ⟨and S. Brigid^B⟩ ⟨and S. Attracta and S. Dympna and S. Ita and S. Marion Calpensis^F⟩ ⟨and the Blessed Sister Teresa of the Child Jesus^B⟩ and S. Barbara and S. Scholastica and S. Ursula with eleven thousand virgins.

(339.12-41)

Joyce incorporated these additions into the structure he had already devised for the episode. He added only two entirely new paragraphs to "Cyclops"; the rest of the revisions expanded existing paragraphs. The additions change the episode's pace, as they give the passages of gigantism an increased life of their own. Unlike Paddy Dignam and his request to Corny Kelleher during the imaginary séance, Joyce did indeed "pile it on."

It is possible to watch Joyce producing one of the major late revisions. We have seen that the parody description of the hanging of an Irish revolutionary (306.24-310.38) represents a crucial point in "Cyclops." The longest passage of gigantism, it separates the episode's first part, where the dominant style parodied is the Butcher and Lang translation of the *Odyssey*, from the remainder, with its greater variety of voices. The parody's length causes us for the first time to forget the "I"-narrator almost completely; our sense of the parody passages' autonomy is stronger here than anywhere before.

When Joyce first wrote the passage (and published it in the *Little Review*) it was only half its final length. Most of the increase consists of one long passage beginning "A posse of Dublin Metropolitan police" (306.35) and continuing through the words "his medical adviser in attendance, Dr Pippi" (308.37-38). The addition, an elaboration of the preceding phrase, "the assembled multitude which numbered at the lowest computation five hundred thousand persons," serves several purposes within the passage: it carries to absurd lengths the sense of the hanging as a social event; it increases Rumbold's presence by delaying his entrance until the end of the fracas; and it obscures the victim who, in the original version, is in danger of becoming a prominent person in the scene before the "*nec* and *non plus ultra* of emotion" (309.28-29) of his farewell to his fiancée. In every sense, the addition is appropriate to the episode's gigantism.

Most of the post-*Little Review* additions to the account, but not the long "posse" passage, were among the "insertions (chiefly verbal or phrases, rarely passages)" which Joyce told John Quinn on November 24, 1920, that he had added to the episode (*Letters*, III, 31). None of these additions is signaled by an entry in the British Museum notesheets. Each one attests to the reporter's care for factual detail, or it increases the bathos; all function in the interests of the episode's technique (all quotations are from pp. 12-13 of Buffalo "Cyclops" typescript V.B.10.a):

when about to pay the death penalty (308.40)

(specially supplied by the worldfamous firm of cutlers, Mssrs John Barber, Sheffield) (cf. 309.10-11)

done to a nicety (309.19)

who was in capital spirits and evinced the keenest interest in the proceedings (cf. 309.22-23)

with an abnegation rare in these our times, rose nobly to the occasion and (309.24-25)

be launched into eternity (309.32; replaces the original "die")

That monster audience simply rocked with delight. (310.4-5)

Big strong men⟨, officers of ~~justice~~ ⟨⟨the peace⟩⟩ and genial giants of the royal Irish constabulary,⟩ were making frank use of their handkerchiefs and it is safe to say that there was not a dry eye in that record assemblage (310.10-13; the bracketed words are an addition to the addition)

requesting her to name the day (310.17-18)

Every lady in the audience was presented with a tasteful souvenir of the occasion (310.18-20)

the gallant young Oxonian (310.22)

fourleaved (310.25)

Two drafts of the long addition survive. The first occurs in the Buffalo notebook containing notes for many late revisions (MS V.A.2). Among the entries on the "Cyclops" page are words or phrases from the "Metropolitan police" passage: "posse," "charabancs," "viceregal party," "hour of five o'clock," "roar of acclamation" and "Catalani," as well as the names of the dignitaries listed in the middle of the passage (307.22-34).[23] On the page facing these notes is a draft of part of the passage containing some, but not all, of the phrases in the notes:

A posse of Dublin Metropolitan police under the command of the Chief Commissioner in person maintained order in the vast throng and the York street brass band under the baton of their capable leader whiled away the time by ~~an~~ admirable⟨y⟩ rendering ⟨rendering admirably⟩ on their ~~?pr~~ blackdraped instruments ~~of Speranza's~~ the matchless melody endeared us [*sic*] to us by the muse

[23] Joyce noted two names that never appeared in the passage: "Pan Poleaxe Paddyrisky" and "the magnate Marhagulyást Paprikát," and his original name for "the Commendatore Bacibaci Beninobenone" was "cav Salvatore Calaberaghi," which Phillip Herring translates as "a trouser-dropping (i.e., cowardly) savior" (*Notes and Early Drafts*, p. 130). One of the names appears as an undeleted entry on a "Circe" notesheet— "Vladimir Pokethankerscheff" ("Circe" 11:25)—a sheet Herring dates from between July 15 and November 1, 1920 (*Notesheets*, p. 527). Joyce probably thought of the name in 1920 but discovered a use for it only in 1921.

of Speranza. Special quick trains and ~~a~~ char-a-bancs had been provided for the comfort of country visitors of whom there were ~~not a~~ large contingents. The viceregal houseparty, ~~was~~ chaperoned by Their Excellencies, was accomodated [*sic*] on the grand stand while directly opposite was ~~a~~ the tribune reserved for the foreign delegation known as the Friends of Ireland. The delegates included the Commendatore Bacibaci Beninobenone (*doyen* of the party [*sic*; no parenthesis], Monsieur Pierrepaul Petitépatant, the Grandjoker Vladimir Pokethankertscheff, the Archjoker Leopold von Schwanzenbad-Hodenberg, Hiram ~~T.~~ ⟨Z.⟩ Bomboost, Count Athanatos Karamelopulos, Ali Baba Bocksheesh Rahat Lokūm Effendi, Señor Hidalgo Caballero Don Pecadillo y de la Malora de la Malaria, Herr Hurhausdirektorpresident Hans Kuechli-Steuerli, ⟨National⟩ Gymnasiummuseumsanatoriumsordinaryprivatedocent ~~Professor~~ ⟨General⟩ Historyprofessordoctor Siegfriedmund Ueberallgemein. All the delegates without exception expressed themselves in the strongest possible terms concerning the atrocious barbarity which they had been called on to witness.

(V.A.2, p. 12v)

Elaborate as this passage is, Joyce augmented it at every step in the revision process. A slightly later version exists in Buffalo MS V.A.9. Typical late revisions occur throughout: the "viceregal houseparty," we now learn, "included many wellknown ladies"; "friends of Ireland" has become "Friends of the Emerald Isle"; the "*doyen* of the party" is now "semiparalyzed," and "had to be assisted to his seat by the aid of a powerful steam crane." These elaborations all exist in the final version. The V.A.9 passage continues that in V.A.2 and incorporates some of the notes not used in the notebook draft:

The arrival of the worldrenowned headsman was greeted by a roar of acclamation from the huge concourse, the viceregal ladies waving their handkerchiefs in their excitement while the even more excitable foreign delegates cheering [*sic*] vociferously in a medley of cries: *hoch, banzai, eljen, vive, Allah,* amid ⟨which⟩ the high ring-ing *evviva* of the delegate of the land of song was easily distinguishable. ~~Signal~~ ⟨The signal⟩ for prayer was then⁄ ~~prom~~ promptly given by megaphone and in an instant all heads were bared, the commendatore's patriarchal som-brero, which has been in the possession of his family since the revolution of Rienzi, being removed by his medical adviser in attendance, Dr Pippi.

(V.A.9, fols. 1r, 2r)

Joyce added significant details to this section of the pas-sage, too, especially the introduction to Rumbold: "Quietly, unassumingly, Rumbold stepped on to the scaffold in fault-less morning dress and wearing his favourite flower the *Gladiolus Cruentus*" (308.19-21). Most of the later additions, like the passage in general, entered the book in stages. Joyce first provided a beginning-to-end skeletal version of the addition, then filled in the details or elaborations be-tween successive *placards* or page proofs. An example of this type of addition within an addition within an addition is the description of the "favourite Dublin streetsingers L-n-h-n and M-ll-g-n" (307.2-3).

The "Metropolitan police" addition does not appear at all on the first *placard*, that pulled by the printer from the typescript on October 1, 1921, but Joyce's additions to the proof tell the printer, "insérez ici, le passage sur les deux feuilles en manuscrit sans interrompre le paragraphe," ap-parently a reference to MS V.A.9. The V.A.9 version oc-curs on the second *placard*, pulled on October 4 (proofs at Harvard). Joyce's work on the passage can thus be placed around this time, very near the end of his work on *Ulysses*. (In mid-December 1921 he wrote to Valery Larbaud and described six passages in "Cyclops," including the "execu-tion" scene, as "new or so amplified as to be new"; *Letters*, III, 55.) The revision process, however, never stopped. Joyce added phrases to the passage on all three sets of *placards* and all but the fourth of the five sets of page proofs.

The final published passage resulted from an arbitrary halt to the expansion processes, a halt caused only by the date of publication, which Joyce in late 1921 decided would be his fortieth birthday, February 2, 1922 (see *Letters*, III, 52). He actually intended the "Friends of the Emerald Isle" passage to be longer than it is. In early November 1921 he sent the following note to the printer:

> If you have not already passed pp. 294 & 295 will you please insert in the list of names *after* "Goosepond Prhtr Kratinabritchisitch" *and before* "Herr Hurhausdirektor-president etc. the name; "Borus Hupinkoff"[24]

The printers received Joyce's "final" additions and corrections to page 294 on November 14 and this note on November 15. Before initialing and dating the note, Darantiere's man wrote "trop tard," and as a result, "Borus Hupinkoff" never became part of *Ulysses*. Had it not been too late, Joyce might have extended the list indefinitely.

By 1922 there was no logical end to Joyce's expansive revisions; the point at which he stopped writing *Ulysses* had to be an arbitrary date. Such a situation was inconceivable in June 1919 when he began "Cyclops," but his work on that episode started the long process that made it almost inevitable. The more we know about *Ulysses* in progress, the more apparent it becomes that Joyce could never have jumped from the type of novel he was writing in the first nine episodes to the elaborations of the last four, especially "Circe" and "Ithaca," without a fairly long transitional middle stage. "Cyclops" made the break with the initial style decisive and final; as such, it prepared the way for the late developments. The turning point in the making of *Ulysses* thus occurred during the summer of 1919 as Joyce "lovingly moulded" the first of Bloom's adventures narrated from an outside, alien, parodic viewpoint.

[24] See *Ulysses*, p. 307.30-32. Joyce forgot to put quotation marks after "etc." The note, which is filed among the final page proofs of *Ulysses*, is reproduced courtesy of the Humanities Research Center, the University of Texas at Austin.

The Last Stage: 1920-1922

JOYCE's early and middle stages of work on *Ulysses* can profitably be studied by a close look at such representative episodes as "Aeolus" and "Cyclops." The last stage requires a more general investigation of all Joyce's work at the time. He encountered different problems in each of the four long, elaborate episodes of the last stage and, in addition to his new writing, he returned to the early- and middle-stage episodes and revised them considerably, almost always by adding phrases and entire passages. When Maurice Darantiere, the Dijon printer, began to set type for the book, Joyce's reading of the successive *placards* and page proofs provided further stimulus for his revisions. The last stage, then, consisted of a complicated mixture of new writing and revision, confused even more during the last six months by the efforts of both Joyce and Darantiere to see the book into print by a fixed deadline.

These complications had been unforeseeable as Joyce began *Ulysses*. He wrote the first nine episodes in a style that he later called the book's "initial style" (*Letters*, I, 129), meaning both the fidelity to the sights and sounds of the Dublin environment and the representation of Stephen's and Bloom's minds. The technique consists of a combination of third-person, past-tense omniscient description and first-person, present-tense recording of the character's thoughts. Variations exist from episode to episode; for example, the sentences of "Lotus Eaters" reflect the theme of sleepiness and drugged forgetfulness, and the opening pages of the original "Aeolus" rhythmically echo the printing machines. But the episodes do not differ from each other to any great extent, nor do they inevitably foreshadow the subsequent elaborations.

Joyce moved toward the middle stage with "Wandering

Rocks" and "Sirens," and he was fully in it when he wrote "Cyclops" in Zurich during the summer of 1919. This stage continued through his writing of "Nausicaa" and "Oxen of the Sun" in Trieste later that year and in early 1920, and included his early work on "Circe" in Trieste and Paris. The techniques of "Cyclops," "Nausicaa," and "Oxen of the Sun"—the three episodes dominated by stylistic parody—probably all resulted from his perfection of the parody methods in "Cyclops" and his consequent discovery of the extensions of such techniques. The "Cyclops" parodies of newspaper accounts, legal and scientific jargon, and heroic language of all kinds may have led him to the extended burlesque of a sentimental novel in "Nausicaa" and to the series of parodies of English writers in "Oxen of the Sun."

Along with the writing of these new episodes, Joyce was accumulating additions for the completed episodes. He first mentioned these in his early letters from Paris. He apparently left most of these additions in Trieste, for he told Harriet Shaw Weaver on July 12, 1920, that he had brought to Paris "an extract of insertions for the first half of the book" (*Letters*, I, 142). These insertions did not actually enter the book until mid-1921. The middle stage therefore consists of Joyce's new work on "Cyclops," "Nausicaa," and "Oxen of the Sun," and of his first group of additions. Although the new work moved away from the realistic concerns of the first nine episodes and toward parody and other forms of exaggeration, the revisions were balanced between Joyce's interest in realistic detail and his growing desire for schematic correspondences, a desire indicated by the schema he sent to Carlo Linati in September 1920, when the middle stage was merging into the last one (*Selected Letters*, pp. 270-71).

Joyce's letters give no indication that, when he began to work on "Circe" in May and June of 1920, he anticipated an episode very different from the ones he had recently completed. His work on "Cyclops," "Nausicaa," and "Oxen of the Sun" fell into three-month patterns, and he assumed that he would need a similar time for "Circe." From Paris he wrote to Claud W. Sykes, "I remain here with my family for 2 or 3 months to write *Circe*" (*Letters*, III, 11). He arrived in Paris also believing in the realistic possibility of the book's publication within the next few months; all that seemed necessary was the completion of "Circe," the insertion of the additions to the earlier episodes, and minor work on the "Nostos." Joyce little realized that Circe's powers would transform *Ulysses* and send him into a new stage of composition lasting over eighteen months.

Work in Progress: 1920

When Joyce arrived in Paris in July 1920 his work on *Ulysses* had reached a crucial point. The *Little Review* was publishing "Nausicaa" (it had begun in the April and May-June issues and would conclude in the July-August number); he had finished "Oxen of the Sun" (by May 12; *Letters*, II, 464); and he had recently begun work on "Circe" (*Letters*, I, 141). Beginning at this time, Joyce repeatedly said that he had partly written the three "Nostos" episodes at an earlier date—he described them variously as drafted, sketched, written in part, written in rough drafts, or written in a plain style (*Letters*, I, 141, 143; II, 459; III, 31)—and because of this the writing of "Circe" meant to his great relief both the end of the long central section of *Ulysses*, the adventures themselves, and the end of the entire book. After sending "Oxen of the Sun" to Frank Budgen he wrote: "Please write to me about *Oxen*. It cost me 1000 hours of work I calculate. There remains *Circe*. The end is plainer sailing" (II, 465).

Joyce arrived in Paris expecting to finish "Circe" (hence, except for minor work, the entire book) within two or three months, and even to begin the publication process. "My intention is to remain here three months in order to write the last adventure *Circe* in peace (?) and also the first episode of the close," he wrote on July 12. "For this purpose I brought with me a recast of my notes and MS and also an extract of insertions for the first half of the book in case it be set up during my stay here" (I, 142). He greatly underestimated the time needed for "Circe," and the inclusion of his additions eventually involved as many as five sets of proofs.

Joyce's optimistic expectations for the completion of "Circe" did not last long. In August he wrote, "I am glad Ulysses had only twelve adventures. Circe herself had less trouble weaving her web than I have with her episode" (III, 15; Circe's spell evidently caused Joyce to confuse her with Penelope). Correcting his allusion, he complained that "the episode of *Circe* has changed me too into an animal" (I, 146). Her transforming powers changed not only Joyce and Bloom, but *Ulysses* itself. The episode was the first to expand far beyond the proportions Joyce originally set for it, and it established a pattern for the rest of his work on *Ulysses*. By the time he finished "Circe," his continuing belief that he had nearly completed *Ulysses* was groundless.

It is tempting to link the conditions of the *Little Review* publication with Joyce's progress on "Circe." A. Walton Litz has speculated that Joyce might never have finished *Finnegans Wake* in its actual form without the deadlines for the *transition* serialization (Litz, p. 88), and a parallel situation probably existed for the episodes of *Ulysses* through "Oxen of the Sun." Beginning in late 1919 and early 1920, however, the episodes grew to lengths requiring three or four issues, and the *Little Review* began to appear less frequently than once a month. In 1920 the *Little Review* published "Cyclops," "Nausicaa," and "Oxen of the Sun," each of which Joyce had finished three to six months before the serialization began. As a result, he spent the entire year of 1920 free from deadlines. The seizure of the July-August 1920 "Nausicaa" issue, long after he had submitted "Oxen of the Sun," made publication of "Circe" unlikely, and the court ruling of February 1921 eliminated the possibility. This lack of deadlines probably affected Joyce's work on "Circe," since no previous episode had developed so far beyond the proportions originally devised. (In 1921 this process would recur, again contrary to his expectations, with "Penelope" and especially with "Ithaca.") The judges in the *Little Review* case may have provided another of the accidents that changed the shape of *Ulysses*.

In his letters Joyce provides a running commentary on his "Circe" progress. He first assumed that the episode would resemble the last few in writing time and in size; then he grew frustrated when his expectations proved inaccurate; finally, he expressed great relief when he completed the episode:

> There remains *Circe*. The end is plainer sailing. (May 18, 1920; II, 465)

> The last adventure *Circe* is being written. (June 22; I, 141)

> My intention is to remain here three months in order to write the last adventure *Circe* in peace (?). (July 12; I, 142)

> [I] want to bore the life out of you about *Circe* which is half written. (July 27; I, 144)

> The final adventure *Circe* is giving me in all ways a great deal of worry. I have written the greater part of it four or five times. (August 16; III, 15)

> I am now writing the *Circe* episode for, I think, the sixth time. (September 3; I, 146)

> I have already written the *Circe* episode some six times. (ca. September 8; III, 19-20)

> Have written *Circe* about five times. (September 14; III, 21)

> *Circe* . . . by the way is a dreadful performance. It gets wilder and worse and more involved but I suppose it will all work out. (Michaelmas 1920; I, 147)

> I am now writing the final version of *Circe*. (November 3; III, 26-27)

> I am now writing out the final (the sixth or seventh) draft of the episode which is about twice as long as the longest episode hitherto, *The Cyclops*. (November 10; I, 149)

I must finish *Circe*. Am making the final draft. (November; III, 30)

I hope to finish the *Circe* episode before Christmas. (November 24; III, 31)

The nerves of my head are in such a bad way that I think Circe must be revenging herself for the unpleasant things I have written about her legend. . . . I shall try to finish the *Circe* episode before Christmas. (December 9; I, 150; he suffered an eye attack in November and early December)

I hope to finish *Circe* (the eighth draft) by Christmas. (December 9; III, 32)

Circe finished this morning at last. (December 20; III, 34)

The earliest extant draft of "Circe" (now Buffalo MS V.A.19) cannot be dated with certainty, but its editor, Phillip F. Herring, suggests the spring and summer of 1920 (*Notes and Early Drafts*, p. 194).[1] It is impossible to determine precisely when Joyce wrote it, but since it ends with a "schema" (Joyce's word) listing six additional scenes, he may have referred to this draft on July 27 when he declared the episode to be half written (I, 144). By this time, he had settled on the basic dramatic form of the episode and had written early versions of some of its scenes. These scenes, like those in the early draft of "Cyclops," include the beginning and end of the episode. The first words of copybook V.A.19 are relatively close to the opening of the final version (see *Notes and Early Drafts*, p. 211, and 429.1-12), but this is not surprising, since the passage is not greatly different from the many naturalistic descriptions in Joyce's works.

The copybook also contains a fairly extended version of

[1] Before Herring, the "Circe" drafts were studied by Norman Silverstein in "Joyce's 'Circe' Episode: Approaches to *Ulysses* through a Textual and Interpretative Study of Joyce's Fifteenth Chapter," Diss. Columbia 1960. Herring's recent work supplants Silverstein's pioneering, but often inaccurate, efforts.

Stephen's encounter with Private Carr at the end of the episode. Although the draft version breaks off with Carr's threat to knock Stephen down, Joyce probably had in mind the subsequent blow, Bloom's rescue, and possibly even Bloom's final vision of Rudy. Joyce includes two of Stephen's and three of Bloom's hallucinations in this draft, thus establishing the basic hallucinatory method, but Bloom's two most important fantasies—his dreams of glory and his transformation into a female slave—developed later. The draft contains the beginning of the transformation hallucination, when Bloom tells Bella, "Enormously I desire your domination" (V.A.19, p. 15r; cf. 528.12-13), but it goes no further. If "transformation scene," an entry on the "schema" at the end of the notebook, refers to this vision, then Joyce must already have planned the scene to some extent. Bloom's dreams of glory, which Joyce called the "Messianic scene" (*Letters*, I, 171), were not added until the summer of 1921.

In the draft, for neither Bloom nor Stephen do the events in "Circe" function as Joyce/Newman in "Oxen of the Sun" announced they would:

> There are sins or (let us call them as the world calls them) evil memories which are hidden away by man in the darkest places of the heart but they abide there and wait. He may suffer their memory to grow dim, let them be as though they had not been and all but persuade himself that they were not or at least were otherwise. Yet a chance word will call them forth suddenly and they will rise up to confront him in the most various circumstances, a vision or a dream, or while timbrel and harp soothe his senses or amid the cool silver tranquillity of the evening or at the feast at midnight when he is now filled with wine. Not to insult over him will the vision come as over one that lies under her wrath, not for vengeance to cut off from the living but shrouded in the piteous vesture of the past, silent, remote, reproachful.
>
> (421.29-42)

As in the "Cyclops" drafts, where there is often little connection between the barroom discussions and the parody
passages, in the "Circe" copybook Joyce had not worked
out the relationship between the "realistic" incidents and
the hallucinations they elicit. The passage from "Oxen of
the Sun," which is in the typescript and would have appeared in the *Little Review*,[2] indicates that Joyce knew
months ahead of time what the relationship would be, but
in the copybook he had not yet transformed intention into
performance.

The draft episode lacks another prominent feature of
the final version: the relationship with the earlier events of
the day, that is, with the earlier episodes of *Ulysses*. The degree to which this was absent is evident in almost any passage from copybook V.A.19. As an example, compare the
draft version of Bloom's entry into the brothel (pp. 9r, 9v,
10r; *Notes and Early Drafts*, pp. 221-23) with the final version (477.1-502.2). By the time the three-page section of
the "Circe" draft appeared in typescript, it had expanded
to six pages (Buffalo TS V.B.13.h, pp. 52-57), and in the
book it occupies twenty-six, twenty of which are the Messianic scene added in the summer of 1921. The Messianic
scene (including a fragmentary version that is part of the
fair copy and typescript) results from Bloom's tendency to
correct other people and to lecture them, as at the end of
"Hades" when he informs John Henry Menton that his hat
is crushed (115.24), or in "Cyclops" when he disputes Joe
Hynes' statement that Nannetti is leaving Dublin for London (315.26-34). In the "Circe" passage Joyce inserted
Zoe's question, "Have you a swaggerroot?" (477.28), and
the results are first Bloom's "lewd" antismoking remark,
then his "stump speech," and eventually the entire fantasy.

As he expanded the scene, Joyce perfected the dialogue
and accompanying stage directions. Zoe's attempts at
seduction increase (Joyce added "She bites his ear gently

[2] "Oxen of the Sun" typescript in the *Little Review* collection at the University of Wisconsin—Milwaukee. (Another copy is at Buffalo, TS
V.B.12.a.)

with little goldstopped teeth"), but so do the physical realities of the brothel ("sending on him a cloying breath of
stale garlic"; 477.19-20). In revising Joyce built up the
dialogue with several phrases from Swift's *Polite Conversation*: "And you know what thought did?" (477.18), "I can
read your thoughts" (499.25-26), "Hog's Norton where the
pigs play the organs" (500.5).[3] "After you is good manners"
(501.30), also from Swift, appears in the draft version, so
Joyce probably had *Polite Conversation* in mind from the
start. Several of the phrases in the draft, as well as some
subsequent additions, appear mixed together on an early
"Circe" notesheet (2:127-41), which suggests that he may
have planned the scene more fully than the copybook
would indicate.

He also added phrases to link the scene with other parts
of "Circe" and with other episodes of *Ulysses*. On pp.
500-01 alone, for example, there are four such additions.
Joyce added the detail that Zoe is "Yorkshire born," thus
bringing in the recurrent song, "My Girl's a Yorkshire
Girl," which will be played later in "Circe" (575-79). In
"Wandering Rocks," the song becomes associated with
Boylan, who walks to the rhythm of its refrain (253.41-
254.2), so when Joyce suggests Zoe is Bloom's "Yorkshire
girl," he provides an ironic echo of Boylan's success with
Molly. (The irony cuts several ways. In the song two men
talk about their "Yorkshire girls," discover disturbing
similarities, and travel to Yorkshire, only to be greeted by
the girl's husband.) Second, Bloom calls Zoe "laughing
witch," a phrase from Philip Beaufoy's story, "Matcham's
Masterstroke," which Bloom reads in "Calypso" and recalls
throughout the day (69.13, 280.21). The third addition occurs in the stage direction as Bloom caresses Zoe's breasts:
"Feeling his occiput dubiously with the unparalleled
embarrassment of a harassed pedlar gauging the symmetry of her peeled pears." With some variations, this
repeats Bloom's "spellingbee conundrum" from "Aeolus"

[3] Mackie L. Jarrell, "Joyce's Use of Swift's *Polite Conversation* in the
'Circe' Episode of *Ulysses*," *PMLA*, 72 (1957), pp. 545-54.

(121.12-16), and the "peeled pears," one of which was part of the original conundrum, also recall the two "head by tail" pears that Boylan sees in Thornton's shop, and that duplicate the sleeping positions of Bloom and Molly (227.17, 731.1-2; these references from the early episodes were in *Ulysses* when Joyce wrote "Circe"; all exist in the fair copy-*Little Review* versions). Finally, the augmented stage direction as Zoe leads Bloom into the house—"With little parted talons she captures his hand, her forefinger giving to his palm the passtouch of secret monitor, luring him to doom"—includes a Masonic sign, one of "Circe" 's recurrent elements.

Zoe's "talons" represent another aspect of "Circe" that Joyce emphasized as he revised the episode. He often discussed "Circe" in terms of animals, an appropriate parallel to the Homeric Circe's transformation of men into swine. Budgen quotes him as saying, "Of course it's an animal episode, full of animal allusions, animal mannerisms" (Budgen, p. 228). Joyce added Zoe's "talons" and four other animal references to these two pages of "Circe" (500-01). (A prominent animal throughout "Circe" is the protean dog, whose species continually changes. At first Joyce always called the animal "dog" or "retriever.")

The "Circe" notesheets reflect Joyce's expansion of the scene with Bloom and Zoe. Some of the many notes appear in the V.A.19 version, but more resulted in subsequent additions, even though Joyce probably had developed many of the ideas to some extent when he wrote out the early draft. Most of the "Circe" notes, like these for the two pages of dialogue, went into his elaborate augmentation of the episode; an example of this is the pair of notesheets, "Circe" 20 and 21, where Joyce listed all the "characters" who had appeared thus far in *Ulysses* to assure their inclusion in "Circe." The characters include concepts like "Parallax" ("Lestrygonians") and subjects of previous discussion, such as "Beresford" ("Cyclops").

In September 1920, shortly after saying that he had written "Circe" five or six times, Joyce began to talk about schematic structurings of his book. On September 3 he sent a "scheme" of *Ulysses* to John Quinn, but this one merely lists the episodes by Homeric title and divides them in two ways, in half (a dotted line separates "Scylla and Charybdis" and "Wandering Rocks") and in three parts (numbered I, II, and III and labeled "Telemachia," "Odyssey," and "Nostos"; *Letters*, I, 145). Joyce sent the first of the real schemata—he called it "una specie di sunto-chiave-scheletro-schema" ("a sort of summary-key-skeleton-scheme")—to Carlo Linati on September 21 (*Selected Letters*, pp. 270-71). The Linati schema contains much information not in the book; these ideas must have been only plans in Joyce's mind. For example, the finished "Ithaca" barely resembles the schema entries:

Time—1-2
Colour—starry, milky
Persons—Ulysses, Telemachus, Eurycleia, The Suitors
Technic—Dialogue, Pacified style, Fusion
Sense (Meaning)—The Armed Hope
Organ—Juices

(Linati Schema)

This "skeleton" of "Ithaca" probably fits the rough plan, sketch, or draft that Joyce claimed he wrote in 1916 (*Letters*, III, 31). If anything, it shows how much work he still had to do on episodes he thought were practically finished.

He qualified this schema to some extent in his accompanying letter:

> I think that in view of the enormous bulk and the more than enormous complexity of my damned monster-novel it would be better to send you a sort of summary-key-skeleton-scheme (for home use only). Perhaps when you have the text my idea will appear clearer to you. . . . I have given only "Schlagworte" in my scheme but I think you will understand it all the same. It is the epic of two races (Israel-Ireland) and at the same time the cycle of the human body as well as a little story of a day (life). The

character of Ulysses has fascinated me ever since boy-
hood. . . . It [the book] is also a kind of encyclopaedia. My
intention is not only to render the myth *sub specie temporis
nostri* but also to allow each adventure (that is, every
hour, every organ, every art being interconnected and
interrelated in the somatic scheme of the whole) to condition and even to create its own technique. Each adventure is so to speak one person although it is composed of
persons—as Aquinas relates of the heavenly hosts.

(*Selected Letters*, p. 271)

The character of Ulysses, the transposition of the myth, the
implication of an organic unity between form and content,
and the explicit statement that the schema cannot substi-
tute for the book all qualify its importance.[4] So does Joyce's
uncertainty in naming his plan; "summary," "key," "skeleton," and "scheme" are not entirely synonymous. He never
placed his later schemata in a context as broad as this one,
at least not explicitly in writing. His later willingness to let
the schema stand alone is an indication of his changing
concept of his book between September 1920 and December 1921.

As "Circe" grew more complex, so did Joyce's plans for
Ulysses. In September the book was not really "a sort of encyclopaedia," but his imagination obviously seized on this
while he worked on "Circe." Growth and expansion became extremely important. In late October 1920 he even
decided to enlarge his plan of eighteen episodes:

Last night I thought of an *Entr'acte* for Ulysses in middle
of book after 9th episode *Scylla & Charybdis*. Short with
absolutely no relation to what precedes or follows like a

[4] Even for the episodes Joyce thought he had completed, the schema
does not reflect his actual practice. For example, the parallel with Aeolus
conditions the technique of that episode as Joyce originally wrote it, since
there is much windiness, and the newspaper office-Aeolian island connection results in echoes of the printing machines in the prose. However,
Joyce did not allow the "adventure" to "create its own technique" until a
year after he wrote to Linati, when he added the newspaper subheads.

pause in the action of a play. It would have to be balanced by a *matutine* (very short) before the opening and a
nocturne (also short) after the end.

(Letters, I, 149)

Although Joyce never implemented this plan, it indicates a
new attitude toward his book inspired by his work on
"Circe."

He was quite conservative, however, in revising *Ulysses* to
conform with his new desire for expansion. Perhaps because of fatigue as much as caution, he continued for several months after finishing "Circe" to feel that "Ithaca" and
"Penelope" would both be fairly short and uncomplicated.
He said this as late as May 2, 1921 (I, 165). Even when he
submitted typescripts to Darantiere in the summer of 1921,
he had revised the first fourteen episodes very slightly
compared to his work of late 1921. The middle stage of the
new work on *Ulysses* ended in early autumn 1920 as "Circe"
grew "wilder and worse and more involved" (I, 147), but
the middle-stage revising lasted until the summer of 1921.
For both his new writing and his revisions of the completed
episodes, though, his six-months' effort on "Circe" was the
impetus for all the expansion and elaboration that characterized his last stage of work on *Ulysses*.

The First Revisions

Compared to the number of words, phrases, passages,
and even scenes that Joyce eventually added to *Ulysses*, his
1920 plans for revision were quite limited. In March, while
discussing publication possibilities with his agent, James
Pinker, he demanded "a revise after the first proof" (*Letters*, II, 462); presumably he needed this to insert the additions he had been accumulating. A November 24, 1920, letter to John Quinn describes the additions, names the most
amended episodes, and repeats the demand for a double
set of proofs:[5]

[5] At this time Quinn was involved with *Ulysses* in three different ways: he
was purchasing the fair copy of the episodes as Joyce completed them, de-

I must stipulate to have three sendings of proofs (pref-
erably a widemargined one must be pulled), namely:

   (1) A galley-page proof of all the book up to and including *Circe*.

   (2) A similar proof of the three chapters of the *Nostos*

   (3) A complete proof of the book in page form.

(Letters, III, 31)

Joyce's phrase "three sendings of proof" is somewhat misleading, since his demand actually involves one set of galley
proofs for the entire book—(1) and (2)—and a complete set
of page proofs—(3). (When Darantiere set the book in
1921, he sent Joyce three copies of each proof, but I assume that the "three sendings" refer to the different pullings.) This implies again that he anticipated only one
round of revisions to the proofs.[6]

In the letters to both Pinker and Quinn, Joyce seems to
assume that the type for the proofs would be set from the
existing typescripts (this meant copies of the same typescripts as those used for the *Little Review*), after which he
would augment the proofs. (When he finally incorporated
the additions he had in mind in 1920, he wrote them directly onto the typescripts.) His nomadic existence made
the two steps necessary. Although he had an "extract of insertions" with him in Paris (I, 142), the additions themselves remained behind in Trieste, sorted and ready for inclusion.

Joyce perhaps began to gather material for additions
and revisions as soon as he finished each episode, but he
probably did not do so in a concentrated way until the period beginning with the writing of "Cyclops." Most likely he
used some variation of the tablet-rough notes-notesheet

---

fending the *Little Review* in its obscenity trial, and talking with B. W.
Huebsch about a possible American book publication of *Ulysses*.

[6] Coincidentally, when publication finally became a reality a year later,
Darantiere pulled *placards* for the "Nostos" episodes separately from those
for the first fifteen episodes. In 1920 Joyce had to ask for separate galley
proofs for the "Nostos," since those episodes were not yet finished.

sequence, as he did for his original work on the last seven episodes. As he told Quinn, he had proceeded as far as sorting the rough notes according to episode before he left Trieste (III, 31). These rough notes have not survived; we can only infer their contents from his additions to the typescripts. Once he received the notes from Trieste, he must have either transferred the information to a notebook similar to the collection of notes for the last revisions (Buffalo MS V.A.2) or, more likely, copied the notes directly onto the typescripts from the sorted sheets or tablets.

The British Museum notesheets for the last seven episodes contain notes that resulted in post-*Little Review* typescript additions to the early episodes. Probably these notes were not among those left behind in Trieste; they may have been some of the "extracts" Joyce brought to Paris. They appear on notesheets for six episodes (all but "Penelope"), with the greatest number concentrated on sheets for "Oxen of the Sun" and "Circe." In all, the notesheets contain about eighty such notes, which is a very low total since, for example, "Lestrygonians" alone contains seventy typescript additions and "Nausicaa" almost 150. Obviously Joyce did not filter most of these additions through the surviving notesheets; rather, these sheets seem to have served as a repository for additions beyond those he had left behind in Trieste—either new ideas that occurred to him in Paris or old ones for which he now discovered a use.

The notesheets reveal several aspects of his concerns and methods in the first stage of revision. Occasionally, though not so often as we might wish, they show a relationship between work on one episode and additions for another. For instance, on a "Cyclops" sheet (7:39-45), he apparently gathered names of illnesses and deformities either to describe Cusack (later the Citizen) or, more likely, for insults to be spoken by Cusack:

yahoo
bludgeon
bear with sore paw (Lestryg)

Cusack
carcinoma of face
cyclostome
elephantiasis

While Joyce developed his list, he must have thought of "bear with sore paw," and he noted the phrase for inclusion in "Lestrygonians," where it appears on the typescript as a handwritten addition to a passage about Sir Frederick Falkiner (see 183.3-4). Similarly, notes on a related topic, clustered together on a notesheet, resulted in additions to the typescripts for widely scattered pages of the book, as in this collection from an "Ithaca" sheet:

Cat rocked on chair to get out   (4:26; not in book)
Wonder mice don't cry   (4:27; cf. 55.36)
Letter on forehead of cat   (4:28; cf. 378.8-12)
cat's shameclosing eye   (4:42; cf. 55.39)
— walks on LB's desk   (4:43; cf. 55.20-21)
Cat ate 'em? What? Fish   (4:61; not in book)

The additions inspired by these notes cause Bloom's cat to become a minor motif in *Ulysses*, culminating in Bloom's comparison in "Ithaca" between the cat and Milly (694.1-15). The basic comparison exists in the earliest extant version of "Ithaca," but Joyce added the parenthetical comparisons—"cf. neckarching cat," "cf. mousewatching cat"—only in the late revisions.

On a notesheet that Phillip Herring has labeled "Circe" Joyce collected notes for additions to several episodes. Two sides of the folded sheet ("Circe" 20 and 21) list the characters in the first fifteen episodes. "Circe" 19, another side of the sheet, contains notes for several different episodes, and he used many of these notes for post-*Little Review* typescript additions to earlier episodes. This sheet contains notes that became additions to "Lotus Eaters," "Lestrygonians," "Cyclops," "Nausicaa," and "Oxen of the Sun," including several that went into the "Cyclops" parody description of the Keogh-Bennett fight (318.29-319.19; see above, pp. 150-51). On the basis of three notes on "Circe"

19 that name people Joyce met shortly after he arrived in
Paris, Herring dates this sheet from the summer of 1921
(*Notesheets*, pp. 526-27). The notes here thus represent
either the "extract of insertions" that Joyce brought to
Paris or new additions that occurred to him after he settled
there.

The typescript additions reflect Joyce's middle stage of
work on the book during his writing of "Cyclops,"
"Nausicaa," and "Oxen of the Sun," and his early work on
"Circe." They are poised halfway between the early
novelistic concerns and the full encyclopedism of his late-
1921 work. Some of the additions increase minute detail
and add to the realism; others point to the schematic elements in the episodes. The intermediate nature of the additions is evident in any episode. A good example is "Lestrygonians," which Joyce named as one of the most heavily
augmented episodes (*Letters*, III, 31). Here the additions
fall evenly into two general types of concern. Many fill in
and expand details in Bloom's mind; examples are "Dock-
rell's, one and ninepence a dozen" (Buffalo TS V.B.6, p. 3;
155.36) and "Not go in and blurt out: what's parallax?
Show this gentleman the door" (TS, p. 9; cf. 167.9-10).
These additions and many others like them serve the interests of realistic detail and seem in no way connected to the
schematic correspondences that were gaining importance
in Joyce's mind.

Balancing the nonschematic additions are an equal
number reflecting Joyce's original and new interests in correspondences. The schema that Joyce sent to Carlo Linati
in September 1920, the one coinciding with the middle-
stage additions, gives the following entries for "Lestrygonians":

Time—1-2
Colour—Blood colour
Persons—Antiphates, The seductive daughter, Ulysses
Technic—Peristaltic prose
Science, Art—Architecture
Sense (Meaning)—Dejection

Organ—Esophagus
Symbol—Bloody sacrifice: Foods: Shame
(Linati Schema)

Most of the typescript additions relating to this schema refer to "foods." There are about twenty-five such additions, ranging from single words like "chawbacon" (TS V.B.6, p. 10; 168.14) to short phrases like "Eat pig like pig" (TS, p. 2; 153.20-21) to longer passages:

No lard for them. My heart's broke eating dripping. ⟨They like buttering themselves in and out. Molly tasting it, her veil up.⟩
(TS, p. 3; 155.12-14; the bracketed words
are an addition to the addition)

The *élite. Crème de la crème.* They want special dishes to pretend they're. Royal sturgeon. High sheriff, Fanagan, the undertaker, right to venisons of the forest from his ex. Spread I saw down in Master of the Rolls' kitchen area. Whitehatted chef. Combustible duck. Curly cabbage à la duchesse de Parme. Geese crammed for them. Lobsters boiled alive.
(TS, p. 13; cf. 175.16-27)

In some of the additions, food is the subject matter, but in most it serves as the kind of metaphor expressing a relationship between the state of the body at different times of the day and the "underthoughts" that result, as Joyce said to Frank Budgen (Budgen, p. 21; see above, pp. 14-15). Examples are "buttering themselves" (TS, p. 3; 155.14), "working tooth and jaw" (p. 10; 169.23), and "crusty old topers" (p. 18; 183.3). Food determines several proverbs and clichés in Bloom's mind—"Bitten off more than he can chew" (p. 10; 169.21), "Eat drink and be merry" (p. 11; 172.4), "God made food, the devil the cooks" (p. 12; 172.13-14)—and it results in a pun, "Poached eyes on ghost" (p. 8; 165.11-12). Passages similar to these exist in the fair copy-*Little Review* version of "Lestrygonians," and Joyce added many more in the late revisions. In the middle-stage revisions, he increased the number of food passages (the "suggestion rather than direct statement" of Bloom's physical and mental condition, as he told Budgen), but he did not overwhelm the episode with references to food, as he did a year later.

One of the typescript additions is an excellent example of this. At one point as he walks down Westmoreland Street Bloom recalls Mrs. Purefoy, who, as he has just learned from Mrs. Breen, has been in the lying-in hospital for three days. In the fair copy, Bloom's thought is limited to "Poor Mrs Purefoy!" (MS, "Lestrygonians," fol. 9). On the typescript Joyce expanded Bloom's thoughts to include Mr. Purefoy and the many Purefoy children:

> Poor Mrs Purefoy! ⟨Methodist husband. Method in his madness. ⟨⟨Saffron bun and milk lunch in the educational dairy. Still his whiskers grew. Hardy annuals he presents her with. ⟨⟨⟨Squallers.⟩⟩⟩ Poor thing!⟩⟩ ⟩
> (TS V.B.6, p. 6)

After the final revisions (see 161.6-16), the paragraph had more details about the Purefoys but even more new references to food.

A few "Lestrygonians" typescript additions combine food and architecture (the "science, art" of the episode, according to the Linati schema), several refer to bloody sacrifice (one of the symbols), and one combines food and peristaltic movement (the technic). Numerically, the typescript additions to "Lestrygonians" divide evenly between novelistic and symbolistic purposes, and even when the subject matter of a passage is food, Joyce's additions show both concerns:

> Perched on high stools by the bar, hats shoved back, at the tables calling for more bread no charge, swilling, wolfing gobfuls of sloppy food, their eyes bulging, wiping wetted moustaches. A man with an infant's ⟨saucestained⟩ napkin tucked round him ~~spooned~~ ⟨shovelled⟩ gurgling soup down his gullet. ⟨Spoonfed⟩ A man spitting back on his plate: gristle: no teeth to chew it. Chump

chop he has. ⟨Bolting to get it over.⟩ Sad booser's eyes.
⟨Bitten off more than he can chew. Am I like that? See
ourselves as others see us. Hungry man is an angry man.
Working tooth and jaw.⟩

(TS V.B.6, p. 10; cf. 169.12-27)

Bloom's thought, "Bitten off more than he can chew," like a
later addition to the passage, "Couldn't swallow it all however," represents the style of the episode dominating
Bloom's mind. His subsequent reflection, though, "Am I
like that? See ourselves as others see us," does not.[7] Joyce
favored neither type of addition over the other; in the
middle stage of revision, he wanted both kinds.

Work in Progress: 1921

Joyce was not sorry to see the end of 1920, with its
"Circe" problems and an eye attack in November and December. On December 30 he wrote Nora's uncle, Michael
Healy, "Renewed good wishes for the New Year, the Devil
being requested by me to take the present one as quickly as
he likes" (*Letters*, I, 153). By early April, though, the new
year too seemed hopeless, and Joyce prepared a typical ex-
planation for the development: "It seems as if this year
$(1 + 9 + 2 + 1 = 13)$ is to be one incessant trouble to me"
(I, 161). The most pressing problem involved "Circe,"
which needed several different typists (there are at least six
changes of typist in the last sixty-five pages of the 145-page
typescript) and suffered one burning before it was fully
typed. By the time the "Circe" typescript was finished on
April 16, he had completed "Eumaeus," and it too was
typed (I, 159, 163). But his luck in the spring of 1921 was
not all bad: around this time he received and accepted Sylvia Beach's offer to publish *Ulysses*.

Besides the typing of "Circe," Joyce's early 1921 problems involved his writing of the last two episodes. He began
"Ithaca" and "Penelope" as he had begun "Circe," expect-

---

[7] This thought becomes a minor motif in *Ulysses*, for it recurs in
"Nausicaa," again as a post-*Little Review* typescript addition (376.2).

ing short, simple episodes, and he believed that he would complete them in little time and without difficulty. Because of "Circe," such expectations quickly proved unrealistic, and by June a familiar complaint began to appear in Joyce's letters: "*Ithaca* is giving me fearful trouble" (III, 46).[8]

Joyce had apparently planned neither "Ithaca" nor "Penelope" very fully in late 1920 and early 1921. As we have seen, when he sent his first schema to Carlo Linati in September 1920, his plans for "Ithaca" were still largely undeveloped. As late as December 10, 1920, he wrote to Budgen, "At first I had not thought of the slaughter of the suitors as in Ulysses' character. Now I see it can be there too. I am going to leave the last word with Molly Bloom— the final episode *Penelope* being written through her thoughts and body Poldy being then asleep" (I, 151-52). Such letters to Budgen are usually reliable indicators of Joyce's recent ideas or progress (as are his letters on "Cyclops" and "Oxen of the Sun"; I, 126, 139-40), so it seems that only in December 1920 did he establish one of the book's climaxes and begin to formulate the last episode.

Joyce's plans for "Ithaca" crystallized early in 1921, but "Penelope" developed even later. At the end of February Joyce described "Ithaca" to Budgen as "a mathematical catechism" in which

> all events are resolved into their cosmic physical, psychical etc. equivalents, e.g. Bloom jumping down the area, drawing water from the tap, the micturition in the garden, the cone of incense, lighted candle and statue so

[8] Two excellent dissertations document Joyce's work on "Ithaca" and "Penelope": Richard Eastman Madtes, "A Textual and Critical Study of the 'Ithaca' Episode of James Joyce's *Ulysses*," Diss. Columbia 1961, and James Van Dyck Card, "A Textual and Critical Study of the 'Penelope' Episode of James Joyce's *Ulysses*," Diss. Columbia 1964. Both Madtes and Card provide a transcription of the Rosenbach Manuscript version of their episode. Madtes indicates Joyce's additions in the Rosenbach Manuscript copybooks of "Ithaca," and Card notes all Joyce's additions to "Penelope" from Rosenbach Manuscript to publication.

that not only will the reader know everything and know it in the baldest coldest way, but Bloom and Stephen thereby become heavenly bodies, wanderers like the stars at which they gaze.

(I, 159-60)

In the same letter Joyce described "Penelope" as the "indispensable countersign to Bloom's passport to eternity," but he apparently did not develop that episode fully until August. (Richard Ellmann says that Joyce thought of "yes" as Molly's last word only in July 1921 after he heard Mrs. Richard Wallace say the word over and over again; *JJ*, p. 531; *Letters*, I, 168-70.) Like "Circe," both "Ithaca" and "Penelope" grew increasingly complex as Joyce tried to write them, and both took longer than he expected. He "finished" neither episode until the autumn of 1921: "Penelope" by September 24 (III, 49) and "Ithaca" by October 29 (I, 175).

In midsummer Joyce suffered a serious eye attack, and there may be a connection between it and his late work on *Ulysses*. The attack lasted five weeks, beginning on July 3 (*JJ*, p. 531). At that time he was working on "Ithaca" and "Penelope," augmenting the typescripts of the early episodes, and beginning to correct the proofs for the book. (He received the first proofs in mid-June; III, 44-46.)[9] He described to Harriet Shaw Weaver his attempts to work on these different aspects of *Ulysses* while recuperating from the eye attack:

I have had five weeks of delightful vacation with my eyes—the strangest but not at all the worst attack because instead of coming to a head in three weeks it did so in three hours. . . . I am now advised to go to Aix-les-Bains but am in Ithaca instead. I write and revise and correct with one or two eyes about twelve hours a day I should

[9] I have provided a census of the *Ulysses* proofs and a chronology of Joyce's work on *Ulysses* from July 1920 until publication as appendixes to my doctoral dissertation, "The Growth of James Joyce's *Ulysses*," Diss. Princeton 1975, pp. 314-65.

say, stopping for intervals of five minutes or so when I
can't see any more. My brain reels after it but that is
nothing compared with the reeling of my readers'
brains. I have not yet quite recovered and I am doing the
worst thing possible but can't help it. . . . I am trying to
make up for lost time.

(I, 168)

When the attack struck, Darantiere had pulled one set of
placards and one or two sets of page proofs for the first five
episodes of *Ulysses*. After the attack he pulled new *placards*
and page proofs for the first five episodes and began to
pull proofs for the other episodes; the first *placards* for
"Hades" date from August 10. Joyce greatly augmented
the episodes from "Hades" on, beginning in late August,
and it is possible that the late revisions originated during
the painful, restless weeks in July and August 1921 when
he could barely read the proofs and could do little work on
"Ithaca" and "Penelope."

During or immediately after his recuperation from the
eye attack, Joyce added an extended scene to "Circe," a
gesture that seems to inaugurate the final revision stage
with its many rounds of new phrases and passages. The
new "Circe" scene, an elaboration of a very short fantasy
already in the episode, depicts Bloom's visionary rise to
glory as the "emperor president and king chairman" of Ireland and as the new Messiah (479.30-499.7; the section
from 478.7-479.29 is part of the fair copy of "Circe"). Two
of the "Circe" notesheets (16 and 17) contain much of the
material for the addition. It is probably not coincidental
that, just as Joyce was about to expand *Ulysses* through in-
numerable revisions, he wrote a scene extending Bloom's
dreams to apocalyptic dimensions. He mentioned that he
had added the "Messianic scene" to "Circe" in a letter to
Valery Larbaud from about August 11 (I, 168-69).

From August 1921 until the book's publication on February 2, 1922, Joyce mixed new work on "Ithaca" and
"Penelope" with corrections and additions to proofs for

other parts of the book, often for several different parts at once. When the printer set type for "Telemachus," "Nestor," "Proteus," "Calypso," and "Lotus Eaters" in June, he pulled one group of *placards* and one group of page proofs (two page proofs for "Calypso" and "Lotus Eaters"). This suggests that in June Joyce still wanted only the one set of galleys and one set of page proofs that he had required the previous November (III, 31; see above, p. 179). By August, though, this number had become inadequate; it turned out that Joyce needed up to four sets of *placards* and up to five sets of page proofs for every page of the book. Ellmann says that "Darantiere's characteristic gesture, throwing up his hands in despair, became almost constant when the type had to be recast time after time" (*JJ*, p. 527).

Beginning in August, just after Joyce recovered from the eye attack, the printers began to work at a much faster pace than in June. Between August and early October they pulled new sets of *placards* and page proofs for the first five episodes, several sets of *placards* and then page proofs for the next five ("Hades" through "Wandering Rocks"), and the first *placards* for "Sirens" and "Cyclops." Much of the "great revision" of the episodes from "Hades" onward occurred in Joyce's additions to the first set of *placards*.

The printers often set type for more than one episode at the same time. On October 1, for example, they pulled the first *placard* for one part of "Cyclops" and the fourth page proof for a section of "Hades." Three of Joyce's letters chronicle Darantiere's and his own progress during this time. On August 30 he told Harriet Shaw Weaver that he had "made a great deal of addition to the proofs so far (up to the end of *Scylla and Charybdis*)" (I, 171); four days later he restated this message to Robert McAlmon in a different idiom: "I have now written in a great lot of balderdash all over the damn book and the first half is practically as it will appear" (III, 48). Third, his well-known letter to Harriet Shaw Weaver of October 7 summarizes his revisions of the first nine episodes while it typically underestimates the work still to be done:

Ulysses will be finished in about three weeks, thank God, and (if the French printers don't all leap into the Rhone in despair at the mosaics I send them back) ought to be published early in November. I sent the *Penelope* episode to the printer. . . . The *Ithaca* episode which precedes it I am now putting in order. . . . I expect to have early next week about 240 pages of the book as it will appear ready and will send on [i.e., through the end of "Cyclops"]. *Eolus* is recast. *Hades* and the *Lotus-eaters* much amplified and the other episodes retouched a good deal. Not much change has been made in the *Telemachia* (the first three episodes of the book).

(I, 172)

As so often happened in 1921, just as Joyce envisioned the end of his work on *Ulysses*, complications developed. Because Valery Larbaud wanted to see "Penelope" for the article he was writing, Joyce sent it to the printers about a month before he finished "Ithaca" (III, 49; I, 175). During the week of October 10, while the printers set "Sirens" for the second time and "Cyclops" for the third, they pulled the first proofs for "Penelope." They were nowhere near "Circe" (they would not begin it until mid-November), but for some reason they now pulled proofs for the "Messianic scene" that Joyce had written only a few months earlier as an addition to "Circe." In late October they simultaneously pulled *placards* for "Nausicaa," "Oxen of the Sun," "Penelope," and one segment from the middle of "Circe," and page proofs of "Sirens" and "Cyclops."

Similar complications occurred in December. On the sixth Joyce told Harriet Shaw Weaver that "the printer has done more in the past three days than in the fortnight before" (I, 177); the new energy was necessary because of Valery Larbaud's December 7 lecture on *Ulysses*. While the printers were pulling the first *placards* for the second half of "Circe," they began to set "Eumaeus" and then "Ithaca." They were also pulling page proofs for the first half of "Circe." On December 10 Joyce expressed his reaction to this situation:

The printer, for some reason, sends me now proofs of *Circe*, *Eumeus* and *Penelope* at the same time without having finished the composition of the first two and I have to work on them simultaneously, different as they are, so that I remind myself of the man who used to play several instruments with different parts of his body.

(I, 178-79)

Darantiere completed the *placards* by January 5, 1922, by which time he had set about two-thirds of "Circe" in page proof. This means that over 200 pages of the book remained to be set in page proof form. He pulled "Ithaca" only on January 19 and "Penelope" within the next day or two. On January 23 Joyce described the state of the proofs for the last episodes as "uncorrected semifinal form" (III, 57), and he returned them to Darantiere during the next week with an incredible number of additions and corrections, "Ithaca" on January 25 and 27, and "Penelope" on January 31 (see Figure 4). To achieve the publication of *Ulysses* on February 2, Darantiere practically reset both episodes in two days to incorporate all Joyce's last-minute changes and additions.

For the early episodes (through "Oxen of the Sun" in this case), where there are several sets of both *placards* and page proofs, the first page proofs seem to follow the first *placards* by about five weeks. Later, beginning around "Circe," there simply was not time for so many proofs or for so great a lag between proofs. Some of the later pages have only one *placard* and one page proof. Joyce's original writing of "Circe," "Eumaeus," "Ithaca," and "Penelope" involved a great deal of work similar to his last-stage revisions of the first fourteen episodes, so the first proofs of the last four represent a much more advanced stage than do those of the earlier ones. But the last four episodes also have the greatest number of additions on the final page proofs. Given the overwhelming number of changes, the chaotic order of the printing, and the difficulties caused by Joyce's handwriting and the printers' lack of English, the accuracy that Darantiere managed to achieve is amazing.

The "final page proofs" of *Ulysses*. Joyce's printer received this corrected and augmented page two days before publication. Reproduced courtesy of the Society of Authors and the Humanities Research Center, University of Texas at Austin. (Figure 4)

Toward the end of his work on the book, Joyce prepared the second of his problematic schemata. He first referred to this plan in a November 6, 1921, letter to Valery Larbaud, while Larbaud was preparing his séance of readings from Joyce's works: "Possibly I may see you tonight. If not I shall post you my scheme of *Ulysses* and proposed programme for the readings" (III, 53). Like *Ulysses* itself, the schema had to be revised and augmented, for around November 15 Joyce wrote to Larbaud requesting the return of the schema, which he would "amplify" and send back (III, 53). On November 26 he wanted to meet with Larbaud "to show you and comment on the new plan" (III, 54). There is no way of knowing what Joyce added to the schema, but the plan that he ultimately showed Larbaud had the same contents as the schema later published.[10]

The Linati schema of a year earlier often contained ideas that Joyce merely planned to include in *Ulysses*, but this one, for better or worse, consists of elements that do exist in the book. The entries for "Ithaca," for example, barely resemble those on the earlier schema:

Scene—The House
Hour—2 A.M.
Organ—skeleton
Art—science
Colour—(none)
Symbol—comets
Technic—catechism (impersonal)

[10] Copies of the schema exist at Southern Illinois University (Herbert Gorman's copy), the University of Texas (Stuart Gilbert's copy), and SUNY at Buffalo (Sylvia Beach's copy). Joyce also gave copies to Harriet Shaw Weaver (*Letters*, I, 178; III, 62) and Edmund Wilson (see *Axel's Castle: A Study in the Imaginative Literature of 1870-1930* [New York: Scribner's, 1931], pp. 211-13). The text of Larbaud's December 7, 1921, lecture appeared in *La Nouvelle Revue Française*, 18 (April 1922), and part of the lecture was translated anonymously as "The 'Ulysses' of James Joyce," *The Criterion*, 1 (Oct. 1922). Larbaud refers to the schema on p. 407 and pp. 101-02, respectively.

Correspondences—Eurymachus – Boylan: Suitors –
scruples: Bow – reason.

(1921 Schema)

This schema derives from Joyce's last stage of work on
Ulysses, as the Linati schema was a product of the middle
stage. The elements in it represent only a part of *Ulysses*,
but a part Joyce was emphasizing in his late revisions of his
book.

The Late Revisions

Joyce overhauled *Ulysses* through his revisions of the last
six months of 1921. Such a complete reworking does not
seem to have occurred to him before the summer of 1921;
even while "Ithaca" and "Penelope" were growing far beyond his expectations, he limited his revisions of the other
episodes to those he had compiled in 1919 and 1920, or to
others like them. But a September 6, 1921, letter shows
that by the time he was finishing his draft of "Penelope" he
knew that the version represented only an outline compared to the dimensions the episode would eventually assume. "This is only the *draft*," he wrote to Budgen, "a great
deal will be added or changed on 3 proofs" (I, 171). A year
earlier, Joyce demanded one extra set of proofs to accommodate the additions he had left behind in Trieste; now he
needed as many as nine sets for all the late revisions.

These revisions serve several functions. Joseph Prescott
has meticulously documented one group of them under
the general term of "stylistic realism."[11] He divides the
changes and additions into several categories: precision,
specification, vividness, dramatization, onomatopoeia, deliberate distortion, rhythm, and neologisms. As an example
of precision, Prescott notes a change in "Ithaca": Bloom
"raised the latch of the area door by the exertion of force at
its ~~free arm~~ ⟨freely moving flange⟩" (669.5-6); and he cites

[11] Joseph Prescott, "Stylistic Realism in *Ulysses*" (1959), in *Exploring
James Joyce* (Carbondale: Southern Illinois Univ. Press, 1964), pp. 106-34.
The following examples come from pp. 107 and 116.

an addition to "Lotus Eaters" as an example of vividness: "With careful tread he passed over a hopscotch court ⟨with its forgotten pickeystone⟩" (77.21-23). Prescott's attention to details like these (he provides nearly two hundred examples) is valuable in that it emphasizes a kind of writing that always concerned Joyce, even in the late stages when other concerns became equally or more important.

However, the concept of "stylistic realism" slights other prominent characteristics of the late revisions, such as Joyce's goal of encyclopedism. This often involved expanding pre-existing facts or motifs to extremes of Cyclopean "gigantism." For instance, Joyce often lengthened fairly short lists completely beyond their original proportions, as in the list of saints in the "Cyclops" parody who respond to Martin Cunningham's request to "bless all here" in Barney Kiernan's (339.12-41; see above, pp. 159-60).

Joyce did not confine his expansion of lists to "Cyclops," but augmented lists primarily in the episodes following "Cyclops" rather than in those preceding it. On the "Circe" proofs, for example, he added most of the responses to Cissy Caffrey's call for the police (598.12-599.8), and on the "Ithaca" proofs he greatly expanded Bloom's dreams of a country house (712.18-714.22). He likewise enlarged in proof the list of the despot Bloom's attempts to eliminate his enemies and to please the crowd around him (485.15-486.7); this forms part of the Messianic scene that he did not write at all until summer 1921. An example of this lengthening process from earlier in the book is the progression of the viceregal cavalcade in the nineteenth section of "Wandering Rocks" (252.3-255.7); Joyce did not expand it to the same extent as these later lists because it describes a realistic event.

In these elaborate lists (which have been seen as part of the Homeric parallel), Joyce worked toward encyclopedism by taking a specific incident and cataloguing its observers or participants. In most cases his techniques of revision caused him to extend the lists to such comical lengths that they eventually assumed a logic of their own beyond any logic in the events that originally inspired them (for example, in the list of saints in "Cyclops," "S. Martin of Todi" leads to "S. Martin of Tours"). By sheer persistence such repeated accumulations ultimately achieved the effect of all-inclusiveness Joyce desired.

While Joyce was elaborating individual lists, he also did a great deal of revising in a way that cuts across the book. One of *Ulysses'* most prominent features is its vast web of interconnections: repeated symbols, recurrent themes and motifs, and fragmented revelation of the history of its characters. Especially in the early episodes, the reader must recognize the various unifying symbols and note and remember the many strands of information about the characters that Joyce introduces indirectly. The symbols and fragments of information both contribute to the aspect of *Ulysses* that Joseph Frank calls its "spatial form":

> All the factual background summarized for the reader in an ordinary novel must here be reconstructed from fragments, sometimes hundreds of pages apart, scattered through the book. As a result, the reader is forced to read *Ulysses* in exactly the same manner as he reads modern poetry, that is, by continually fitting fragments together and keeping allusions in mind until, by reflexive reference, he can link them to their complements. . . . The reader is intended to acquire this sense as he progresses through the novel, connecting allusions and references spatially and gradually becoming aware of the pattern of relationships.[12]

From the start of his work on *Ulysses*, Joyce's interior monologue technique produced a gradual revelation of the characters through their fragmentary thoughts and memories, but much of the "spatial" aspect of the book resulted from his 1921 revisions. During his last six months of work, he intensified the patterns of symbols, motifs, and

[12] Joseph Frank, "Spatial Form in Modern Literature" (1945), in *The Widening Gyre: Crisis and Mastery in Modern Literature* (New Brunswick: Rutgers Univ. Press, 1963), pp. 18-19.

personal histories. His work on the symbols relates to the schema he prepared in late 1921; that plan essentially reflects this aspect of the late work. In some cases he took elements already in the book and found symbolic and schematic values for them. For example, Stuart Gilbert gives fourteen examples of architectural and "alimentary allusions" in "Lestrygonians" (Gilbert, p. 209). Half of them existed in the fair copy of the episode, three others first appear as handwritten additions to the typescript after the *Little Review* publication, and the other four were late revisions. Joyce did not have the details of his elaborate schema in mind in 1918 when he first wrote "Lestrygonians," but he later found many appropriate symbols already in the episode, and he added many others.

Joyce added over eighty "alimentary allusions" to "Lestrygonians" after he sent the typescript to Darantiere; all are extensions of the schema entries for the episode's "organ" and "correspondences"—the esophagus, and hunger, food, and teeth. Similarly, he added numerous references to the heart in "Hades" and new musical puns in "Sirens." In another extension of the schema, he revised several episodes to achieve a greater "expressive form"; examples of this are the flower imagery in "Lotus Eaters" and the newspaper subheads in "Aeolus." (A. Walton Litz has discussed this type of revision in detail; pp. 44-52.)

The late revisions built up the "web" of the book's realistic details. The great increase in the number of minor leitmotifs interconnected different parts and, even more important, provided many more examples of the consistency of Bloom's mind. As with the elements from the schema, Joyce usually increased the realistic linkages by exploiting details he had already put into *Ulysses*. One example is the bee sting that Bloom suffered on May 23, 1904, and that he recalls throughout June 16. In the fair copy, the incident appears twice: in the distorted language of "Oxen of the Sun" (MS, "Oxen," fols. 6-7; cf. 386.25-33) and in "Circe" (MS, "Circe," fol. 41; 515.35-36). Then, beginning in the summer of 1921, Joyce elaborated the incident to turn it

into a minor motif. It appears as an addition to the Rosenbach Manuscript version of "Penelope" (which Joyce probably wrote in September 1921): "Whit Monday is a cursed
day too no wonder that bee bit him" (MS, "Penelope," p.
15v; 764.34-35). It also occurs in the "Ithaca" copybook
that forms part of the Rosenbach Manuscript, the earliest
extant version of that episode (probably written in October): "He compressed between 2 fingers the flesh circum-
jacent to a cicatrice ⟨in the left infracostal region below the
diaphragm⟩ resulting from a sting inflicted 2 weeks and 3
days previously (23 May 1904) by a bee" (MS, "Ithaca,"
copybook II, p. 14r; 710.37-711.2).

Joyce included the incident in the last two episodes; at
the same time, he planted allusions to it in the earlier ones:

> Still gardens have their drawbacks. That bee or bluebot-
> tle here Whitmonday. (68.18-19; added to first page
> proofs of "Calypso," which were pulled in June but
> which Joyce probably did not revise until August)

> Nice young student that was dressed that bite the bee
> gave me. He's gone over to the lying-in hospital they told
> me. (97.28-30; added to first *placards* of "Hades" in
> mid-August)

> Still I got to know that young Dixon who dressed that
> sting for me in the Mater and now he's in Holles street
> where Mrs Purefoy. Wheels within wheels. (163.5-7;
> added to first *placards* of "Lestrygonians" between mid-
> August and early September)

In November and December of 1921 Joyce added two
more references to the incident on the proofs of
"Nausicaa" and "Circe" (378.21, 515.23). In the final version of *Ulysses*, the incident provides one of the strands of
Bloom's history that Joyce allows the reader to pick up a bit
at a time. Likewise, as a recurring memory of both Bloom
and Molly, it contributes to the presentation of their shared
experience.

A similar process occurred with the minor character,

Professor Maginni, the dancing master. Joyce first put him in *Ulysses* in "Circe" (575.17ff) during the summer of 1920. At first he spelled the name "Maghinni," as at "Circe" notesheet 6:19; it appears this way in the earliest extant draft of "Circe" (V.A.19, p. 17r; see Phillip Herring's discussion of early names for characters in *Notes and Early Drafts*, pp. 198-99). In late September and early October 1921 Joyce added Maginni to "Lestrygonians" and "Wandering Rocks" to prepare for his part in "Circe" (153.34-35, 220.24-29, 235.24-26, 253.39-41).

Even extremely significant motifs entered the book in this way. For example, the phrase "agenbite of inwit" appeared once in the fair copy (MS, "Scylla and Charybdis," fol. 24; now 206.26), but Joyce expanded it into a major motif in Stephen's mind only in the summer and fall of 1921 when he added it in five different places (16.7-8, 17.3, 189.27, 243.27, 31). In the library episode Stephen uses the phrase as part of his biographical argument ("Venus had twisted her lips in prayer. Agenbite of inwit: remorse of conscience. It is an age of exhausted whoredom groping for its god"), but in the last rounds of revision Joyce changed an isolated phrase into one that runs through Stephen's tormented mind both before and after the Shakespeare discussion. When the phrase appears only in "Scylla and Charybdis," it serves as an example of Stephen's tendency to display his erudition in front of willing listeners; as one occurrence of a repeated motif, it functions as Stephen's natural and less arrogant verbalization of a phrase that has been in his mind all day.

Occasionally Joyce introduced a phrase into a late episode and simultaneously planted preparations for it in earlier ones. For example, in the earliest extant version of "Ithaca," he provided the complete address of the scene of Bloom's father's suicide: "The Queen's Hotel, Ennis, county Clare" (MS, "Ithaca," copybook II, p. 3r; cf. 684.33). From the start Joyce located the suicide in the Queen's Hotel in Ennis, but he added two references in "Hades" to link Ennis with County Clare (92.41-42,

101.31-33). Obviously, even the most minute consistencies were essential. Along the same lines, he included the phrase "the Parable of the Plums" as Stephen's subtitle for his "Pisgah Sight of Palestine" in the Rosenbach copybook of "Ithaca" (MS, "Ithaca," copybook II, p. 4r; 685.18) at about the same time that he was adding it to "Aeolus" (149.26). He even added a stylistic preparation for Gerty MacDowell's episode in the summer of 1921 when he inserted a phrase in her idiom into the last section of "Wandering Rocks" (252.39-253.6).

Joyce's expansion of the interconnecting web of symbols and motifs differs from the revisions that Joseph Prescott classifies as "stylistic realism," but in late 1921 Joyce was occupied with both. His concern with "stylistic realism" is a carryover from his early and middle stages of work, and it indicates that he never entirely rejected his old aesthetic goals as he developed new ones. But it was the expansion of the symbolic network, a last-stage phenomenon, that he documented in his 1921 schema with its categories of "organ," "art," "colour," "symbol," and especially "correspondences." Along with the new episodes of "Ithaca" and "Penelope," these additions are the final result of "Circe" 's transforming powers that initiated the last stage of Joyce's work.

Conclusion

Joyce's urge to expand *Ulysses* was contained only by his stronger desire to see his book in print. So, on January 31, 1922, two days before his fortieth birthday, he stopped writing it. Once he finished the book—or "abandoned" it to his publisher and the public[13]—the tasks of interpreting

---

[13] "*Ulysses* provides a perfect illustration of Paul Valéry's remark that a work of art is never finished, but only abandoned." Litz, p. 7. Litz summarizes the events leading to publication in "The Last Adventures of *Ulysses*," *Princeton University Library Chronicle*, 28 (1967), pp. 63-75; rpt. in Ulysses: *Cinquante Ans Après*, ed. Louis Bonnerot (Paris: Didier, 1974), pp. 1-12.

and assessing the complete work necessarily take precedence over any questions about the methods of composition. We may know that Joyce added the "Aeolus" subheads two years after he wrote the episodes they are de-
signed to foreshadow, but we must ultimately deal with
their degree of success as a foreshadowing device, however
they entered the book.

Several major problems in interpreting *Ulysses* unfortunately gain little or no illumination from a study of Joyce's
work on the book. For example, the massive collection of
notes, drafts, typescripts, and proofs reveals hardly anything about the Homeric parallel. Phillip Herring has
shown that the notes for an episode like "Eumaeus," where
the structure and content are less complicated than in the
other middle- and last-stage episodes, emphasize the
Homeric parallel (*Notesheets*, pp. 49-57). Occasionally Joyce
revealed his attempts to develop a Homeric motif, as in his
notes about "moly" (see Litz, pp. 25-26; *Notesheets*, pp. 40-
41). And Joyce's 1918 Zurich notebook (Buffalo MS
VIII.A.5) suggests that, to a greater extent than we have
heretofore realized, the details of the "Homeric" parallel
may actually be derived from commentators like Victor
Bérard.[14] But Joyce's workshop gives us no help in dealing
with the meaning of the parallel or in assessing the various
contradictory interpretations, such as those of Harry Levin, who sees the relationship as one of "parallels that
never meet" and that "convert a realistic novel into a
mock-epic," and of Richard Ellmann, who describes one
meaning of the parallel as "the ennoblement of the mock-
heroic" and argues that "Bloom *is* Ulysses in an important
sense."[15] The subtle heroic/ironic relationship between
Homer's world and 1904 Dublin was so basic to Joyce's
conception of *Ulysses* that he did not need to express his in-

[14] For a fascinating study of Joyce's use of Bérard, see Michael Seidel,
Epic Geography: James Joyce's Ulysses (Princeton: Princeton Univ. Press,
1976).

[15] *James Joyce: A Critical Introduction*, rev. ed. (Norfolk: New Directions,
1941, 1960), p. 71; *JJ*, pp. 370, 371.

tentions in his notes or to work them out through false starts and revisions in the drafts. So we are left with copious documentation for the Homeric details but little information about the parallel's meanings.

The prepublication documents are similarly limited concerning the problem of Joyce's sympathy or irony toward his characters. We can watch him gradually break away from the representation of their minds and turn to a succession of parody styles, but his attitude toward the characters is as ambiguous in the worksheets as in the final version. I believe that several additions to Stephen's interior monologue imply a softening of Joyce's attitude toward him, but Bloom is more problematical. If a reader sees Bloom's mind as "a compost of objects" reflecting "his complete, narcotic immersion in his environment," then Joyce's presentation of him at every stage of *Ulysses*' development would serve to reinforce the condemnation. However, if Bloom's mind seems to possess "the power . . . to infuse common things with uncommonness" and to be "unsubduable," then the early versions and revisions would all show these qualities.[16] The documents carry us no closer to Joyce's basic assumptions than the final version.

Despite these limitations, though, an investigation of Joyce's making of *Ulysses* can be extremely rewarding. With its eighteen different episodes and over ten versions of some sections, Joyce's book was composed in ways so idiosyncratic as to be interesting in themselves. More important, his refusal to confine the contents of *Ulysses* to a closed fictional world forces us to look beyond the book for its meaning. (For instance, Stephen remembers fragments of incidents from *A Portrait of the Artist as a Young Man*, and certain elements in the book can be "explained" only by referring to Joyce's own life.) Our understanding of *Ulysses* benefits immensely from a knowledge of Joyce's earlier works, the real Dublin of 1904, the prototypes of the characters, and the history of Joyce's work on the book. As a

[16] Hugh Kenner, *Dublin's Joyce* (1956; rpt. Boston: Beacon, 1962), pp. 174, 170; *JJ*, pp. 372, 371.

result, it often happens that critics who are not actually studying Joyce's writing of *Ulysses* turn to the drafts and early versions to support their arguments. At the least, I have attempted in this study to present an accurate account of the entire complex process.

The notebooks and drafts may be less helpful than we might wish regarding the meaning of the Homeric parallel and Joyce's attitude toward his characters, but they provide extremely useful documentation of *Ulysses'* growing complexity as he wrote the last nine episodes and revised the entire book (that is, his work from 1919 to 1922). The "Cyclops" drafts show the precise point at which he abandoned the interior monologue technique that he had used through the first eleven episodes and turned irrevocably to nonrepresentational styles. His progress from that time in the summer of 1919 to February 1922 was a gradual movement through a series of parody styles (what I have called the middle stage) before he attempted the elaborate psychofantasy of "Circe" and the complex mixture of fact and myth in "Ithaca." Richard Ellmann's biography portrays a man whose tastes, interests, and life style were surprisingly conservative, and Joyce's drafts show that the great artistic innovator proceeded with caution before taking each major step in his writing and revising. Thus, the postulation of a middle stage between the early "novelistic" work and the late "schematic," "symbolistic" writing seems necessary for both biographical and artistic reasons: Joyce was incapable of leaping from his early goal of compression to the opposite extreme of expansion without passing through a series of intermediate steps, and in the middle-stage episodes he combined his waning interest in the human story of Bloom and Stephen with his growing attraction to parodic style.

I have suggested that Joyce wanted *Ulysses* to be a record of all the stages he passed through and not merely a product of the last one. This means that the processes by which he wrote the book cannot be separated from other aspects of its meaning. The processes seem to me to support readings of *Ulysses* that emphasize its ambiguity, which in this case seems best defined as a desire to hold opposing meanings or values in permanent suspension. Gradually and cautiously, Joyce moved from the interior-monologue technique of his early stage of work to the parody styles of the middle stage, and finally to the complex intermixture of realism and symbolism in both the new work and the revision of the last stage. This progression meant a shift from verisimilitude to symbolism and from the characters to the schema. But Joyce retained his entire range of concerns in the final version of *Ulysses*, and all need to be recognized in his "chaffering allincluding most farraginous chronicle" of one day in Dublin.

Appendix—The Early Texts of *Ulysses*

The Rosenbach Manuscript

A major *Ulysses* document, the holograph manuscript owned by the Philip H. and A.S.W. Rosenbach Foundation, was published in facsimile in 1975. Because of the publication, a manuscript that could previously be used only in Philadelphia is now easily accessible. The reproduction is outstanding, so close to the original that it is usually possible to distinguish between Joyce's original text (generally in ink) and his subsequent additions (often in pencil). On many occasions, it is even possible to read both an original word and its correction, one on top of the other. It is ironic, then, that the close inspection of the manuscript made possible by this facsimile, particularly collation with the extant typescripts, casts serious doubt upon its place in the textual development of *Ulysses*. In view of the complex textual situation, it is worthwhile to rehearse in detail the early development of *Ulysses* and to establish the position of the Rosenbach Manuscript as precisely as possible.[1]

Scholars working on the text of *Ulysses* hoped that the facsimile publication would make accessible the key document in the book's early textual development. This devel-

[1] While investigating the Rosenbach Manuscript, I participated in a regular four-way communication involving Hans Walter Gabler, Philip Gaskell, and A. Walton Litz. Each of us had come to the independent conclusion that, for several episodes, something was missing between the Rosenbach Manuscript and the typescripts, and we shared ideas and examples as they occurred to us. Inevitably, some of the observations offered here originated with them, and my main arguments and some of my examples will also be found in their reviews of the facsimile: Gabler's in *The Library*, 32, 5th ser. (1977), pp. 177-82; Gaskell's in *TLS*, June 25, 1976, p. 803, as well as several follow-up letters between July 30 and November 12; and Litz's in the *James Joyce Quarterly*, 14 (1976), pp. 101-11. In his current work on the development of "Nausicaa," Myron Schwartzman has found that the Rosenbach Manuscript was probably not the direct ancestor of that episode's typescript.

opment seemed clear: (1) notes and early drafts led to a holograph manuscript of each episode; (2) from this manuscript a typescript (in three or four copies) was made; (3) all copies of the typescript were corrected and slightly augmented, and, for the first fourteen episodes, one copy was used for the *Little Review* serialization; and (4) in 1921, another copy was further augmented for submission to the printer Darantiere, after which processes the many sets of proofs were pulled, corrected, and augmented. It was assumed that the Rosenbach Manuscript was the holograph manuscript of step (1), making it the only complete early version in the direct line of textual descent. When the facsimile appeared, its editor, Clive Driver, included a "Bibliographical Preface" that assumed, without demonstration, that the typescripts for all episodes were indeed prepared directly from the document at hand, the "author's final manuscript" (MS, I, 13).

For nine episodes, this is certainly the case. The three "Telemachia" episodes were typed by Joyce's Zurich friend Claud Sykes in late 1917 and early 1918, during which time Joyce sent him several cards and letters with corrections (see *Letters*, I, 109; II, 413, 415-16). Many of these changes and additions are written onto the manuscript in a hand not Joyce's, presumably Sykes' (MS, "Nestor," fols. 7, 10, 15; "Proteus," fol. 9). Further, in "Telemachus," where Stephen drags his ashplant along the ground and thinks, "My familiar, after me, calling, Steeeeeeeeeeeephen!" Joyce added a marginal note, certainly for his typist: "N.B. There are 12 e's here" (MS, fol. 26). And in the margin of fol. 11 of "Proteus" Joyce wrote "p. 7," presumably a reference to the typescript. There is nothing in the few surviving typescript pages (one page each for "Nestor" and "Proteus") to contradict the assumption that the typist used the extant manuscript for these three episodes.

For two of Bloom's episodes, "Wandering Rocks" and "Cyclops," there is abundant proof that the typescripts were made from the Rosenbach Manuscript. The manuscript for each episode is filled with marginal additions and

corrections; all are incorporated into the body of the typescript. More important, the two typescripts contain no
phrases or passages that are not in the manuscript: the
manuscript text plus the additions and corrections on the
manuscript equal the typescript text. As with the manuscript of the first three episodes, there are signs here that
indicate use by a typist. For example, in "Wandering
Rocks" there is an "X" in the margin of fol. 34, a "Λ" on fol.
45, and a line under a word on fol. 47; these marks correspond to the beginnings of typescript pages 20, 24, and 25.
There are even more marks on the "Cyclops" manuscript:
"X"'s on fols. 21, 30, 37, 44, and 48 match the beginnings
of typescript pages 13, 18, 22, 26, and 28. And in several
places in "Cyclops" Joyce clarified in the margin a word
that was not legible in the text (as on fols. 29, 30, and 31).

The last four episodes complete the group. Only "Circe"
involved complications at the manuscript stage, but they
were serious enough to make up for the simpler episodes.
The first half (fols. 1-45) was typed directly from the
Rosenbach Manuscript, but then the typist's father had a
heart attack (*Letters*, I, 159). The rest of the manuscript was
copied in longhand by a group of amanuenses, primarily
Sylvia Beach, and the typists then worked from this longhand copy. The situation was further complicated when
the husband of one typist read the manuscript (in the
longhand copy) and, scandalized, threw part of it into the
fire. Joyce had already sent the original to John Quinn
(who by then was purchasing the manuscript), so he asked
Quinn to return the lost pages (*Letters*, III, 40-41). Quinn
sent photocopies of fols. 73-80, which were transcribed in
longhand and typed, apparently more than once. One
typescript of three of these pages was merged with the rest
of the "Circe" typescript, which was prepared from the
Rosenbach Manuscript and the amanuenses' copy made
from it.

The three "Nostos" episodes were also typed directly
from the Rosenbach Manuscript. "Eumaeus" was the last
episode Joyce wrote out in the loose-sheet format of the

previous fifteen episodes. For some reason, this episode's typist regularized the appearance of the text by changing all dashes indicating speeches to quotation marks. This typist also acted as a censor, leaving blanks whenever a word or phrase gave offense. Joyce had to restore these omissions by hand.

Unlike the other episodes, Joyce copied "Ithaca" and "Penelope" in notebooks with the basic text on the right-hand pages and additions on the left; George Joyce, who wrote to Quinn for his father on May 25, 1922, described them as "written verry [*sic*] legibly, to save trouble with typists in a large copybook."[2] "Ithaca" moves back and forth between two notebooks, with the breaks carefully marked, probably because Joyce was copying one section while the typist worked on another. "Penelope," which is written in the first "Ithaca" notebook, beginning upside down at the back, is complicated only because the last sentence is not in the notebook. Joyce neglected to send this to Quinn, although he apparently thought he had: on June 3, 1922, George Joyce told Quinn that "the concluding paragraph of the Penelope episode beginning 'No that's no way' and ending 'Yes I will yes' will be found on turning back the page after the words 'do about him though.' " This last sentence was typed from a clean holograph draft written on five foolscap sheets.

The direct connection between the Rosenbach Manuscript and the typescripts unfortunately breaks down in the other episodes. The typescripts for almost half the text were probably not prepared from the extant manuscript, but from a working manuscript from which were made both the Rosenbach fair copy and, after changes and additions, the typescripts. The episodes involved are: "Calypso," "Hades," "Aeolus," "Lestrygonians," "Scylla and Charybdis," "Sirens," "Nausicaa," and "Oxen of the Sun." For these parts of *Ulysses* the Rosenbach Manuscript, like

[2] Joyce's letters to Quinn are in the Manuscripts Division of the New York Public Library and are quoted by permission. All subsequent letters to and from Quinn in this Appendix are from the same collection.

the entire *Little Review* version, stands outside the main line of textual transmission.

The many reasons behind this assertion involve both the appearance and the content of the Rosenbach Manuscript. First, the extant fair copies for these eight episodes do not look like those for the other episodes on loose sheets. For example, although "Wandering Rocks" and "Cyclops" in the Rosenbach Manuscript are filled with marginal additions and corrections (29 in the former, 54 in the latter), these eight episodes are almost totally devoid of such changes. There are none in "Calypso," "Hades," "Aeolus," or "Scylla and Charybdis," and only one in "Lestrygonians" and four in "Sirens." These episodes do contain corrections within the text (rather than in the margin), where they are less immediately noticeable.

The nature of certain mistakes in the Rosenbach Manuscript contributes to the doubts about its standing. These same eight episodes appear to have been copied hastily, with little concern for the legibility of individual words, and not from notes or partial drafts but from a pre-existing complete draft. They are filled with the kind of transcription error that results from hasty copying: an omitted "him" in "While he unwrapped the kidney the cat mewed hungrily against" ("Calypso," fol. 8) or "said" in "—There it is, John Murray. Alexander Keyes" ("Aeolus," fol. 1); a misspelled "two" in "Mr Bloom smiled O rocks at too windows of the ballast office" ("Lestrygonians," fol. 4) and "hat" in "Has that silk that ever since" ("Hades," fol. 10). These are, of course, minor errors, inevitable in the copying of a long text, but none of these or similar mistakes is corrected on the Rosenbach Manuscript, suggesting that Joyce not only copied hastily but neglected to proofread the manuscript. Again, it seems that appearance counted more than accuracy.[3]

---

[3] When Robert Martin Adams looked at the Rosenbach Manuscript, he came to a similar conclusion: "One possible theory . . . is that Joyce kept the early chapters of *Ulysses* in a number of MSS, on which he entered corrections and improvements, as opportunity offered, without systematic

However, it is a comparison between the Rosenbach
Manuscript and the typescripts that most undermines its
authority for these eight episodes. In his "Bibliographical
Preface" to the facsimile, Clive Driver notes that there are
many places where, though the *Little Review* and final versions agree on a reading, the Rosenbach Manuscript differs
from both. He explains that Joyce made the changes "in
typescript," presumably implying that corrections were
made to a text typed from the Rosenbach Manuscript (MS,
I, 32). He does not note, though, that the typescript frequently agrees with the *Little Review* and final versions and
not with the manuscript, meaning that Joyce made the
changes some time before the preparation of the typescript.

I offer four corresponding passages from the Rosenbach
Manuscript (including Joyce's corrections and additions)
and the typescript (before he provided any additions). If
the Rosenbach Manuscript were the typist's copy, the second version of each example would follow directly from
the first. I have underlined all words and punctuation
marks in the typescripts that differ from the manuscript.
Similar passages occur throughout these eight episodes;
they are the rule rather than the exception.

> Who was telling me? Mervyn Browne. Down in the vaults
> of saint Michan's they have to bore a hole in the coffin
> after ~~the~~ ⟨a⟩ few months to let out the gas and burn it.
> Out it rushes: blue. One whiff of that and you're a doner.
> (MS, "Hades," fol. 24)

collation. The MS now in the Rosenbach Foundation was copied from one
or several of these early documents; *Little Review* and the final text resulted from a separate editorial operation. Everything about the Rosenbach MS indicates that the first sections of it, particularly, were copied out
mechanically (not without boredom) from pre-existing MSS, perhaps with
the specific notion that it could be sold to a collector, perhaps for use by a
typist, but certainly at a decided remove from the ardors of creative synthesis" (*Surface and Symbol: The Consistency of James Joyce's* Ulysses, Galaxy
ed. [New York: Oxford Univ. Press, 1962, 1967], pp. 274-75). Curiously,
Adams seems to base his argument on the "Telemachia" episodes, which
were certainly typed directly from the Rosenbach Manuscript. His conclusion, however, applies very well to the eight problematic episodes.

Who was telling me? Mervyn <u>Brown</u>. Down in the vaults of saint <u>Werburgh's lovely old organ hundred and fifty</u> they have to bore a hole in the coffins <u>sometimes</u> to let out the <u>bad</u> gas and burn it. Out it rushes: blue. One whiff of that and you're a doner.

(Buffalo TS V.B.4, p. 9; cf. 104.1-5)

His downcast eyes followed the silent veining of the oaken slab. Beauty: it curves: curves are beauty. Shapely goddesses. Juno. Venus. Their curves the world admires. I will call into the museum, see them standing in the round hall, naked, goddesses they don't care who looks at them, all parts. Never speaking. I mean to say to fellows like Flynn. Quaffing nectar at mess with the gods golden dishes all ambrosial. Not like a lunch for a tanner, we have boiled mutton, carrots and turnip, bottle of Allsopp. Nectar imagine it like drinking electricity: gods' food. Lovely forms of women. ⟨Junonian.⟩ bodies. Immortal. And we stuffing food in one hole and out ~~the other~~ ⟨behind⟩. They have no. I never looked. I'll look today. Keeper not looking. Bend down let something ~~drop~~ ⟨fall⟩. See if she.

(MS, "Lestrygonians," fols. 21-22)

His downcast eyes followed the silent veining of the oaken slab. Beauty: it curves: curves are beauty. Shapely goddesses, <u>Venus, Juno:</u> curves the world admires. <u>Can see them museum library</u> standing in the round hall, <u>naked goddesses.</u> They don't care <u>what man</u> looks. All <u>to see</u>. Never speaking. I mean to say to fellows like Flynn. Quaffing nectar at mess wit<u>h gods</u> golden dishes all ambrosial. Not like a <u>tanner lunch</u> we have<u>,</u> boiled mutton carrots and turnips<u> </u>bottle of Allsop. Nectar imagine <u>it</u> drinking electricity: gods' food. Lovely forms of woman Junonian<u>.</u> Immortal <u>lovely</u>. And we stuffing food in one hole and out behind. They have no. <u>N</u>ever looked. I'll look today. Keeper <u>won't see</u>. Bend down let some<u>_</u>thing fall<u> </u>see if she.

(Buffalo TS V.B.6, p. 14; cf. 176.24-39)

First night I met her no Mat Dillon's in Roundtown.
Yellow, black lack [*sic*] she wore. Musical chairs. We two
the last. Fate. Fate. After her. Round and round. Slow.
Quick. Round. We. All looked. Halt. She sat. Yellow
knees.

—*Charmed my eye* . . .

Then singing. *Waiting* she sang. I turned her music.
Full voice of perfume of the lilactrees. Bosom I saw, both
full, throat warbling. When first I saw. She thanked me.
Why did she me? Spanishy eyes. At me. Luring. Ah, alluring.

(MS, "Sirens," fol. 25)

First night <u>when first I saw her at</u> Mat Dillon's in
<u>Terenure</u>. Yellow, black <u>lace</u> she wore. Musical chairs.
We two the last. Fate. <u>After her. Fate.</u> Round and round
slow. Quick round. We <u>two</u>. All looked. Halt. <u>Down</u> she
sat. Yellow knees.

—*Charmed my eye* . . .

<u>Singing. Waiting</u> she sang. I turned her music. Full
voice of perfume of <u>what perfume does your</u> lilactrees.
Bosom I saw, both full, throat warbling. <u>First</u> I saw. She
thanked me. Why did she me? <u>Fate.</u> Spanishy eyes. At
me. Luring. Ah, alluring.

(Buffalo TS V.B.9, p. 13; cf. 275.17-28)

Malachi's tale froze them with horror. The secret
panel ⟨beside the chimney⟩ slid back and in the recess
appeared—Haines. He had a bag full of ⟨Irish⟩ poems
in one hand, in the other a phial marked *Poison*. Surprise, horror, loathing appeared on all faces while he
eyed them with a ghastly grin. I anticipated this reception, he began, for which, it seems, history is to blame.
Yes, it is true. I am the murderer of Samuel Childs. ~~Hell~~
⟨The future inferno⟩ has no terrors for me. Like the
modern Irish ~~I carry~~ ⟨my hell⟩ is in this life. I have tried
to obliterate my crime. Distractions, rookshooting, the
Erse language (he recited some), laudanum (he raised
the phial to his lips) camping out. In vain! Hie spectre

stalks me. Dope is my only hope. . . . Ah, the black panther. With a cry he suddenly vanished and the panel slid back. An instant later his head appeared in the door opposite. Meet me at Westland Row Station at ten past eleven. He was gone. Tears gushed from the eyes of the dissipated host. The seer raised his hand to heaven, murmuring: 'Tis the vengeance of Mananaan. The sage repeated: Lex Talionis. The sentimentalist is he who would enjoy without incurring the immense debtorship for a thing done. Malachi ceased, overcome. The mystery was unveiled. Haines was the third brother. His real name was Childs. The black panther was himself the ghost of his own father. He drank drugs to obliterte. For this relief much thanks. The lonely house by the graveyard is uninhabited.

(MS, "Oxen of the Sun," fol. 42v)

But Malachias' tale began to freeze them with horror. He conjured up the scene before them. The secret panel beside the chimney slid back and in the recess appeared—Haines! He had a portfolio full of Celtic literature in one hand, in the other a phial marked *Poison*. Surprise, horror, loathing were depicted on all faces while he eyed them with a ghastly grin. I anticipated some such reception, he began, for which, it seems, history is to blame. Yes, it is true. I am the murderer of Samuel Childs. And how I am punished! The inferno. has no terrors for me. What way would I be resting at all and I tramping Dublin this while back and himself after me the like of soulth?My hell, and Ireland's, is in this life. I have tried to obliterate my crime. Distractions, rookshooting, the Erse language (he recited some), laudanum (he raised the phial to his lips) camping out. In vain! His spectre stalks me. Dope is my only hope. . . . Ah! Destruction! The black panther! With a cry he suddenly vanished and the panel slid back. An instant later his head appeared in the door opposite and said: Meet me at Westland row station at ten past eleven. He was gone!

Tears gushed from the eyes of the dissipated host. The
seer raised his hand to heaven, murmuring: 'T̶i̶s̶ ̶t̶ The
vendetta of Mannanaun! The sage repeated Lex
talionis. The sentimentalist is he who would enjoy without incurring the immense debtorship for a thing done.
Malachias, overcome by emotion, ceased. The mystery
was unveiled. Haines was the third brother. His real
name was Childs. The black panther was himself the
ghost of his own father. He drank drugs to obliterate.
For this relief much thanks. The lonely house by the
graveyard is uninhabited. No soul will live there. The
spider pitches her web in the solitude. The nocturnalist
peers from his hole. A curse is on it. It is haunted. Murderer's ground.

(Buffalo TS V.B.12.a, p. 18; cf. 412.5-39)[4]

The changes between manuscript and typescript could
have been accomplished in three ways: (1) The typist used
the Rosenbach Manuscript and Joyce sent his changes by
card or letter (his procedure with Claud Sykes during the
typing of the "Telemachia"), or he included pages of corrections with the manuscript (see the pages following
"Circe" fols. 40 and 43). Undermining this theory is the
fact that it would have required a superhuman effort on
the part of the typist to incorporate all the changes in the
typescript without making a mark on the manuscript or a
mistake in typing. The typist must have used a manuscript
version that included Joyce's additions and corrections,
probably as marginal additions linked to the text by lines or
superscripts. (2) Typescripts were prepared from the
Rosenbach Manuscript, Joyce corrected and augmented
these typescripts, and a second set of typescripts (the sur-

[4] This text is the same as that in the "Oxen of the Sun" typescript in the
Little Review collection at the University of Wisconsin—Milwaukee. In the
Rosenbach Manuscript, Joyce copied this paragraph (without indenting
the first line) onto the back of fol. 42: he had evidently omitted it from fol.
43 in preparing the fair copy. However, there is no indication (as for a
typist) of where the passage belongs in the text.

viving set) was made.[5] This sequence has the advantage of keeping the Rosenbach Manuscript in the line of textual descent, but it cannot account for the physical appearance of the manuscript for these eight episodes. Nor does there seem to have been time between Joyce's completion of the fair copies and the completion of the typescript for the preparation of two typescripts. Given the lack of evidence, the existence of a second typescript seems to me far less likely than the existence of a working manuscript, as proposed in theory (3). (3) After completing the working manuscript of each episode, Joyce made copies of the eight in question with the idea of eventually selling them.[6] After preparing the copy (the Rosenbach Manuscript), he made changes and additions on the working manuscript, and gave this augmented manuscript to the typist. There is no concrete proof for this assertion, but there is at least Sylvia Beach's controversial statement in *Shakespeare and Company* that "as soon as Joyce completed an instalment, he made a fair copy and sent it off to Quinn, who, in return, sent Joyce the sum agreed on—small sums, but they helped."[7]

[5] This theory was suggested by Philip Gaskell in his review of the facsimile (*TLS*, June 25, 1976, p. 803), but later rejected by him (letter to *TLS*, August 6, 1976, p. 986).

[6] At first, Joyce would have made the fair copy not specifically for Quinn, but for eventual sale to an unknown buyer. Quinn offered to buy the manuscript of *Ulysses* in a letter of June 26, 1919, during Joyce's early writing of "Cyclops," but the offer was accepted only on February 5, 1920, during "Oxen of the Sun."

[7] (New York: Harcourt, Brace, 1959), p. 39. In his "Bibliographical Preface" to the facsimile, Clive Driver rejects Sylvia Beach's assertion with scorn and blames it for creating a "myth" that has resulted in "neglect" of the Rosenbach Manuscript. He castigates scholars whose views have been

colored by this myth. Walton Litz, for example, in his *The Art of James Joyce*, states: "The episodes to 'Oxen of the Sun' are substantially the same as those which appeared in the *Little Review*, and bear few revisions" [Litz, p. 130]. Anyone familiar with Joyce's method should be suspicious of an assessment that precludes Joyce's making substantial revision in typescript. (MS, I, 32)

Driver has compared the Rosenbach Manuscript, *Little Review*, and final

Except for the likelihood that, at first, Joyce made the fair copy not specifically for Quinn but for a hypothetical prospective buyer, this statement now appears to be true and the document we have was never used for the preparation of eight of the typescripts.

There are indications on some of the typescripts that the text of the typist's copy was indeed identical with the Rosenbach Manuscript, with additions and corrections probably indicated by lines or superscripts. On the typescript of "Calypso," for example, the last words of the first paragraph read "a fine tang of ~~urine~~ faintly scented urine" (Buffalo TS V.B.3, p. 1; cf. 55.5). And in "Aeolus," the typescript reads, "He took out his handkerchief to dab his nose. ~~Almond ? Cirt ?~~ Citronlemon? Ah, the soap I put there" (Buffalo TS V.B.5, p. 4; 123.6-7). In both cases the typist first omitted a revision (and in the process typed a text identical to the Rosenbach Manuscript version) and then went back and corrected the error. These mistakes are infrequent and easily explained given an original that was heavily marked; for me, they support the probability that theory (3) is correct.

The remaining episode, "Lotus Eaters," is a curiosity. The first five pages (fols. 1-5) contain many more corrections (interlinear rather than marginal) than the remaining eleven (fols. 5b-15), which are extremely clean. And fol. 5 contains two sets of pencilled numbers, evidently instructions to the typist regarding the number of spaces to indent:

> [9]What is home without
> [5]Plumtree's Potted Meat?

versions, but in his determination to explode the "myth," he has either failed to make the crucial comparison between manuscript and typescripts, or, having made it, has chosen to ignore the evidence entirely. In his preface Driver brings together much useful factual information about Joyce's writing of the Rosenbach Manuscript, but he is misleading and often mistaken when he discusses the document's place in the total composition of *Ulysses*.

[18]Incomplete.

[5]With it an abode of bliss.

[9]Love's.
Old.
Sweet.
Song.
Comes love's old . . .

The "Lotus Eaters" typescript is not extant, but these passages do appear with this spacing in the *Little Review*, which was set from the typescript (5, iii [July 1918], pp. 40-41). It is possible that the first part of the Rosenbach Manuscript is the typist's copy, and the second part is a clean fair copy prepared for sale.

To summarize, for nine episodes—"Telemachus," "Nestor," "Proteus," "Wandering Rocks," "Cyclops," "Circe," "Eumaeus," "Ithaca," and "Penelope"—the Rosenbach Manuscript lies in the direct line of textual transmission. For eight others—"Calypso," "Hades," "Aeolus," "Lestrygonians," "Scylla and Charybdis," "Sirens," "Nausicaa," and "Oxen of the Sun"—it appears to lie outside the direct line. For "Lotus Eaters," it lies partly in and partly out of the line. In terms of pages, this means that of the 792 holograph pages in the Rosenbach Manuscript, 454 (or 57 percent) are in the line of descent and 338 (43 percent) are not.

The Typescripts

Each episode's early development culminated in a typescript. The typescripts for the fourteen episodes that appeared in the *Little Review* were all prepared and used in a similar fashion. The typist, working from Joyce's holograph manuscript, made three copies of each episode (four for "Oxen of the Sun"). Joyce corrected and slightly augmented all copies, mixing up top copies and carbons and sometimes neglecting to make all changes on all copies. He retained one copy and sent two to Ezra Pound, one for Margaret Anderson and the *Little Review* and one for Harriet Shaw Weaver and the *Egoist*. The typescript used by the *Little Review* was lost; all that has survived is the part of "Oxen of the Sun" the *Little Review* was enjoined from printing.

When Joyce sent typescripts for the book publication to Maurice Darantiere in 1921, he sent copies of the same typescripts used for the *Little Review* serialization. He had two copies available: the one he had kept originally and the one he had given to Pound for Harriet Shaw Weaver. He wrote his latest additions and corrections onto one copy and sent this to Darantiere. For none of these episodes was a new typescript made specifically for the book publication.[8]

The typescripts for the last four episodes, however, were prepared directly for the book publication. Considering the immensely complicated process of producing the "Circe" typescript, the use of the resulting documents was fairly straightforward: four copies of the typescript were made, and one was used by the printer. In the summer of 1921, after the typing of "Circe" but before Darantiere began setting it, Joyce wrote a "Messianic scene" for the episode. He expected the typescript of this scene to be inserted into the printer's copy of "Circe" (he put crayon marks on p. 54 to indicate the placement of the insert), but Darantiere must have received the insert separately, since he set it six weeks before beginning "Circe."

"Eumaeus" and "Penelope" were even simpler. For "Eumaeus," an original and three carbons were made, and one set was corrected (with dashes and offensive language restored), augmented, and sent to the printer. "Penelope" seems to have involved only an original and one carbon; again one copy was corrected and augmented for Darantiere.

[8] I have discussed the typescripts for the first fourteen episodes in much greater detail in my article, " 'Cyclops' in Progress, 1919," *James Joyce Quarterly*, 12 (1974/75), pp. 158-60. See also Driver, "Bibliographical Preface," MS, I, 18-19, 24.

Finally, "Ithaca" presents increased complications. Two copies of a typescript were prepared directly from the copybooks that form part of the Rosenbach Manuscript, but as Joyce augmented one copy, it became necessary to retype many pages. There were three rounds of revisions and three partial retypings. The final typescript is thus a mixture of the first, second, third, and fourth typings. Besides this, Joyce wanted to show excerpts of the episode to Valery Larbaud, so when about half the episode was typed for the first time (but before he made any corrections or additions), he went through the typescript and the copybooks for those parts not yet typed and starred certain questions and answers. These were typed separately, one question and answer to a page, and sent uncorrected to Larbaud.[9]

During the writing of most of *Ulysses*, Joyce thought of the typescripts as the culmination of his work on each episode, and once each typescript was prepared and corrected, he was ready to move on to the next episode. It was the typescripts, with their texts more developed than in the Rosenbach Manuscript, that Joyce sent to the *Little Review*, and it was the typescripts that he submitted to Darantiere. Philip Gaskell has described them as "the ultimate fair copy" of *Ulysses*,[10] and I believe he is correct.

The Little Review

The *Little Review* serialization of the first fourteen episodes is the final early text of *Ulysses*. As I explained in the Introduction, the *Little Review* version lies outside the line of transmission and, except in a few cases, has no textual significance. Joyce corrected and slightly augmented

[9] See Peter Spielberg, *James Joyce's Manuscripts and Letters at the University of Buffalo: A Catalogue* (Buffalo: Univ. of Buffalo, 1962), pp. 70-76. TSS V.B.15.c-h contain the four typings of the episode. 15.a-b are the separate partial typescript (top copy and carbon) prepared only for Larbaud; 15.c was not, as Spielberg claims (p. 71), "based in part on this typescript." Joyce told Larbaud about the special typescript on October 30, 1921 (*Letters*, III, 51).

[10] *TLS*, June 25, 1976, p. 803.

all copies of the typescripts for these episodes (though occasionally he neglected to make all changes on all copies), and then sent one copy to Ezra Pound for the *Little Review*. He never saw the *Little Review* proofs, so he had no control over the many printer's errors or editorial deletions.

In 1921 Joyce prepared a text of these episodes for the book publication by taking a copy of the typescript made for the *Little Review* and inserting more revisions. (In most cases, this copy also contained the same corrections and additions as the copy used by the periodical.) So the line of transmission bypasses the *Little Review*, progressing from the typescript with the first set of revisions to the typescript with the first and second sets.

The *Little Review* installments nevertheless retain some textual significance, especially for those pages where no typescripts have survived. Here, the serial installments stand as the only indication of certain revisions made at the typescript stage. The *Little Review* can be collated with the first *placards* (the other version set directly from the typescripts); words in the *Little Review* but not in the *placards* are especially important, since Joyce may have neglected to register an addition on the copy he sent to Darantiere. The *Little Review* is similarly significant in the few places where a word or phrase appears there but not on the extant printer's copy of the typescript. The typescript used by the *Little Review* has not survived, leaving the printed serial version as the only evidence for such a word or phrase. The *Little Review* contains many errors, and so can be used only with caution, but it occasionally must be considered as the most authoritative extant evidence of Joyce's intentions.

Each of these early texts of *Ulysses*—Rosenbach Manuscript, typescripts, and *Little Review* version—thus contains major complications for anyone hoping to sort out the development of the book. Joyce knew that there was a kind of immortality to be had in keeping the professors busy with the enigmatic content of his work, but he would be equally delighted to know that he has so successfully confounded the efforts of his editors and textual critics as well.

Bibliography

Bibliographies and Catalogues

Scholes, Robert E., comp. *The Cornell Joyce Collection: A Catalogue*. Ithaca: Cornell Univ. Press, 1961.

Slocum, John J., and Cahoon, Herbert. *A Bibliography of James Joyce: 1882-1941*. London: Hart-Davis, 1953.

Spielberg, Peter, comp. *James Joyce's Manuscripts and Letters at the University of Buffalo: A Catalogue*. Buffalo: Univ. of Buffalo, 1962.

Works by James Joyce: Published

The Critical Writings of James Joyce. Ed. Ellsworth Mason and Richard Ellmann. New York: Viking, 1959.

Dubliners. 1914; text corrected by Robert Scholes. New York: Viking, 1967.

Exiles: A Play in Three Acts, including Hitherto Unpublished Notes by the Author, Discovered after his Death, and an Introduction by Padraic Colum. New York: Viking, 1951.

Finnegans Wake. New York: Viking, 1939, 1958.

Giacomo Joyce. Ed. Richard Ellmann. New York: Viking, 1968.

James Joyce's Scribbledehobble: The Ur-Workbook for Finnegans Wake. Ed. Thomas E. Connolly. Evanston: Northwestern Univ. Press, 1961.

Joyce's Notes and Early Drafts for Ulysses: *Selections from the Buffalo Collection*. Ed. Phillip F. Herring. Charlottesville: Univ. Press of Virginia, 1977. Includes the following documents (numbers refer to Peter Spielberg's catalogue, except for the Cornell document, which refers to Robert Scholes' catalogue):

   Ulysses notebook V.A.2.
   Ulysses notebook VIII.A.5.
   "Cyclops" MSS V.A.6, V.A.7, V.A.8, V.A.9.
   "Cyclops" MS, Item 55. Joyce Collection, Cornell University.
   "Circe" MSS V.A.19, V.A.20.

Joyce's Ulysses *Notesheets in the British Museum*. Ed. Phillip F. Herring. Charlottesville: Univ. Press of Virginia, 1972.

Letters of James Joyce. Vol. I, ed. Stuart Gilbert. New York: Viking, 1957, 1966. Vols. II and III, ed. Richard Ellmann. New York: Viking, 1966.

A Portrait of the Artist as a Young Man. 1916; text corrected by Chester G. Anderson and ed. Richard Ellmann. New York: Viking, 1964.

Selected Letters of James Joyce. Ed. Richard Ellmann. New York: Viking, 1975.

Stephen Hero. Ed. Theodore Spencer. New York: New Directions, 1944, 1963.

Ulysses. 1922; New York: Random House, 1961.

Ulysses (*Little Review* version). Serialized in the *Little Review* (New York). IV, xi (March 1918)-VII, iii (September-December 1920).

Ulysses: *A Facsimile of the Manuscript*. 3 vols. New York: Octagon, and Philadelphia: The Philip H. and A.S.W. Rosenbach Foundation, 1975.

Ulysses schema. Transcribed and trans. Richard Ellmann. Appendix to *Ulysses on the Liffey*. Galaxy ed. New York: Oxford Univ. Press, 1972, 1973. [The 1920 Linati schema.]

Ulysses schema. Reproduced photographically in *A James Joyce Miscellany: Second Series*. Ed. Marvin Magalaner. Carbondale: Southern Illinois Univ. Press, 1959, opposite p. 48. Partly transcribed in Stuart Gilbert. *James Joyce's* Ulysses: *A Study*. 1930; rpt. New York: Vintage, 1952, p. [30]. [The 1921 schema.]

The Workshop of Daedalus: James Joyce and the Raw Materials for A Portrait of the Artist as a Young Man. Ed. Robert Scholes and Richard M. Kain. Evanston: Northwestern Univ. Press, 1965.

"The V.A.8 Copybook: An Early Draft of the 'Cyclops' Chapter of *Ulysses* with Notes on Its Development." Ed. Myron Schwartzman. *James Joyce Quarterly*, 12 (1974/75), 64-122.

Works by James Joyce: Unpublished

The Buffalo collection numbers refer to Peter Spielberg's catalogue.

Ulysses placards and page proofs. V.C.1, V.C.2, V.C.3, V.C.4. Poetry Collection, Lockwood Memorial Library, State University of New York at Buffalo.

Ulysses placards and page proofs. Sylvia Beach Collection, Princeton University.

Ulysses placards. Houghton Library, Harvard University.

Ulysses page proofs. Humanities Research Center, University of Texas at Austin.

"Nestor" TS V.B.1. SUNY at Buffalo.

"Proteus" TS V.B.2. SUNY at Buffalo.

"Calypso" TSS V.B.3.a, b. SUNY at Buffalo.

"Hades" TS V.B.4. SUNY at Buffalo.

"Aeolus" TS V.B.5. SUNY at Buffalo.

"Lestrygonians" TS V.B.6. SUNY at Buffalo.

"Scylla and Charybdis" TS V.B.7. SUNY at Buffalo.

"Wandering Rocks" TSS V.B.8.a, b. SUNY at Buffalo.

"Sirens" MS V.A.5. SUNY at Buffalo.

"Sirens" TS V.B.9. SUNY at Buffalo.

"Cyclops" TSS V.B.10.a, b. SUNY at Buffalo.

"Nausicaa" TSS V.B.11.a, b. SUNY at Buffalo.

"Oxen of the Sun" MS V.A.13. SUNY at Buffalo.

"Oxen of the Sun" TS. *Little Review* Collection, University of Wisconsin—Milwaukee.

"Oxen of the Sun" TSS V.B.12.a, b, c. SUNY at Buffalo.

"Circe" TSS V.B.13.a, b, c, d, e, h, i. SUNY at Buffalo.

"Eumaeus" TSS V.B.14.a, d. SUNY at Buffalo.

"Ithaca" TSS V.B.15.a, b, c, d, e, f, g. SUNY at Buffalo.

"Penelope" TSS V.B.16.b, c. SUNY at Buffalo.

Finnegans Wake notebook VI.C.7. SUNY at Buffalo.

Secondary Sources

Adams, Robert Martin. *Surface and Symbol: The Consistency of James Joyce's* Ulysses. Galaxy ed. New York: Oxford Univ. Press, 1962, 1967.

Aristotle. *La Rhétorique d'Aristote*. Trans. François Cassandre. 1654; Amsterdam: J. Covens and C. Mortier, 1733.

Beach, Sylvia. *Shakespeare and Company*. New York: Harcourt, Brace, 1959.

Benco, Silvio. "James Joyce in Trieste." *The Bookman* (New York), 72 (1930), 375-80.

Bérard, Victor. *Les Phéniciens et l'Odyssée*. 2 vols. Paris: Librairie Armand Colin, 1902-03.

Bonnerot, Louis, ed. Ulysses: *Cinquante Ans Après*. Paris: Didier, 1974.

Briskin, Irene Orgel. "Some New Light on 'The Parable of the Plums.' " *James Joyce Quarterly*, 3 (1966), 236-51.

Budgen, Frank. *James Joyce and the Making of* Ulysses. 1934; rpt. Bloomington: Indiana Univ. Press, 1960.

Card, James Van Dyck. "A Textual and Critical Study of the 'Penelope' Episode of James Joyce's *Ulysses*." Diss. Columbia, 1964.

Dalton, Jack P. "The Text of *Ulysses*." *New Light on Joyce from the Dublin Symposium*. Ed. Fritz Senn. Bloomington: Indiana Univ. Press, 1972, 99-119.

Driver, Clive. "Bibliographical Preface." Ulysses: *A Facsimile of the Manuscript*. New York: Octagon, and Philadelphia: The Philip H. and A.S.W. Rosenbach Foundation, 1975, I, 13-38.

Ellmann, Richard. *James Joyce*. Galaxy ed. New York: Oxford Univ. Press, 1959, 1965.

———. *Ulysses on the Liffey*. Galaxy ed. New York: Oxford Univ. Press, 1972, 1973.

Frank, Joseph. "Spatial Form in Modern Literature." 1945; rpt. in *The Widening Gyre: Crisis and Mastery in Modern Literature*. New Brunswick: Rutgers Univ. Press, 1963, 3-62.

French, Marilyn. *The Book as World: James Joyce's* Ulysses. Cambridge: Harvard Univ. Press, 1976.

Gabler, Hans Walter. Review of Ulysses: *A Facsimile of the Manuscript*. *The Library*, 32, 5th ser. (1977), 177-82.

Garrett, Peter K. *Scene and Symbol from George Eliot to James*

Joyce: Studies in Changing Fictional Mode. New Haven: Yale Univ. Press, 1969.

Gaskell, Philip. Review of Ulysses: *A Facsimile of the Manuscript. TLS*, June 25, 1976, p. 803, plus follow-up letters between July 30 and November 12.

Gilbert, Stuart. *James Joyce's* Ulysses: *A Study*. 1930; rpt. New York: Vintage, 1952.

Goldberg, S. L. *The Classical Temper: A Study of James Joyce's* Ulysses. London: Chatto and Windus, 1961.

Goldman, Arnold. *The Joyce Paradox: Form and Freedom in His Fiction*. London: Routledge and Kegan Paul, 1966.

———. Review of Adams, *Surface and Symbol. Essays in Criticism*, 13 (1963), 282-92.

Gorman, Herbert. *James Joyce*. New York: Rinehart, 1939, 1948.

Groden, Michael. " 'Cyclops' in Progress, 1919." *James Joyce Quarterly*, 12 (1974/75), 123-68.

———. "The Growth of James Joyce's *Ulysses*." Diss. Princeton, 1975.

———. "Toward a Corrected Text of *Ulysses*." *James Joyce Quarterly*, 13 (1975), 49-52.

Hart, Clive. *James Joyce's* Ulysses. Sydney: Sydney Univ. Press, 1968.

——— and Hayman, David, eds. *James Joyce's* Ulysses: *Critical Essays*. Berkeley and Los Angeles: Univ. of California Press, 1974.

Hayman, David. Ulysses: *The Mechanics of Meaning*. Englewood Cliffs: Prentice-Hall, 1970.

Hurley, Robert Edward. "The 'Proteus' Episode of James Joyce's *Ulysses*." Diss. Columbia, 1963.

Jarrell, Mackie L. "Joyce's Use of Swift's *Polite Conversation* in the 'Circe' Episode of *Ulysses*." *PMLA*, 72 (1957), 545-54.

Kenner, Hugh. "Circe." *James Joyce's* Ulysses: *Critical Essays*. Ed. Clive Hart and David Hayman. Berkeley and Los Angeles: Univ. of California Press, 1974, 341-62.

———. *Dublin's Joyce*. 1956; rpt. Boston: Beacon, 1962.

Kenner, Hugh. "Homer's Sticks and Stones." *James Joyce Quarterly*, 6 (1969), 285-98.

Keogh, J. G. *"Ulysses'* 'Parable of the Plums' as Parable and Periplum." *James Joyce Quarterly*, 7 (1970), 377-78.

Klein, A. M. "The Oxen of the Sun." *Here and Now*, 1 (1949), 28-48.

Larbaud, Valery. "James Joyce." *La Nouvelle Revue Française*, 18 (1922), 385-407.

————. "The 'Ulysses' of James Joyce." Trans. anon. *The Criterion*, 1 (1922), 94-103. [Portion of "James Joyce."]

Levin, Harry. *James Joyce: A Critical Introduction*. Rev. ed. Norfolk: New Directions, 1941, 1960.

Litz, A. Walton. *The Art of James Joyce: Method and Design in* Ulysses *and* Finnegans Wake. Galaxy ed. New York: Oxford Univ. Press, 1961, 1964.

————. "Ithaca." *James Joyce's* Ulysses: *Critical Essays*. Ed. Clive Hart and David Hayman. Berkeley and Los Angeles: Univ. of California Press, 1974, 385-405.

————. "The Last Adventures of *Ulysses.*" *Princeton University Library Chronicle*, 28 (1967), 63-75. Rpt. in Ulysses: *Cinquante Ans Après*. Ed. Louis Bonnerot. Paris: Didier, 1974, 1-12.

————. Review of Ulysses: *A Facsimile of the Manuscript*. *James Joyce Quarterly*, 14 (1976), 101-11.

Madtes, Richard Eastman. "A Textual and Critical Study of the 'Ithaca' Episode of James Joyce's *Ulysses.*" Diss. Columbia, 1961.

Magalaner, Marvin, ed. *A James Joyce Miscellany: Second Series*. Carbondale: Southern Illinois Univ. Press, 1959.

Mullach, Friedrich Wilhelm August, ed. *Fragmenta Philosophorum Graecorum*. 3 vols. Paris: Firmin-Didot, 1883.

Owen, Rodney W. "James Joyce and the Beginnings of *Ulysses*: 1912 to 1917." Diss. Kansas, 1977.

Pound, Ezra. *Pound/Joyce: The Letters of Ezra Pound to James Joyce*. Ed. Forrest Read. New York: New Directions, 1967.

Prescott, Joseph. "Stylistic Realism in *Ulysses.*" 1959; rpt. in

Exploring James Joyce. Carbondale: Southern Illinois Univ. Press, 1964, 106-34.

Roscher, W. H., ed. *Ausführliches Lexikon der Griesischen und Römischen Mythologie*. 6 vols. Leipzig: Teubner, 1884-1937.

Seidel, Michael. *Epic Geography: James Joyce's* Ulysses. Princeton: Princeton Univ. Press, 1976.

Senn, Fritz, ed. *New Light on Joyce from the Dublin Symposium*. Bloomington: Indiana Univ. Press, 1972.

Silverstein, Norman. "Joyce's 'Circe' Episode: Approaches to *Ulysses* through a Textual and Interpretative Study of Joyce's Fifteenth Chapter." Diss. Columbia, 1960.

Stanford, W. B. *The Ulysses Theme: A Study in the Adaptability of a Traditional Hero*. 2nd ed. 1954, 1963; rpt. Ann Arbor: Univ. of Michigan Press, 1968.

Sultan, Stanley. *The Argument of* Ulysses. Columbus: Ohio State Univ. Press, 1964.

Thornton, Weldon. *Allusions in* Ulysses: *An Annotated List*. Chapel Hill: Univ. of North Carolina Press, 1968.

Tolomeo, Diane. "The Final Octagon of *Ulysses*." *James Joyce Quarterly*, 10 (1973), 439-54.

Wilson, Edmund. *Axel's Castle: A Study in the Imaginative Literature of 1870-1930*. New York: Scribner's, 1931.

Index

Library of Congress Cataloging in Publication Data

Groden, Michael.
  Ulysses in progress.

  Bibliography: p.
  Includes index.
    1. Joyce, James, 1882-1941. Ulysses.   2. Joyce,
James, 1882-1941—Technique.   I. Title.
PR6019.09U6533   823'.9'12   77-1217
ISBN 0-691-06338-9